D1715158

The
State Park Movement
in America

The
State Park Movement
in America

A CRITICAL REVIEW

Ney C. Landrum

UNIVERSITY OF MISSOURI PRESS
COLUMBIA AND LONDON

Library of Congress Cataloging-in-Publication Data

Landrum, Ney C., 1931–
    The state park movement in America : a critical review /
Ney C. Landrum.
        p. cm.
Includes bibliographical references (p.   ).
        ISBN 0-8262-1500-9 (alk. paper)
    1. Parks—United States—History.   I. Title.
SB482.A4L36 2004
333.78'3'0973—dc22
                                        2003019599

Designer: Kristie Lee
Typesetter: Crane Composition, Inc.
Printer and binder: Thomson-Shore, Inc.
Typefaces: Minion, Bodoni Highlight

B2142030

For Matilde Hume Landrum, my wife and companion of forty-five years, for always being by my side;

For the thousands of men and women in state parks work, who perform such important public service with never the recognition they deserve; and

For my grandchildren—McKenzie, Robert, Cassie, Alex, and Ellie—who represent the generations of tomorrow that also have a vital stake in how America's state parks are managed today.

Contents

Preface xi

Acknowledgments xv

Prologue 1

1. "Parks Americana" 3

2. The Nature of Parks 14

3. The States Begin to Stir
State Park Initiatives in the Nineteenth Century 27

4. The Momentum Builds
State Parks Expansion in the Early Twentieth Century 48

5. Coalescence
The First National Conference on Parks 74

6. "A State Park Every Hundred Miles"
The National Conference on State Parks Goes to Work 90

7. Dubious Progress
Assessing the Relevance of the National Conference on State Parks . . . 111

8. An Unexpected Boon
Economic Recovery and a New Deal for State Parks 124

9. Recovery and Beyond
   Depression-Era Initiatives Look to the Future 141

10. A Major Interruption
    Wartime Distraction and Postwar Rebound 155

11. The Continuing Search for Direction
    The Ever-Resilient National Conference on State Parks 169

12. A New Era of Federal-State Cooperation 182

13. Signs of Maturity 201

14. A Look behind the Scenes
    Issues and Influences that Shape the State Park System 220

15. Anything Goes
    An Age of Expansion, Experimentation, and Expediency 233

16. Looking to the Future
    The View from One Observer's Soapbox 253

Appendix
   Selected Data on America's State Parks 262

Selected Bibliography 267

Index 273

The Need for State Parks

It is becoming increasingly difficult for men and women in great cities to go back to the great outdoors and there renew the springs which nourish and sweeten their lives. The real wilderness lies too distant from them. The only countryside they know is hedged in and fenced and offers no opportunity for a real taste of that hardship or at least that absence of the more softening influences of city life which their inner being craves. City parks do not fill the gap. They are necessary and useful in their place, but they are often all art, not nature, and it is nature which man wants. He must have somewhere to go outdoors, not too far away where he can entirely forget the city and all its ways.

National Parks partly fill this need but they are remote from the great masses of population; consequently the great movement for *State Parks* in recent years has come from a realization of the need and of the remedy. The *State park* has come to stay. It is a growing factor in modern American life, and it is one of the most hopeful, for it is a reaction of the inner instincts of humanity against a wholly new and artificial environment which threatens not only the impairment of its life but the mutilation of its soul. Modern man was building himself a prison. The *State Park* is one way out and the way which leads to those open fields not only of life but of thought where high, clean air may some day reinspire mankind to a truer vision of what this world might become.

— Adapted from the introduction to the
Proceedings of the Second National Conference on State Parks

Preface

This is not—nor was it intended to be—the definitive history of America's state parks. In fact, it might not properly be regarded as a history at all. Although I have attempted to trace the course of the state park movement over the past hundred years or so, and to fully acknowledge the many successes it has achieved, a collateral purpose of this "critical review" has been to raise concerns about questionable developments of the recent past and the influence they might have on the movement's future direction. These are my personal views, of course, based on forty years of direct participation and observation in state parks work. I certainly do not expect everyone to agree with my assessment, but I hope they will at least do me the favor of hearing me out.

My primary object in undertaking this study was simply to take a critical look at the central idea of the state park "movement" in the United States; to track its evolution, examine its causes, note its many divergent paths, and perhaps assess what might be called its successes and failures. In doing so, I was not concerned directly with individual state parks—of which there are thousands—or even with discrete state park *systems*. I have sought to keep my focus on the *movement* itself, involving all fifty of the state park systems, as a major social and environmental phenomenon primarily of the twentieth century.

State parks occupy a central position in the overall gamut of public outdoor recreation, bridging the critical gap—often a yawning chasm—between the largely playground types of recreation provided by America's cities and towns and the contrasting backcountry recreational experiences available in the vast national parks. Because the national parks are still relatively few and generally remote, the types of recreation they provide would likely never be accessible to much of the population except through the similar offerings of the more numerous and closer-to-home *state* parks. Providing this vital link is, or should be, the essential purpose of every state park system.

Prototypes of the state park actually started springing up here and there long before the term itself came into use. Before anyone—even the most farsighted of the conservation pioneers—had a clear notion of what a state park system might be, numerous unrelated efforts were under way around the country to preserve special places of natural or cultural importance. Many of these early preservation projects were accomplished through state legislation or with other direct assistance from the state governments, and thus signified a growing recognition and acceptance of state responsibility in a relatively new field of public service. Through these early successes, such American landmarks as Niagara Falls, the California redwoods, and the San Jacinto Battleground were saved for posterity.

A few scattered, unrelated successes, however, do not a park *movement* make. Even though word of these accomplishments was getting around, still the momentum was slow to build, especially in the less populous areas of the country. By the time of the first National Conference on Parks (subsequently, *State* Parks), in 1921, only nineteen of the states reported having anything resembling a state park, and many of those had but one such area. If this meager progress yet constituted a movement, it was indeed a sluggish one.

It was not long thereafter that exciting things began to happen. According to Herbert Evison—who, as the second executive secretary of the National Conference on State Parks, knew a thing or two about the subject—"the automobile fairly launched the state park movement." Although Evison's assertion might be a bit simplistic, it is certainly true that the rapid growth of automobile travel in the early part of the twentieth century stimulated great interest in tourism generally, including parks of all kinds. Thus, the economic potential of state parks as travel destinations, or at least for overnight stopovers, provided a practical incentive for state park development more persuasive for some than merely "preservation for preservation's sake." The prospect of stimulating tourism and making money with state parks undoubtedly fired the imagination of many a state official and private entrepreneur alike, and the clamor for more state parks grew louder and louder.

To imply that the economic stimulus, while undeniably powerful, caused interest in state parks to coalesce into a true movement, however, would be not only inaccurate, but also unfair. For every budget-minded legislator or profit-minded concessionaire that saw entrepreneurial potential in state parks, there surely were just as many equally motivated individuals who looked to state parks as a means of saving the best of their states' scenery and cultural heritage. Both of these incentives, the *economic* and the *preservation,* contributed mightily to the growing momentum for state park development, and they were soon joined by still a third of equal importance: the need to provide wholesome and healthful outdoor *recreational* opportunities for a rapidly expanding population. With such a combination of motivating forces, the emergence of a strong national movement for state parks was almost inevitable.

The state park movement that finally took shape, though, was never as cohesive as it might have seemed. As a matter of fact, it was eventually manifested as a movement with fifty different fronts—or at least that many variations—one for each state. With the interest and excitement generated by the 1921 National Conference on Parks, it appeared that a national consensus on what a state park and a state park system should be might actually develop. Certainly, definite efforts were made to bring that about. Then, as the inchoate consensus started to unravel due to strong differences of opinion among the movement's leaders, another major event took place to bring the nation's state park programs back into a measure of conformity. Through participation in the public works initiatives of Franklin Roosevelt's New Deal, many, if not most, of the state parks of that time came under the influence of the still relatively new National Park Service, with something of a "cloning" result. Applauded by many, perhaps resented by some, vestiges of the national park imprint persist today, especially in the numerous parks developed by the legendary Civilian Conservation Corps.

By the time government services returned to a semblance of normality following the Second World War, state parks were a firmly established program in all but five of the forty-eight states. By that measure, it may fairly be said that the movement was an obvious success. In the surge of innovation and development that took place in the post-war era, however, state park programs were quick to explore and pursue disparate philosophies, management objectives, and recreational offerings. As a result, the fifty state park programs today may be characterized as much by their differences as by their similarities. For almost all other state government functions—education, transportation, social services, whatever—there appears to be a high degree of similarity, even uniformity, in the way they deliver their services. By contrast, in their diverse approaches and myriad configurations, the fifty state park programs are uncommonly individualistic.

The independent, "do-it-my-way" spirit that has pervaded the state park movement over the past several decades may be seen as a "mixed bag." It has certainly produced much creativity and innovation in the field of park management generally, and especially in the ways and means of delivering outdoor recreational opportunities to the public. On the other hand, this free-for-all approach may well have led some states down a dubious path of harmful resource use and questionable service to their principal clienteles. Because there are few, if any, universally accepted norms for state park development and management, no one—especially not another state park agency—is in a position to point an accusing finger and say, "you're doing things wrong!" There are no arbiters for the inexact science (or is it an art?) of state parks.

I certainly do not presume to be such an arbiter. As a longtime observer and practitioner in the state parks field, though, I hope through this study to cast a perceptive and critical "insider's" eye on the situation as it exists today, how it got that way, and what it might bode for the future. This is, admittedly, a large order, and I do not fancy that I am the person best suited for the task. But as one who cares deeply for America's state parks and wants to see them all prosper, I offer my comments for what they may be worth.

Ney C. Landrum
Director Emeritus
Florida State Parks

Acknowledgments

I am indebted to many people and organizations for assistance in bringing this project to fruition—far too many, regrettably, to acknowledge them all individually. Foremost among them, though, are the National Association of State Park Directors, which sponsored the project from its inception, and the numerous individuals who served as state park directors during this time and who responded so promptly and completely to my many requests for information and assistance. I want to thank especially the four NASPD presidents with whom I worked during this period—David Weizenicker of Wisconsin, Fran Mainella of Florida, Ken Travous of Arizona, and Phil McKnelly of North Carolina—and also the members of the editorial advisory committee appointed by NASPD to hold my hand along the way: Jerry Pagac of Indiana, Wayne Perock of Nevada, and Chazz Salkin of Delaware. As executive director of NASPD, Glen Alexander graciously assisted me with numerous administrative details.

Many individuals in the Department of the Interior and the National Park Service provided valuable assistance. Principal among these were Tom Ross and Wayne Strum of the Park Service's National Center for Recreation and Conservation, Joe DuRant of the Harpers Ferry Center, and all of the courteous and helpful staff of the Department of the Interior Library. Lee Furr, the able overseer of the Joseph Lee Memorial Library at the National Recreation and Park Association, provided absolutely indispensable help during my many days rummaging through the collections there. My thanks also to Dr. Rebecca Conard of Middle Tennessee State University for the use of photographs from her collection.

As this was my first real venture into the esoteric world of book publishing, I would have been completely lost without the constant guidance and advice of the staff of the University of Missouri Press. I am grateful for their invaluable assistance, as well as their infinite patience.

And, finally, my greatest debt is owed my long-suffering wife, Matilde, without whose continuing interest, encouragement, and support this book would never have seen the light of day.

The
State Park Movement
in America

Stephen Tyng Mather, whose uncommon vision and dynamic leadership profoundly influenced the successful development of both the national park and the state park movements in America. NATIONAL PARK SERVICE

Prologue

Steve Mather was not happy.

How could anybody, especially members of Congress, expect him to build a national park system of the highest quality if they kept pressuring him to include properties of such questionable suitability? After all, just any old piece of land, even of modest scenic or historic interest, would not meet the lofty standards for a *national park*. Interior Secretary Lane had been very specific in laying down those standards: A national park must have "scenery of supreme and distinctive quality or some natural features so extraordinary or unique as to be of national interest and importance." The words could easily have been Mather's own; in fact, they were.

Stephen T. Mather had come to the nation's capital in 1915 at Lane's request to accept the challenge of administering the world's first national parks program—a program at that time with no funds, no staff, and no clear-cut mandate or policy direction. By dint of considerable personal charm and dogged perseverance, however, he was soon able to persuade Congress to create a national park *service* and give it the means to do the job. Appointed the first national parks director in 1917, Mather lost no time in molding the nation's handful of parks into a true system according to his own noble ideas. He was eminently successful, probably far beyond anyone's realistic expectations—but the road to success had been fraught with obstacles and frustrations.

In a relatively few years, the national parks concept had truly captured the nation's fancy; it seemed that every locality not only wanted its own park, but also had an energetic group ready to lobby for it. Congress was all too eager to oblige. In 1916 alone, the year that the National Park Service organic act was passed, Congress considered sixteen proposals for new national parks. Only two of those were deemed worthy of enactment, but the nominations for new parks—a few good, most marginal, and some bordering on the ridiculous—continued unabated. One congressman eventually introduced a bill to "establish a . . . national park in every state." Mather, who was now spending much of his time and energy trying tactfully to discourage and derail so many questionable proposals, decided that the situation was desperate. Something had to be done.

1

Director Mather was not the only one concerned about the lowering of national park standards, of course, and in late 1920 he arranged a brainstorming session in Chicago with some of his like-minded advisors. While there was a strong consensus that the integrity of the national park system had to be protected, there also was general agreement that many of the properties found lacking for national park status still had substantial merit and deserved protection through some other appropriate means. The most appropriate means, they concluded, was through inclusion in some other type of public park program, preferably at the state level. That, Mather decided, was an idea that all national park advocates should actively promote.

What happened next almost defies credibility. In barely two months' time, with Stephen Mather lending every bit of his prodigious prestige and influence, a national conference to promote state and other public parks was conceived, planned, organized, and convened. Supported nominally by an ailing President Woodrow Wilson and actively by practically every park and conservation luminary in the country, the first National Conference on [State] Parks became a stunning reality. Held in Des Moines, Iowa, in January 1921, it brought together some two hundred highly motivated delegates and ignited a "prairie fire" for development of public parks across America.

This was exactly the catalyst needed at the time, and out of this auspicious convocation emerged the modest beginnings of a nationwide *state park movement* that would achieve unimaginable success in the years to come.

Steve Mather was well pleased.

1

"Parks Americana"

The Genesis

America is truly a land of parks. Look anywhere across this vast, sprawling continent—from the city centers to the suburban neighborhoods to the remotest hinterlands—and you will find those special places where Americans like to roam, romp, or relax. As different as these sundry properties may otherwise be, they are all still affectionately known by the people as their "parks."

While the idea did not originate here, it most certainly achieved the pinnacle of its expression in the myriad forms of parklands that grace our countrysides from one ocean to the other. In numbers and variety, the parks of America put this country in a class by itself. Not only have they helped shape our landscapes and preserve our national heritage, but, as an exciting and universally popular concept, parks have become permanently ingrained in the American psyche and helped mold us as a people.

Almost from the time European settlers established themselves on these shores, they began setting aside various plots of land for their common use and enjoyment. Dictated at first by practicality, the preservation of public spaces in time became a form of aesthetic expression as towns and cities continued to grow and develop. Most of these early efforts evidenced a strong European influence, of course, following the ideas and models that had been brought over from the Old World countries; but adaptation to new and challenging conditions on this continent soon brought about distinctly American variations. Such modest beginnings hardly constituted a foundation for an American parks legacy, but they did establish valuable precedents for public open space preservation that have served us well to this day.

America's parks as we now know them, however, were not entirely—not even primarily—an inherited idea. But neither were they envisioned during their formative years as the quintessential part of our national character they were destined to become. Springing up randomly here and there, America's parks were at first merely part of a slowly coalescing idea—an obscure concept that had yet to be nurtured and nourished by a succession of visionaries for another two centuries in order to attain its present state of refinement.

Today, we take great pride, and justly so, in America's magnificent national parks—over 125 thousand square miles of forest and mountains, wetlands and desert, along with sites containing the most important shrines from our nation's dramatic past. It was "the best idea America ever had," opined the British Ambassador James Lord Brice in 1912. "Absolutely American, absolutely democratic, [the national parks] reflect us at our best rather than our worst," concurred the writer Wallace Stegner decades later. While probably no area of government endeavor has been able to escape controversy altogether, our national parks seem to have been unanimously applauded and admired almost from the very beginning.

As important as they are, however, the national parks are only one component of America's vast public park estate. Probably best known and certainly most widely used of all parks are those countless areas, large and small, provided by local and regional governments. These close-to-home playgrounds and green spaces cater to millions of users every day, wherever people have clustered, from the tiny hamlet to the huge metropolis. Impressive, too, in their own right are the thousands of state parks—some of them older than the first national park—which collectively comprise almost twenty thousand square miles of scenic landscapes and cultural treasures. Sharing characteristics of both the national and the local parks, state parks nevertheless occupy their own special niche and have their own devoted clientele. Whatever their identity—national, state, or local—among this smorgasbord of parklands there are special places to satisfy the needs and desires of every American. For a park-loving people, we are indeed abundantly blessed.

But what happened along the way to make the United States of America the preeminent land of parks—the world's leading exponent of the modern parks concept? What social forces came into play to motivate the settlers, planners, and developers of this new land to create our unique "Parks Americana"? It is a long, involved, but eminently gratifying, story—a fascinating drama in several acts—and well worth a quick review.

Yellowstone National Park, created by act of Congress in 1872, not only inaugurated America's unprecedented national parks program, but also served as the inspiration for numerous other natural area preservation efforts around the country. YVONNE FERRELL

The European Contribution:
Parks as Urban Landscape Features

America's first "parks" were merely expressions of borrowed urban planning doctrines that had influenced the design of European cities for centuries. The Spaniards brought with them to the New World the concept of the *central plaza,* which served as the hub and focal point for the development of their towns and cities. Soon afterward, the English arrived with a similar idea, the *commons,* sort of a communal "front yard" to serve the needs of the newly settled townspeople. Originally the domain of the city planners, such landscape features as these were standard fixtures in most of the towns of the period.

Some of the more progressive colonial cities, however—again borrowing from precedents brought from Europe—went much further, adopting sophisticated plans that incorporated squares, boulevards, ornamental gardens, and fountains. Although many of these more elaborate projects never got off of the drawing board, cities such as Philadelphia, Savannah, and Washington were meticulously planned and eventually became showpieces to rival their older sisters in England, France, and Italy.

Today, virtually every city and town in America has designated open spaces—whether as part of a formal plan or not. They all follow in the tradition of the early prototypes of the seventeenth and eighteenth centuries, which in retrospect may be seen as the informal beginning of a public park movement in America.

As the practice of urban planning evolved and began to rely more and more on the inclusion of open spaces, landscape architecture emerged in the mid-nineteenth century as a whole new field of professional endeavor. The principal exponent of this new school was none other than the legendary Frederick Law Olmsted, who, with his collaborator Calvert Vaux, first made his mark with the design of New York City's famous Central Park. With this precedent-setting project, Olmsted departed from the European tradition of parks—which saw them primarily as passive art objects—by taking advantage of the natural terrain features to incorporate a variety of uses, both passive and active. In this regard, Central Park was an important turning point in the emergence of a clearly American style of urban parks, and it was to become a major influence on park planning and design throughout the country.

Urban America and the Playground Movement

Although by the early 1800s a goodly number of open spaces had been formally set aside in America's growing cities, very few of them were designed with active recreational use in mind. They were created as landscape ornaments to be passively admired and enjoyed, and to help define the city's desired growth pattern. They also might be used for public gatherings and for outdoor events such as fairs and expositions, and even for drilling the local militia; but the occasional recreational use as a bowling green or a football field (probably for a form of rugby or soccer) was the exception. Recreation for personal enjoyment was simply at odds with the strong, even harsh, work ethic that the Puritans and other abstemious Protestant sects had brought with them from Europe. (As Thomas Macaulay put it: "The Puritan hated bear-baiting, not because it gave pain to the bear, but because it gave pleasure to the spectators.")

This widespread attitude was to change rapidly and drastically, however, as the nineteenth century progressed. As the nation flourished economically and its population became more urbanized, cities and towns continued to grow and to assume broader responsibilities for their citizens. Among those responsibilities of course was the need to provide for public health, safety, and social well-being. Response to this important need took many forms, but one of the first was the improvement of schools and the extension of educational opportunities to the masses. This expansion of public education programs not only produced a more enlightened populace but also introduced the concept of health and physical fitness into the schools. From there it was only a short jump to intramural, and then to intermural, athletics and the eventual spread of active recreation programs to every town and city in the country.

The sports and recreation phenomenon that started with school physical fitness programs was accompanied by a gradual increase in personal leisure time—available not just to the wealthy, but to the common folk as well. By the end of the century, active recreational pursuits had taken on many forms (tennis, golf, baseball, cycling, skating, gymnastics—to mention a few), and a substantial part of America's population was participating with gusto. This transformation from an "all work–no play" society was phenomenal in its impact—a dramatic succession of events characterized by L. H. Weir of the National Recreation Association in 1946: "By slow degrees over a period of more than three centuries, culminating rapidly within the past two generations, the American people have captured an entire new conception of life—a new philosophy of living."[1]

1. L. H. Weir, "Historical Background of Recreation Movement in America," 242.

The tremendous growth in active recreation participation in due course created a commensurately huge demand for places to play and facilities to support the more specialized activities. Obviously, mere open spaces would not suffice in most cases; new types of play areas, or "recreational parks," were needed. The response—first by local governments and then by public schools and private organizations—was quick in coming. Countless play fields of every size and description popped up across the country in a groundswell of public recreational interest that, even after another full century, has yet to subside.

In the wake of this recreation explosion, a whole new industry was quickly created to supply facilities and equipment for an expanding array of leisure activities. This in turn ushered in a new field of professional endeavor, the park and recreation specialists. Clearly, new types of expertise were needed to manage and maintain the play areas and facilities and to conduct the numerous organized programs being offered—not only by municipalities and schools, but in time by private organizations such as the YMCA as well.

In 1885, the American Physical Education Association was founded to promote athletics in the schools and elsewhere, and this was soon followed by creation of the American Association of Park Superintendents, in 1898, to enhance professionalism in that growing area of specialization. Thus it came to be that a nationwide boom in active recreational pursuits resulted in a new concept of "parks" and in the process created a new, important, and lasting area of public service responsibility.

The American Frontier and the Preservation Movement

As important as the active outdoor recreation phenomenon was, it was not by any means the only factor that helped shape the concept of American parks. Equally instrumental was the people's newfound interest in nature and the timely awakening of the post-pioneer generation to the pressing need to preserve some of the country's magnificent scenic wonders. Although their origins and purposes were independent, these two very different, yet complementary, park movements generally paralleled each other, both culminating with impressive and irreversible successes by the end of the nineteenth century.

The idea of preservation did not take hold immediately, of course. American colonists of the seventeenth and eighteenth centuries, faced with the rigors of life in a harsh wilderness environment, no doubt had priorities other than parks on their minds. To them, the great outdoors that we now value so highly would have been viewed not as an opportunity for recreation or aesthetic gratification, but rather as a serious challenge to their very survival. The vast, unbroken forests provided materials for shelter, fuel, and food; beyond that, they were simply an impediment, a formidable obstacle that had to be overcome. Thus preoccupied, the early American pioneer had precious little time for civic-improvement projects and scant inclination toward noble visions for the future. Towns might be made more livable by setting aside a central plaza or a commons, but saving any of the spectacular countryside for posterity would have to wait another century or two and the further advance of civilization.

General acceptance of the idea of wildland preservation may have been a long time in coming, but when the momentum finally did shift in the latter part of the nineteenth century, there was no turning back. The pioneers' westward advance across the continent succeeded in taming a once awesome land, but it also began to raise a new consciousness about the lasting impact of such a drastic transformation of the landscape. Settlement and development were destroying the very resources that had lured the settlers west in the first place. Where once the prairies, forests, and wildlife had seemed inexhaustible, the plow, the axe, and the gun had now taken a devastating toll. And with the consequent loss of the prairie flowers, the virgin timber, and the herds of free-ranging bison, much of America's scenic beauty and charm had vanished as well.

Absent some timely intervention, it would take but a few more decades before virtually all of America's virgin landscapes would be irreparably defaced. If anything could be done to spare some part of this magnificent land, it had to be done quickly. Fortunately, the wake-up call sounded in the nick of time.

Public attitudes did not miraculously change from "development" to "preservation" overnight, but midway through the nineteenth century an increasing number of concerned voices began to be heard, preaching the importance of saving some of the most spectacular western landscapes just because they were beautiful to behold. Among the early travelers through the western territories were prominent explorers such as Jim Bridger, John C. Fremont, and John Wesley Powell, who waxed eloquently about the breathtaking sights they had encountered in the Yellowstone Basin, the Yosemite Valley, the Grand Canyon of the Colorado, and elsewhere. Bridger's early reports of the Yellowstone geysers, in fact, were deemed so incredible they were contemptuously dismissed as "Jim Bridger's lies." Such luminaries as Frederick Olmsted (who had moved to California in 1863), John Muir, and Theodore Roosevelt soon took up the cause, however, validating the earlier accounts and adding momentum to the call for preservation.

Although these word-of-mouth reports succeeded in capturing the public's fancy back East, probably just as influential were the contributions of artists such as the landscapists Albert Bierstadt and Thomas Moran, American Indian painter George Catlin, and a host of others. Their sweeping canvases—long before the age of color photography—conveyed images of wondrous scenes that words alone could never adequately describe. In due course, this combination of word and picture was sufficiently impressive to fire the public imagination and prod the country to action.

And with a newfound enlightenment spreading across the country, the concern for preservation was not limited to the frontier West. Back East, also, a call was being heard from influential citizens to save this or that special area before it was too late. The call was soon followed by action—slowly and randomly at first, but ever accelerating, so that by the end of the century successful preservation projects had been accomplished at every level of government. Most noteworthy of course was the inauguration of America's celebrated national parks program with the designation of Yellowstone National Park in 1872, but state and local governments and various citizens' interest groups were also becoming increasingly active by that time.

As early as the 1820s and 1830s, recognition of the value of mineral springs and hot springs for public recreational and therapeutic use led to the reservation of such resources in the state of Georgia and in the territory of Arkansas—possibly the first instances of state-administered "park" projects in the country. By 1853, the city of New York was busily acquiring land for its Central Park, and, in 1864, the state of California ventured into the "public use, resort and recreation" business on a substantial grant of public domain land in the Yosemite Valley. Back East, in the mid-1870s, a long-held civic dream was being realized through the acquisition of thousands of acres of "forest reserves" in New York's Adirondack and Catskill Mountains. These few examples serve merely to illustrate the steadily growing interest in natural area preservation that pervaded the country over the latter half of the nineteenth century—a strong and persistent interest that bespoke even greater things to come.

Another Awakening: The Need for Historic Preservation

Closely related to natural area preservation, the public's interest in saving historic sites and commemorating past deeds and events also gained great momentum as the nineteenth century progressed. Even before the century began, concern was being expressed over the casual destruction of older buildings, such as Green Spring in Virginia, which in 1796 was reputed to be the oldest occupied house in North America. As the country grew and aged, redevelopment of older sections was of course inevitable. Many quaint structures and places that had been taken for granted were lost before public sentiment could be aroused. Fortunately, the national conscience was sufficiently stirred by midcentury to bring about a number of notable historic preservation successes. Prominent among those was the Hasbrouck House, George Washington's military headquarters in Newburgh, New York, acquired in 1850 and believed to be the first such project in the country to be opened for public visitation.[2] This was soon followed by Mount Vernon, in 1858, and an increasing number of others.

It was the War between the States, however, that really sparked popular interest in preserving historic—or certain to become historic—sites. The almost cathartic desire of the war's survivors, civilian as well as military, to honor their fallen heroes was manifested in a clamor for saving the battlefields and erecting monuments. In both the victorious North and the vanquished South, patriotic fervor required that brave deeds be recognized and dead comrades remembered. Literally thousands of commemorative projects were undertaken, ranging from simple stone markers on a lonely roadside to vast fields of engagement such as Manassas and Gettysburg. Many of these projects became popular visitor attractions and were maintained through a variety of public and quasi-public agencies as forerunners of the park concept as we know it today.

Although the motivations for preserving natural areas (such as Yellowstone) and historic sites (such as Mount Vernon) were somewhat different, the resulting projects were in fact very similar, all sharing common characteristics of planning, acquisition, development, and operation. They also have kindred recreational objectives and mutually dependent functional relationships. It was, therefore, neither inappropriate nor surprising that in many instances they eventually were placed together administratively for public management as "parks." Many park systems today include both types, the natural and the historic, and any distinction between them has been largely ignored or deliberately minimized through years of compatible joint management.

The State Parks—One Part of the Whole

From a hostile wilderness in the seventeenth century, America has been transformed today into a land of abundant amenities, and not the least among these

2. Michael Nadel, "Scenic, Historic, and Natural Sites," 162.

Interest in preserving historic sites paralleled that of natural areas in the late nineteenth century. Here, an 1880s survey team marks the location for a monument commemorating the famous battle of San Jacinto in Texas—a project that would lay the groundwork for a vast state park system yet to come. THE SAN JACINTO MUSEUM OF HISTORY, HOUSTON

are its parks. From the tiniest of tot-lots to the most expansive of wilderness areas, these parks are our national treasures. To use them properly, to obtain from them the full measure of enjoyment, will require a respect and care for them that likely will not be forthcoming without a concomitant understanding of what they are and why they exist.

Toward that end, much has been written about parks in general, and about certain types of parks in particular. America's spectacular national parks, for obvious reasons, have been the subject of countless books and articles, dealing in infinite detail with every conceivable aspect of that ever-popular topic. Similarly, the nation's city parks and playgrounds—because they so directly and intimately affect the multitudes of the urban population—have been scrutinized through every possible medium and to every possible end. For some reason, however, there remains one major category of parks that, as a whole, has received relatively little attention by either scholars or the public at large—certainly far less attention than its importance in the hierarchy of American parks would deserve. That category, of course, is the *state parks* of the United States.

In the following chapters we will take a closer look at the state parks to examine their collective role as a protector of resources and provider of public recreation in America. If we accept the premise that parks are an essential part of our national experience—in a physical, social, and even spiritual sense—then how, where, and by whom those parks are provided should be of more than passing interest to the American people. Where, for instance, do the state parks fit into the overall picture? The state governments are the basic building blocks of our federal system, and therefore are the first line of response to all legitimate public domestic needs. It is only logical, then, that parks should be a state government priority. But are state parks merely duplicative of other park programs, or do they have their own distinct and important role? And if they do, are they filling it adequately and effectively?

Before we can analyze the state parks—or any category of parks, for that matter—in terms of their effectiveness as parks, it is necessary that we first seek to clarify what it is we are talking about. In other words, what on earth is a *park*, anyway? Let's see if we can shed a little helpful light on this ambiguous subject.

2

The Nature of Parks

Parks: The Search for Meaning

America's public park movement was firmly established in the nineteenth century, but the impressive accomplishments of that time could not even hint at the explosive growth that would take place in the century that followed. Over the past five decades, especially, the numbers and forms of spaces that have taken on either the name or the identity of "parks" have increased dramatically in this country, at every level of government. This very proliferation, though, while no doubt producing much public benefit, also generated more than a little confusion about the fundamental purpose being served. Indeed, with so many projects undertaken with such widely variant objectives, one might reasonably wonder just what a park *is,* and what it is really supposed to do.

Ask a dozen people to describe a "park," and you'll likely get twelve different answers. But even if individual perceptions vary, there will surely be almost unanimous agreement that parks are "good." They conjure up pleasant images of peaceful surroundings, of happy children at play, of spectacular natural scenery, of contented seniors relaxing on a bench, of vast open spaces, of welcome patches of green amidst the city concrete, of serious nature lovers plying their various avocations, of stately formal gardens—the variations on the theme are endless.

Through all of this variety, though, where is the common thread? Why are there so many different kinds of parks, and so many programs to provide them? All of them are manifestly popular with the people, so they obviously require no further justification from the user's standpoint. On the other side of the coin, though, the numerous providers of parks, public and private, seem always to be seeking a clearer identity and purpose, sorting out their missions and mandates, trying almost desperately at times to establish their own special niche in a confused mosaic of often overlapping and competing programs.

Logically, the public interest will be best served if all of the various programs are clearly delineated and fully coordinated in order to avoid wasteful duplication and needless competition. To the extent that each program justifies its existence on the assumed public necessity for "parks," it would seem that the starting point for clearing some of the air would be to take a look at, first the term, and then the concept, of a park itself. If it serves no other purpose, such an exercise in semantics should help us better understand how we arrived at the situation we find today.

Parks: A Historical Perspective

The essential idea of parks as specific places to relax, play, and enjoy the surroundings is certainly not a new one, even by Old World standards. Various prototypes have been attributed to the Sumerians, the Babylonians, the Greeks, the Romans, and a number of other ancient civilizations. The eminent professor of landscape architecture Laurie Davidson Cox traced the separate concepts of *recreation* and *preservation* back to Greece and Babylon, respectively. In one case, he cites the *Academia* and the *Lyceum* of Athens as examples of Greek facilities used for public recreation, in the sense of the modern "play field," and adds: "It has always seemed to me that park people were caught napping when they permitted the collegiate world to appropriate the word *'academic,'* which really should be the English word of classic origin to designate the park and recreation idea rather than education." In a second attribution, Cox asserts that what we now think of as "natural area" parks had their origin in a type of "naturalistic" park found among the Babylonians.[1] Various sources—even the Bible (was the Garden of Eden perhaps the very first park?)—have been cited for examples of ancient beautification works such as floral gardens, pathways, fishponds, and the like, as well as for sports and hunting grounds.

While it may be gratifying to project the parks' pedigree back into antiquity, most scholars seem content to use a much later starting point for the evolution of the modern park concept. Even so, various versions of the present English word *park* date back at least to the early Middle Ages. In medieval England a *parke* was

1. Laurie D. Cox, "The Nature of State Parks and Parkways," 51.

an enclosed preserve where "beasts of the chase" could roam freely and be hunted at leisure by the landed gentry. There was no such thing as a public park, of course; the unfortunate serf caught poaching the local lord's game might likely end up with his severed head skewered on the castle gate!

These parks were all owned and used by the wealthy aristocracy, usually with the specific permission of the sovereign. In fact, at one time three express conditions had to be met in order to qualify as a park: a grant from the king, a fence or other barrier to enclose the area, and the game animals—usually deer—for the containment of which the park was established in the first place.[2] From this original meaning, it is easy to see how the term was broadened and extended through the years to other, increasingly divergent uses.

To be sure, the word *park* did not leap directly from the English nobleman's private hunting preserve to anything akin to the parks we know today. But the original use of the term did embrace a number of elements that closely relate to our contemporary ideas of a park: open space, natural landscapes, wildlife, recreational use, defined boundaries, protective management, and so forth. In this sense, it is easy to make the connection between the two concepts, even after a thousand years.

On the other hand, other derivative uses of the same term create problems for us in trying to clarify the meaning and produce a suitable consensus definition of *park.* How can a park be a scenic open space—or even an active playground— and also be a place where we stash our automobiles, store military equipment, or concentrate industrial activities? While a complete etymological examination of this diverse term might be interesting, for the present purpose it seems that we are stuck with the word *park,* as imprecise as its meaning might be, and it is up to us who use the word to define it for each specific application. Thus, after centuries of evolution, the term *park* may be less useful to us today than it was when it was first coined.

When the very term *park*—as opposed to the *concept* of "park"—eventually reached America, it apparently was used in the same sense that it had been in England. Reference was made as early as the eighteenth century to "small parks of deer" in Connecticut. Other related terms were being used at the time, of course— such as the *commons,* the *great ponds* of Massachusetts, the village *greens* and so forth—dating to the mid-1600s. Areas thus labeled were especially common throughout Puritan New England, where the paternalistic concern of town fathers

2. *Oxford English Dictionary,* 2d ed., s.v. "park."

for their constituents seems to have been an influence. Many such areas still exist as public spaces today and could loosely be called "parks," even though such use would not help much in our search for a fully workable definition.

In our review of likely park ancestry we must fast-forward well into the nineteenth century before finding any real claim to legitimacy. The examples from ancient Greece and Babylon are a bit too tenuous, and enclosures for "beasts of the chase" are more likely the progenitors of the present-day wildlife preserve or game management area than of the park per se. The town commons and the city square are at least worthy cousins, if not direct forebears. So, we still have not fully come to grips with this carelessly used term and the elusive concept it purports to represent. It seems obvious that the answer we seek cannot simply be extracted verbatim from historical example or analogy. Rather, it would appear that we must look to more contemporary usage and a deeper analysis of the subject matter to which the term *park* is applied.

Looking for a Common Denominator

In Chapter 1, we traced the development of America's interest in parks along two main, and generally parallel, lines: the *urban playground* movement and the *preservation* (including both natural and historic) movement. While the purpose in each case was clear and distinct, there was no standard or consistent terminology yet in use to denote either similarities or differences between them. Even by the end of the nineteenth century the term *park* itself still was not in common, much less universal, use. It is significant, though, that the principal exponents of these two broad movements did acknowledge some kinship with each other, and this was reflected by the mix of participants in the growing number of organizations and conferences dealing with themes of common interest. One important reason for this, of course, was the rapid increase in parks, especially in the city suburbs, that combined both playground and preservation features.

But we are still left searching for that one essential factor, the common denominator, that will legitimatize our characterizing all of the diverse areas of both playground and preservation movements as "parks." What *do* they all have in common? In the one case, these areas are usually smaller and closer to population centers, rely on spaces and equipment of human design, and are used to a much greater extent for active play and organized sports. In the other, the areas are generally more remote, depend more on a natural or historic setting, and are enjoyed through more passive means. Taking these diverse, yet in some ways

similar, features into consideration, one might very easily conclude that the unifying factor is that they all involve the use of leisure time for fun, fitness, or ful-
fillment of some kind—in a word, *recreation.*

Any park deserving of that distinction will provide recreation, or leisure activities, of some description—but therein lies a major part of the puzzle we are trying to solve. The concept of recreation is itself so broad and inclusive that using
the provision of recreation as the essential criterion for a park would enable just
about any parcel of land to be so called. Such a definition is so general as to be almost useless for any analytical purpose. Thus, to further refine and qualify the
meaning of *parks* requires that we first take a closer look at *recreation.* After all,
the two elements form a mutually dependent relationship, in which recreation is
the end product and parks are the means of delivering it.

Many definitions have been advanced over the years for the term *recreation.*
Almost as many synonyms have been suggested: *amusement, diversion, entertainment, pastime,* and *sport,* to mention the most common. Such elasticity allows
the term to be variously defined or interpreted to suit the purpose at hand. My
personal preference is to take the word literally as it was originally used: to *re-
create,* to create anew, to revive or refresh. Only in that sense can recreation properly be regarded as a true public responsibility, a legitimate role for government
to play. Let the individual seek entertainment or diversion for himself; certainly
there is an endless variety of offerings (the "abounding inanities," as Indiana's
Richard Lieber called them) available through the private commercial sector. Governments, though, out of an appropriate concern for the health and welfare of
their citizens, have a fundamental duty to provide an adequate level of healthful,
wholesome, and socially acceptable leisure-time outlets for the people. That is
both the rationale and the essence of a public recreation program.

The Recreation/Parks Relationship

If, as has been submitted, parks presuppose recreation, then we should be concerned here only with those types of recreation that do indeed depend on parks
for their delivery. Normally, this would be limited to *outdoor* recreation, omitting
the infinite number of customarily indoor activities such as performances, arts
and crafts, many games, and various forms of personal enrichment that might or
might not be called recreation, depending on your point of view. But outdoor
recreation is itself an almost boundless category, a spectrum of activities potentially so broad that one extreme bears little or no resemblance to the other. What

connection is there, for example, between children playing hopscotch in the town square and wilderness hikers exploring the hidden recesses of remote backcountry? The answer, of course, is that both parties are engaging in forms of healthful, wholesome, socially compatible outdoor recreation. But is that enough of a similitude to help us understand the true nature of, and the need for, public parks? Surely, there must be some more precise and insightful way to categorize recreation, and thus the parks necessary for the support of this important activity.

Recreation professionals have been wrestling with the problem of classification for many years. Different classes of recreation would suggest different kinds of parks, but to propose a separate park design for each of the myriad forms of recreation is an obvious impracticality. How, then, should recreation be subdivided and reduced to a manageable and meaningful number of basic, nuclear groupings? Various contrasting dichotomies have been proposed: indoor/outdoor, active/passive, intensive/extensive, participant/spectator, urban/rural, individual/group, organized/casual, and the like. While each of these might serve some useful purpose in specific, limited applications, clearly none of them alone is suitable as a means of breaking down the complex organism of "recreation" into components we can use, in turn, to establish corresponding classes of parks. Some technique that is practical, yet still all-inclusive, is needed.

In the late 1950s, Marion Clawson, a public lands scholar then with the Washington-based think tank Resources for the Future, found himself confronted by a problem. How could he, or anybody, plan intelligently for future recreational land needs when the term *recreation* itself was so broad and amorphous as to be almost meaningless? He acknowledged the distinction between indoor and outdoor recreation, and he proposed that the latter class, which was his immediate concern, be subdivided into three categories: user-oriented, resource-based, and intermediate.[3]

This pioneering work produced probably the most useful method of analyzing recreation—or, more specifically, outdoor recreation—published up to that time. But Clawson based his categories on factors of concern more to the recreation *user* than to the professional recreation *planner*. For instance, his user-oriented category seemed to be determined largely on the basis of convenience and easy accessibility (minimal travel distances), while the quality, and thus consequent visitor appeal, of the resources at the destination site was the main criterion for the resource-based category. The intermediate category was just that: not as

3. Marion Clawson, "The Crisis in Outdoor Recreation."

convenient as user-oriented and not as spectacular as resource-based. No real consideration was given to the specific types of development or kinds of activities provided. As Clawson saw it, most of the national parks would qualify as resource-based and most of the state parks would fall into the intermediate category.

Grappling with a similar problem several years later, in 1962, I attempted to adapt Clawson's three-category system to deal more specifically with the physical factors necessary for the *support* of broad classes of outdoor recreation. In doing so, I found that, to my way of thinking, there really were only two fundamental groupings: one that relied on artificial, man-made facilities, and a second that required one or more elements of the resource base for its support. To describe these two groups, I borrowed Clawson's terminology and called the first *user-oriented* and the second *resource-based*. The terms seemed to fit perfectly. Others, of course, have devised similar methods and used like terminology for breaking down recreation into its basic parts, although there is still no universal agreement as to which recreational activities belong in which category.

The User-Oriented/Resource-Based Distinction

To me, the user-oriented/resource-based breakdown is the most important, even essential, distinction for the professional to make in understanding recreation and the parks on which recreation depends. Before designing any park, the planner must first determine which of these two main classes of recreation—or what mix thereof—the park is to provide. The rest, shall we say, is easy.

But before making the determination of what type of park is to be provided, the planner must have a good understanding of the distinctions, sometimes subtle, between user-oriented and resource-based. In the first case, it is necessary only to have a suitable plot of land, a good design and adequate funding for construction. The park, because it is entirely man-made, may be placed almost anywhere for the convenience of the users (hence the name *user*-oriented). The park might be single-purpose, as a golf course, or it might contain any combination of compatible facilities: ballfields, tennis courts, swimming pools, landscaped grounds, and the like. The only real limitations are space, funding, and intent.

Contrasted with user-oriented outdoor recreation is the other major category, *resource-based*. To be sure, human involvement is necessary also to bring a resource-based park into being, but the recreational activity is dependent not primarily on the man-made adaptations but on the resources themselves (again,

as the name implies). Even with special ventures made possible by human tech-
nology and determination (wave pools and snow machines, for example), man
still cannot truly replicate the outdoor recreational experiences provided by nature. Such activities as surfing and skiing may require the use of man-made
equipment, but the exhilaration comes essentially from the setting itself, and this
is true of the many other forms of resource-based outdoor recreation, from
mountain climbing, wilderness camping, or big game hunting, on one extreme,
to simple picnicking, beachcombing, or trout fishing on the other.

It would, of course, be folly to try to oversimplify something as inherently
complex as recreation. There are bound to be a few odd pegs that just won't fit
into the available holes, and this indeed happens to be the case with the user-
oriented/resource-based dichotomy. First, there is the matter of "historic sites"
and the tremendous amount of recreation they provide through public visitation. On which side of the fence do they (along with closely related "archaeological," or "prehistoric," sites) fall? While it is true that the interest provided by such
sites is attributable to human activity, I have no trouble at all calling the products
of that activity (a pioneer settlement, a battlefield, and so on) "resources" and as-
signing the dependent recreational activity to the resource-based category. I justify this on the grounds that historical and archaeological resources, while not
natural in origin, still are fixed in number and location by virtue of their status as
antiquities. In other words, as much as some of us might like to try, we still can't
go out and create our own authentic Mount Vernon, Gettysburg Battlefield, or
Moundsville. It just won't work. Such irreplaceable, one-of-a-kind properties are
clearly *resources*.

Another gray area that must be dealt with in this analysis is what to do about
those outdoor recreational activities that may be *either* user-oriented *or* resource-
based, depending on their setting or purpose. Such cases tend to suggest a hybrid
category we might call "conditional" outdoor recreation (not to be confused with
Clawson's "intermediate" category, however). This possibility exists with many
activities, such as swimming, which may be in a man-made pool or in a lake or
ocean; walking, which may be around the block just for exercise or along a wood-
land trail in search of nature; or picnicking, which may be a lunch break taken on
a city park bench or as a family outing to the seashore. Because so many typically
resource-based activities may be alternatively enjoyed in a user-oriented setting
(the reverse is true also, but it does not create the same dilemma—a user-oriented
activity will always be that, regardless of where it takes place), it is sometimes
necessary to assign the activity to one category or the other based on the locale

and the type of experience sought by the participant. After all, a cyclist taking his exercise on a remote national park trail may still be an example of user-oriented outdoor recreation simply because it is the physical endeavor, rather than the park's natural scenery, that he seeks.

Parks: Whose Responsibility?

After our digression into the finer points of outdoor recreation anatomy, how do we now relate this knowledge to the matter of parks, particularly state parks? It is abundantly clear that both basic forms of outdoor recreation—user-oriented and resource-based—are important, perhaps vital, to the well-being of the American people. Both forms are in great demand, and it is impossible to say that one is more important than the other. This being the case, it is essential that suitable parks be provided in sufficient numbers at appropriate locations to satisfy the demand for both major classes of outdoor recreation—a gargantuan task that requires a comprehensive approach by all potential outdoor recreation providers.

While all forms of outdoor recreation may be important and each activity may have its own body of enthusiasts, it is nevertheless unfortunately true that many of these activities are not compatible with each other. In a user-oriented park, active forms of play might be very disruptive to users who prefer to sit quietly and contemplate the beauty of landscaped surroundings. Likewise, in a resource-based setting, a powerboat pulling a water-skier might be anathema to the canoer or kayaker. Obviously, parks should be provided for the support of all legitimate types of outdoor recreation, but in many cases they will have to be *different* parks, or at least different areas of a sufficiently large single park. Meeting this important qualification will therefore require not only many parks with great diversity, but also widely differing management philosophies and planning approaches, with specialized programs and staffing. Experience has shown that it is impractical for a single park authority, or even a single level of government, even to attempt a program so vast and comprehensive as to satisfy every one of these wide-ranging needs.

In the early part of the twentieth century, when the separate park preservation and active recreation movements seemed to be converging, it was widely held that they should indeed be merged into one program. Undoubtedly stimulated by the tremendous success of New York's Central Park, many leaders in the field (probably most of whom were already Olmsted disciples) openly advocated the development of parks that would cater to the needs of all potential users. But the Central Park model proved not to be practical in many situations, and it eventually became apparent that a layered program with different areas of specialization was the better approach. That lesson holds true today—even more so with the still increasing diversity and complexity of the outdoor recreation field.

Recognizing that the diversity of outdoor recreation required an equal diversity of responses was a major step forward, but it did not automatically result in a clarification of roles for the potential respondents. The consequent scramble by different governmental and private entities to secure their own special places in the hierarchy of outdoor recreation supply served not to clarify but to further confuse the matter. In one extreme case it was reported that "in one single community we have as many as 21 different agencies, created by law and supported by the people's money, for the handling of parks and public recreation."[4] The lack of any clear division of responsibility among the several levels of government was just as bad. The obvious inefficiency in the situation was soon recognized, and the call went out at least as early as the 1924 White House–sponsored National Conference on Outdoor Recreation (more about this in Chapter 6) for a coordinated national policy in this field of public service.

Even today, after diligent efforts by such formal task groups as the Outdoor Recreation Resources Review Commission in the 1950s and the President's Commission on Americans Outdoors in the 1980s, we still do not have a universally accepted, practical blueprint to guide the nation's combined outdoor recreation programs. But that is grist for another chapter; what is important here is to note that the problem was at least recognized fairly early, and that recognition did succeed in influencing to some degree the directions various governmental outdoor recreation programs took for the final three-fourths of the twentieth century. In time, a practical accommodation came about—perhaps as much by chance as by design—that produced a more or less identifiable tradition for each of the principal levels of government. Those traditions, although not totally distinct nor mutually exclusive, have evolved essentially along the lines of the user-oriented/resource-based outdoor recreation dichotomy.

User-oriented outdoor recreation, by its very nature, should be placed conveniently close to the users, typically in or around centers of population. An individual seeking just a few hours of play will not want to travel any great distance to the tennis court, golf course, swimming pool, or whatever. Parks designed for such activities can, and frequently do, utilize relatively small spaces handily located for short-time, often impromptu participation. Clearly, this kind of outdoor recreation

---

4. "Introduction and Summary," in National Conference on Outdoor Recreation, *Proceedings of the National Conference on Outdoor Recreation,* 2.

is best suited for programs at the local level, and the municipal and county governments have responded admirably. No city or town in America of any appreciable size is without a parks and recreation program of some sort, and they are all heavily weighted toward the user-oriented category. Some of them, as do many of the counties, have expanded programs that offer resource-based recreational activities as well, but boundary restrictions and the limited resource base available have militated against large-scale ventures of that type.

In contrast with the user-oriented type, resource-based outdoor recreation cannot be provided at just any handy location, and usually not on smaller parcels of land. Rather, it must be located with the supporting resources, wherever they may be found. Often these resources will be extensive, as a mountain range or a wild river system, and desirably they will contain spectacular scenery and unusual natural or historic features. Considering these requirements, resource-based outdoor recreation areas, or parks, will almost always be found at some distance from their potential users, and they will probably range from many hundreds to many thousands of acres in size. These two factors, combined with the specialized management and visitor programs normally associated with large, remote natural areas, practically necessitate that the federal and state governments assume primary responsibility for resource-based outdoor recreation. And, interestingly, the exacting management required to maintain the often delicate physical properties of these areas tends to preclude or at least discourage the provision of user-oriented outdoor recreation, with its heavy emphasis on manmade facilities and intensive use. Thus the line of responsibility for national and state parks is fairly cleanly drawn, on the opposite end of the spectrum from city and county programs.

But while both the national parks and the state parks may be devoted principally to serving resource-based outdoor recreation needs, they differ in one very major respect—flexibility. Although the national parks are aimed at a nationwide clientele, they are not numerous enough or appropriately distributed to serve much of the country's population except as major vacation destinations, typically involving a commitment of considerable time and money on the visitor's part. From a practical standpoint, this places the Yellowstones, Yosemites, and Grand Canyons beyond the reach of much of America. State parks, on the other hand—many of them equal in quality to their national counterparts—are much more numerous and widely distributed, and thus are readily accessible to people everywhere, usually on a single day's outing. Filling this void and ensuring the practical availability of resource-based recreational opportunities to every American is the essential purpose of every state park program.

Outdoor recreation—the provision of which is the essential purpose of every public park—takes many forms. State parks are primarily concerned with the preservation of areas that support *resource-based* recreation, such as camping in New Hampshire's scenic Crawford Notch State Park. NEW HAMPSHIRE STATE PARKS

Although we have grouped the national and state parks together as having similar responsibilities in the supply of public outdoor recreation, that does not mean that they necessarily have identical missions. Far from it. There are substantial differences between the states and the United States in scope and capabilities, of course, but the real reason they cannot be directly compared is because the fifty individual states themselves are too diverse in every way. While acceptance of some responsibility for providing resource-based outdoor recreation for its citizens may establish a basic similarity for the fifty state park programs, still each state, for reasons it has deemed entirely sufficient, has chosen to define its mission and pursue its program in its own way.

In later chapters, we will take a look at some of the similarities and differences among the states and how these factors have influenced the direction state park programs have taken.

A Natural Progression: From Parks to Park Systems

It would be convenient, if erroneous, to look at all of the thousands of public parks in America today and imagine that they had all neatly come into existence and found their exact places with the aid of some preconceived master plan. In actuality, though, this impressive assemblage of parks came about more by happenstance than by design. Up until the middle twentieth century, especially, most of the nation's parks were selected, acquired, and developed on a largely individual basis, with little, if any, systematic guidance. This certainly was not all bad, of course—not by a long shot. If highly motivated citizens, interest groups, and government leaders had not acted when they did to take advantage of opportunities as they arose, we would have far fewer parks to enjoy today.

By degrees, however, various park-related professions evolved, and the need for planning, coordination, and balance—not only in the acquisition of new park sites, but also in the management of existing ones—was clearly recognized. With this important recognition, the random approach of the past gave way to a new concept, that of the integrated park *system*. This was an extremely important turning point that marked the coming of age of America's public park movement.

It was almost a half-century after the establishment of the first national park before Congress passed legislation to create the National Park Service and provide for systematic management of the sixteen park properties already on hand. So it was, for the most part, with the fifty state park programs that came into being over the course of almost a century, from the 1880s to 1970. Many of them began in the early years of the park movement when there was little experience and few precedents to guide them; they were the real pioneers. Others joined the ranks over ensuing decades, often striking out in new directions rather than following in the paths already established. The last states to come in had the advantage of a highly evolved parks profession and many years of others' accumulated experience on which to draw, and thus were able more quickly to define their missions and pursue their goals than had been the case with their predecessors.

The fact remains, however, that today's state park systems, like the national park system, started with random, unrelated efforts across the country to acquire and preserve exceptional properties for public use and enjoyment. Each of these efforts is an important part of our story, and a brief look at a selected few of them will serve to provide historical perspective for our examination of America's state park movement.

3

The States Begin to Stir
State Park Initiatives in the Nineteenth Century

The Stage Is Set

The United States at the middle of the nineteenth century was still a very young nation. Although its territorial limits had essentially been reached (only Alaska and Hawaii were missing), still only thirty-one states had been formally established. Most of the vast area west of the Mississippi River was being administered as largely unsettled territories. Back East, much of the nation was preoccupied with the growing schism over slavery and states' rights, but even such dire domestic problems did not dampen the enthusiasm for territorial expansion and development in the farther reaches of the continent. America seemed bound and determined to fulfill its "manifest destiny."

That destiny, of course, did not at the time envision the preservation of any of America's abundant land resources as public parks. There was no precedent for such an idea anywhere in the world, and as yet no recognition of a need to save anything—especially if doing so might stand in the way of total subjugation of the beckoning frontier.

Still, almost in contravention of the times, serendipitous exceptions began to occur here and there around the country. The states and territories were increasingly being confronted with situations dealing with public land disposition that called for innovative solutions. As luck would have it, sometimes the best solution was actually (and perhaps surprisingly) determined to be retention of the property for public use. From such random beginnings, the long and desultory course of an incipient state park movement was set slowly in motion.

Small Beginnings

By the early 1820s, travelers through central Georgia were already well aware of the supposedly healing qualities of certain springs in the Indian territory that was later to become Butts County. The wide popularity of its mineral waters for drinking and bathing prompted the state to include this area—by then known as Indian Springs—in a treaty negotiated with certain factions of the Creek Indians in 1825. Under this treaty, Creek Chief William McIntosh (his father was a Scotsman) personally ceded to the state a thousand acres around the spring, thus conveying it into general public ownership.

Although the state proceeded to offer most of the McIntosh tract for public sale, it specifically provided by law that ten acres including the springs be retained for public use. Soon thereafter, the state legislature passed another act authorizing a private entrepreneur to "erect a bath house on [the retained site], being the reserve near the Indian Spring, for the use of the public, provided he shall permit any individual to use the same without charge." Both the retention of the springs in public ownership and the provision for continuing public use (without charge, yet) offer clear evidence of the state's intent to establish a special status for this popular recreational resource. The Indian Springs property—now greatly expanded and improved—has continued in public ownership and use to this day, providing the basis for Georgia's claim of having the "oldest state park in the nation." Whether or not it was the first "state park" can be argued, but Indian Springs undeniably stands out as one of the earliest examples of a state acting to preserve a piece of land specifically for public recreational use.

Mineral springs and hot springs have long been recognized as having exceptional interest and potential for public recreational purposes. Another case in point is the salt springs and the hot springs of the Arkansas Territory, which early on caught the fancy of various promoters and entrepreneurs. With covetous eyes being cast on these unusual resources (long before the more spectacular thermal features of the Yellowstone basin were widely known), the United States Congress was moved, in April 1832, to enact legislation for their interim preservation and orderly disposition. This act has been cited as "the beginning of federal assistance to states for outdoor recreation," but, if it was so, much of that significance must be inferred. There was no actual mention of an "outdoor recreation" purpose.[1]

In fact, the act provided that all of the salt springs—the ones already known

---

1. Phillip O. Foss, "Recreation," 225.

By the time these turn-of-the-twentieth-century ladies refreshed themselves with a cool drink at Georgia's Indian Springs, this popular site (an eventual state park) already had been a public recreation area for some seventy-five years. GEORGIA DEPARTMENT OF NATURAL RESOURCES

and those yet to be discovered—would be withdrawn from disposition and made available to the Territory of Arkansas to be rented or leased for private use for periods of not more than five years. Although all revenues from such rentals were earmarked for road construction and improvement in the territory, it is assumed that the uses made of the springs by the renters would have served primarily health and recreation purposes. Thus, the Territory of Arkansas presumably became an indirect provider of outdoor recreation areas for its people, in much the same way that some states today lease out public park areas for private management.

As a related point of interest, the same act that turned the *salt* springs over to the Territory of Arkansas also reserved all of the *hot* springs in the territory for later disposition by the United States. In 1880, the most famous of those hot springs—forty-seven in all—were incorporated into a park, and formally designated as *Hot Springs National Park* in 1921. In this respect, the act of 1832 may be seen not only as a vehicle for assisting the Arkansas Territory in developing its recreation potential, but also as a precursor of America's national park system.

Specific examples of state action to set aside parklike properties for public use prior to the late nineteenth century are regrettably few. More common were the successes in preserving historic sites, although relatively few of those early projects were conceived as or ever became part of a formal state park system. There were notable exceptions, of course, such as the Washington Headquarters State Historic Site in New York, acquired in 1850, and the San Jacinto Battleground State Historic Site in Texas, established in 1883. In the final decades of the century, though, examples of a *true* state park—those embodying the elements of both large-scale resource preservation and planned outdoor recreational use— gradually emerged, starting in California and eventually spreading to a handful of other states. Interestingly, the one man most responsible for lighting this spark was none other than the illustrious Frederick Law Olmsted himself.

Yosemite Valley: California's Noble Experiment

Olmsted had come to California in 1863 to manage the Mariposa Estate, a huge private landholding owned in part by the noted explorer John C. Fremont. He brought with him of course the reputation as probably the country's foremost park planner, earned largely through his innovative work on New York City's famous Central Park. Surrounded by the awe-inspiring scenery that abounded in California's Yosemite Valley, Olmsted surely must have felt that he had found heaven on earth—"the greatest glory of nature," he exclaimed. He lost no time in allying himself with other prominent individuals in the area who saw the vast potential of this unique resource and shared his enthusiasm for its preservation. It was an interesting and diverse alliance. In addition to Olmsted and other like-minded preservationists, the coalition of supporters of a state-managed park also included representatives of road-building and railroad companies and other commercial enterprises whose interest lay primarily in the prospects for a booming tourism business in the area.

Considering the motley mix of protagonists in the Yosemite drama, it is indeed remarkable that their immediate goal was realized so quickly and so successfully. The first step, of course—and it was a major one—was to seek a transfer of the desired property from the federal government, which held it as part of the public domain. It proved to be remarkably easy, however. On June 30, 1864, the United States Congress, almost without comment, passed an unprecedented piece of legislation entitled "An Act authorizing a grant to the State of California of the Yosemite Valley, and of the land embracing the Mariposa Big Tree Grove." The boundaries of the authorized grant were very loosely defined, but it has been estimated that they embraced some twenty thousand acres—a significant chunk of real estate.

This act was important in several major respects. Although it did not use the term *park* itself, it did specify that the subject property "shall be held for public use, resort and recreation," and that it "shall be inalienable for all time"—both relatively new ideas in such a context. Further, the act provided that "all incomes derived from leases of privileges [were] to be expended in the *preservation and improvement of the property* [my emphasis], or the roads leading thereto"—also a very modern concept. It is interesting, too, that the act took the trouble to specify that the property was "to be managed by the Governor of the State *with eight other commissioners* [my emphasis], to be appointed by the Executive of California." Clearly, Congress—or, more likely, the actual author of the bill—foresaw a need to place management responsibility with a collegial executive rather than entrust it to any one individual, even the governor.

The Yosemite experience with state-managed property is generally regarded as the creation of America's first state park. In most respects it is deserving of that recognition, but as an experiment it proved to be less than a glowing success. In the end, it was re-ceded to the United States in 1905 and became part of the Yosemite National Park. But its forty years under state control provides an interesting study in the difficulties and challenges of pioneering such a new field of public endeavor as park management.

The state of California actually assumed management responsibility for the Yosemite property in 1866, and the governor quickly appointed the required eight-person commission to oversee it. Olmsted was named chairman of the commission, but he soon left to return to his landscape architecture practice back East. With two thousand dollars in start-up funds provided by the legislature, the commission proceeded to hire a manager, survey the park boundaries, and evict the few settlers in the valley—whose claims were deemed to be invalid because the area they were in had never been opened to homesteading. It seemed that the new "state park" was off to a good start.

In spite of a well-intentioned manager and, by all accounts, a reasonably competent board of commissioners, however, the situation at Yosemite quickly deteriorated and was never to recover under state management. Whereas there had been an original expectation that the park would draw enough visitors to make it financially self-supporting, that quickly proved not to be the case. The valley was a long way from the nearest railhead, at Stockton, and its formidable topography made access by any means extremely difficult. The visitors did not come, and

funding support from the state soon dwindled to nothing. Faced with a mounting dilemma, the commissioners turned to a variety of strictly nonpark commercial ventures to make ends meet. As historian John Ise put it: "The commissioners
turned the Valley into a farm, allowed some of the land to be cultivated or fenced
for pasturage, permitted the cutting of trees, dammed Mirror Lake for irrigation,
with little regard for the tourists or the preservation of the scenic values of the
Valley."[2] Contemporary critics—many reacting from their own personal obser-
vations—were even more harsh. In spite of sporadic efforts by the state of California to deal with the mounting management problems—spending a total of
almost a half-million dollars in the process—the situation only got worse, leading eventually to a general consensus that the whole undertaking was simply beyond the means and capabilities of the young state at that time.

As the state of California struggled with management of the Yosemite Valley,
growing interest in preserving the surrounding "high country" prompted the
U.S. Congress to take further action in 1890. In that year, almost two decades
after the creation of the first national park at Yellowstone, three additional areas
were set aside for special protection, all in the vicinity of the already existing
"state park." These three areas—later to be identified as "Sequoia," "Yosemite,"
and "General Grant"—were eventually folded into the one we now call Yosemite
National Park. The timing of the congressional action was significant, because it
introduced a direct federal land management role into the same locale where the
state was already in business. According to Ise, this resulted in friction between
the two governments and created new problems for the state—which controlled
the more habitable lands in the valley but lacked the means (and possibly the determination) to carry out an effective management program.[3] The straws were
beginning to accumulate on the camel's back, and critics of the state's efforts in
the Yosemite Valley grew more vociferous as well as numerous.

Concerns over the state's alleged mismanagement inevitably reached the nation's capital. In 1891 an investigation ordered by Secretary of the Interior John
W. Noble produced a long list of serious problems and concluded, "these acts of
spoliation and trespass have been permitted for a number of years, and seem to
have become a part of the settled policy of the [state's] management."[4] Other
prominent voices chimed in, most notably that of the eminent naturalist John

2. John Ise, *Our National Park Policy: A Critical History,* 71.
3. Ibid., 72.
4. Ibid., 73.

Muir, who had been advocating re-cession of the valley to the federal government practically since he arrived in the area in 1868. Although there was widely divided opinion among Californians as to whether the state should give up the property, the inescapable financial demands of park management combined with ramifying public relations problems eventually forced a decision. In early 1905, the California legislature voted to re-cede the property to the United States. The re-cession was accepted the following year, and the Yosemite Valley, after four decades of state management, was immediately absorbed into the surrounding national park.

Judging it as a single, isolated case, California's initial venture into the "state park" business would have to be deemed an obvious failure. Yet seen as a harbinger of a nationwide movement soon to emerge, it must be viewed in a far more favorable light. Bear in mind that in its scope and in its avowed preservation purpose the Yosemite Valley undertaking was truly precedent-setting. Not only were there no real state parks in 1864, there were no national parks, either. California's experiment pioneered a new field of public land management and provided valuable lessons—positive as well as negative—for other park advocates who would soon follow. The many problems faced by the state, along with its successes and failures in dealing with them, were widely recognized and fully documented. Taken as a whole, that forty-year experience embraced just about every aspect of park planning, administration, and management, and the lessons learned—or that should have been learned—could have filled a classic textbook on the subject. In that respect alone, California's Yosemite Valley "park" experience made a truly valuable contribution; but the mere fact that such a nobly conceived and logistically challenging project was undertaken at all in 1864 is an even greater acknowledgment of the state's vision and leadership in this field.

In the Yosemite Aftermath

It would be unrealistic to assume that any one experience—no matter how noteworthy—would have had any immediate impact on other states taking on the challenge of park management in the late nineteenth century. In such an inchoate field of endeavor, it seemed that all of the pioneers, at every level, were destined to repeat many of the same mistakes. Not long after Congress put California tentatively in the park business with the cession of the Yosemite Valley, it proceeded with the establishment, in 1872, of the first national park in the Yellowstone region of the Wyoming Territory. Unfortunately, the federal government initially fared little better than California had in protecting and managing its new "park."

Yellowstone was a vast area in a remote part of the country, with unmarked boundaries and wide-open opportunities for trespass, poaching, highway robbery, and any number of other criminal acts. Clearly, Congress and federal authorities did not understand or anticipate the needs of effective park management any more than had the state of California before. Hardly any funds were appropriated, and only a handful of men could be hired to police the area. It seemed that Yellowstone was destined to be a national park more in name than in fact. Ironically, it was this deplorable situation with America's first national park that set the stage for another state (actually, a territory) to try its hand at park management.

Driven by desperation, Secretary of the Interior Henry M. Teller wrote to the governor of Wyoming in 1883, asking for the territory's help in dealing with the rampant lawlessness in the Yellowstone park. Taking on any such responsibilities was probably the furthest thing from the Wyoming legislature's mind at that time, but it passed a law the next year with a small appropriation to create a number of law enforcement and judicial positions to deal with the worst problem areas. Unfortunately, in its subsequent execution, the whole arrangement seemed to be motivated more by greed on the part of the individual officials (who were compensated by a system of fees) than by any idea of public service. Flagrant abuses by both the constables in the field and the justices of the peace that assessed the fines soon discredited the entire territorial effort. As described by one account:

> The common verdict, as gathered from official reports and other sources, is that the body of police, styled assistant superintendents, were not only inefficient, but positively corrupt. They were, for the most part, creatures of political favoritism, and were totally unused to the service required of them. Commissioned as guardians of the rarest natural wonders on the globe, they not infrequently made merchandise of the treasures which they were appointed to preserve. Under their surveillance, vandalism was practically unchecked; and the slaughter of game was carried on for private profit almost in sight of the superintendent's quarters.[5]

After only two years of questionable service, the Territory of Wyoming bowed out of the park protection business in 1886, when, apparently reacting to the

5. Ibid., 31.

growing criticism of its performance, the territorial legislature repealed its earlier law. Ironically, this abrupt action had unexpected and unintended consequences. As noted by Ise, "The effect of the withdrawal of the Wyoming guardians was, however, to advertise the fact that the park was entirely without protection, and conditions became even worse than they had been before."[6] The federal government, of course, proceeded to take other measures for the protection of Yellowstone, and Wyoming—soon to be a state—would wait another decade before venturing again into the public park arena.

The less-than-satisfactory experiences with state management of public domain lands (which, in view of the fact that the federal government could not, or would not, do any better, should not be regarded as an exclusive indictment of state capabilities) apparently did not discourage other states from seeking federal land grants for park-related purposes. In the mid-1870s a proposal to place Mackinac Island, in Michigan, under state control came before Congress but was not approved, presumably because of the controversy then brewing over California's handling of the Yosemite Valley. Instead, it was made a national park in 1875, only to be reconsidered more favorably for state management two decades later (as we will see).

Similar overtures were made by state "park" advocates in Colorado (for Royal Arch, Garden of the Gods, and Pagosa Springs), Oregon (for Crater Lake), and possibly others, all unsuccessfully. Ise noted: "There was a fairly widespread notion that federal lands in any given state should at least be handled in accordance with the wishes of that state, if not given to the state," and further speculated that:

> The states wanted these state parks because they had no conception of the expense that would be involved in administering them, believed that they would be self-supporting or even assets to the state. When in later years they saw that national parks and state parks could not be self-supporting they turned to a demand that scenic areas be set up as national parks, so that the federal government would pay the expenses.[7]

While this may well be an accurate assessment of the situation existing at the time, it should not be attributed simply to greedy motivation on the part of the states. The Yosemite Valley undertaking—the first of its kind—was clearly motivated at its conception by a sincere desire to preserve a truly spectacular natural

6. Ibid., 31–32.
7. Ibid., 50.

area, and it is very likely that there was at least some element of purely preserva-
tionist ardor behind most of the other projects as well.

Back East: Different Approaches

At the same time that random attention was being focused on possibilities for
state use of public domain lands in the West, visionaries back East were also getting bright ideas of their own. In the older parts of the country, however, the situation was quite different. While there still were many scenic properties well
suited for park use, almost all of the land was by then held in private ownership.
Rather than simply petitioning Congress for a choice tract of land, if a state wanted
to create a park, it would more likely have to acquire the site through other, usually complicated and expensive, means. There was precious little money available
for park acquisition in those days, and very few precedents for actually purchasing park lands anyway. As often as not, enthusiastic park advocates had to pursue
their causes through other devices, such as private donations and innovative uses
of the state's police powers. Still, if a spectacular piece of property was deemed
sufficiently worth saving, a group of persistent and imaginative champions could
usually find a way.

Notwithstanding the determination and resourcefulness of the growing number of zealous park advocates, however, it clearly was easier to pursue such a goal
if at least some of the desired property was already in public ownership and not
otherwise committed. This truism no doubt contributed to the birth of the state
park idea in the state of Wisconsin. There was still a good bit of state-owned land
in northern Wisconsin in 1878, when the legislature, for reasons that are not entirely clear, passed an act designating a half-million-acre tract as "The State Park"
(certainly an early, if not actually the first, statutory use of that term). The subject
lands were "hereby dedicated and set apart for a state park, and no such lands not
now sold or contracted to be sold shall hereafter be sold, nor shall any privilege,
license or authority be given to any person or persons whomsoever, to cut down
or destroy any timber growing on such lands." While some had their doubts, the
act was applauded by one Madison newspaper, which called the proposed park
"one of the wildest and most beautiful spots in the lake region . . . and if preserved in its natural perfection will be one of the finest bequests the present
could possibly hand down to coming generations."[8]

8. George Rogers, "The Might-Have-Been State Park," 24.

As it turned out, however, just over fifty thousand acres, or one-tenth, of the huge dedicated area (three-fourths the size of Rhode Island) was actually owned by the state. Further, there was very little population in that remote part of Wisconsin, and no apparent organized public support for the park project. Even those responsible for implementing the act were dubious that the remaining property could ever be acquired, especially in the face of opposition from the private timber interests that were the dominant economic force in that part of the state.

Not much is known about any management or public use of "The State Park" after its designation, but in 1897, after only nineteen years, the legislature effectively abolished the "park" and authorized the sale of most of the state-owned land for timber purposes. This action led to charges at the time that the sale had been politically engineered to "benefit friends in the lumber industry." A much later critic found the whole project to be suspect, and accused "The State Park" of being nothing but a "clever holding action to keep timber off the market until a later and more opportune time."[9] Whatever the truth, Wisconsin still points to "The State Park" episode as the beginning of its state park movement. It would be only a few years later that Wisconsin would emphatically demonstrate its foresight and leadership in the state parks field with a series of other trendsetting developments.

New York Weighs In: Niagara Falls

Meanwhile, New York State, always in the vanguard of the scenic preservation movement, was also making important state park history. Official concern over the loss of New York's natural landscape had surfaced as early as 1820, when Governor DeWitt Clinton, in a message to the state legislature, urged retention of the Adirondacks in state ownership. Clinton's interest was primarily in preservation of the watershed rather than in parks per se, but his call for action foreshadowed a broader and more urgent public interest to come. Legislation to preserve the Adirondacks would, unfortunately, have to wait another sixty years, and during that time an even more famous—and imminently endangered—New York scenic treasure was attracting the attention of the state's preservationists: the incomparable Niagara Falls.

By mid-nineteenth century, Niagara Falls was fast becoming a major tourist attraction, and its increasing popularity was accompanied by rampant com-

9. Judith Joy Borke, "Wisconsin's State Park System, 1878–1994: An Oral History," 7.

mercialism. The sheer number of commercial establishments was obstructing the best views of the falls and changing the character of the once-serene area. Growing concern over the situation resulted in calls for remedial action as early as 1867. The "Free Niagara Movement," a carefully orchestrated campaign to save the falls, enlisting the aid of many of the state's prominent citizens (Olmsted, again, was one), succeeded in convincing a substantial majority of the legislature in 1883 to pass an act that created the Niagara Reservation. Governor Grover Cleveland signed the act into law and quickly appointed the "Commissioners of the State Reservation at Niagara," whose charge was for the "selection, location and appropriation of certain lands . . . to preserve the scenery of the Falls of the Niagara."[10]

The Niagara Reservation was not yet a "done deal," however. Lengthy litigation instituted by many of the affected private property owners around the falls delayed further progress. The crux of the dispute apparently was the amount of compensation the owners would receive for their holdings, which, they contended, were made eminently more valuable because of a "patent of nobility" that the falls themselves imparted. The state's commissioners of appraisal seemed to agree that the lands did indeed enjoy that special quality, but they held that "the rushing water, the spray, the rainbow and the roar of the cataract were 'not subject to human proprietorship.'"[11] With the litigation finally settled, the legislature floated a precedent-setting million-dollar bond issue to purchase the property. The Niagara Reservation State Park, as it is now known, was officially dedicated on July 15, 1885, and remains as the oldest natural area state park continuously in operation to this day.

Ironically, some time after it rescued Niagara Falls from all of its unwanted commercial attention, the state decided to go further and enhance the breathtaking natural spectacle by adding colored lights to illuminate the falls. Criticism of this gaudy excess by Princess Kikuko of Japan, the emperor's sister-in-law, on a visit in 1931, prompted the National Conference on State Parks to adopt a resolution at its meeting that year expressing disapproval of New York's attempts to "gild the lily."[12]

---

10. It is interesting to note that the same legislature also took action to prohibit further state land sales in the Adirondacks, laying the groundwork for eventual establishment of a park— actually, a "forest preserve"—in the Adirondack and Catskill Mountains.

11. *Fifty Years: New York State Parks* [6].

12. National Conference on State Parks, minutes of the board of trustees, May 27, 1931, in Minutes of Policy Making Bodies, series 1 and 2, box 1, National Recreation and Park Association Library, Ashburn, Va. (hereinafter referred to as NRPA Library).

The urgent need to protect its famous Niagara Falls (shown here in 1905) motivated New York to establish the first fully successful state park in America, in 1885. NEW YORK STATE OFFICE OF PARKS, RECREATION AND HISTORIC PRESERVATION

The Park Idea Spreads

While Niagara may have been the *first* state park, it did not remain long as the *only* state park. In the final decade of the nineteenth century, at least a half dozen other states took concrete steps toward establishing their first "natural area" parks. As mentioned earlier, the Texas legislature had set aside the famous San Jacinto battle site, near present-day Houston, in 1883, and it remains as the first of that state's impressive inventory of park properties; but the motivation in that case was clearly a desire to commemorate an important historic event (Sam Houston's defeat of Santa Anna in 1836, which won for Texas its independence from Mexico). Other states, though, principally in the Northeast and the Midwest, were picking up on the examples provided by California and New York and launching their own efforts to preserve special places of exceptional natural beauty.

Minnesota weighed in early. In name, anyway, its first "state park" dates back to March 1885, when the legislature passed a law authorizing the creation of a "State Park at Minnehaha Falls." Actually, Minnesotans had been kicking around the idea of establishing such a park at least since 1867, but— just as with the case of New York's Niagara—it required some time to mobilize supporters and convince the government to act. Interestingly, the establishment of the Yellowstone National Park in 1872 was cited in support of the cause. "Is not there just as good reason for the state to own and preserve the beautiful Falls of Minnehaha and adjacent grounds as for the national government to retain ownership of and preserve Yellowstone park?" asked one of the advocates.[13] In the final analysis, the city of Minneapolis stepped in to help acquire a 173-acre site and assume management responsibility for the "Minnehaha State Park."

But a true Minnesota state park was not far in the offing. After another tentative venture in 1889, involving a historic memorial site known as "Camp Release" (from the release of captives after the Dakota Indian War of 1862), the state of Minnesota staked a solid claim as "number two" with the authorization of its renowned Itasca State Park in 1891. In the spring of that year, the Minnesota legislature, reacting to a growing public clamor, narrowly passed a bill providing for establishment of a thirty-five-square-mile park at Lake Itasca, the headwaters of the Mississippi River. It was the culmination of a relatively brief, but nonetheless intensive, campaign that no doubt had drawn much of its inspiration and guidance from the Minnehaha Falls experience of a few years prior. "Why cannot we," one prominent supporter asked in a letter to the St. Paul newspaper, "have a real wild park, one far from the hum and bustle of large cities, like the national park of the Yellowstone, and that [one] once proposed, I believe, for the Adirondack region in New York?"[14] These and similar sentiments were echoed by other influential voices, even adding the practical argument that protecting the river's source would help ensure the flow of water that powered the area's mills (an argument apparently borrowed from New York, where it had been propounded in support of preserving the Adirondacks as the headwaters of the Hudson River).

In a very real sense, Itasca was envisioned more as a true state park (again, my term) than was Niagara Falls. Whereas Niagara dealt primarily with the preservation of a single natural feature (albeit a most spectacular one!), in scale and purpose Itasca was more like California's Yosemite, seeking to preserve a large and diverse area capable of supporting a range of compatible uses—scientific and educational as well as recreational. Even so, as nobly conceived as it was, Itasca was opposed by commercial timber interests and might well have suffered the fate of

13. Roy W. Meyer, *Everyone's Country Estate*, 2.
14. Ibid., 5.

Wisconsin's "State Park," except for the determination and perseverance of a few dedicated individuals.

One such individual was Jacob V. Brower, who not only had played a key role in getting the park authorized, but also was appointed the state's first park commissioner that same year, 1891. Brower worked hard over the next several years, always with limited and undependable means, to acquire the needed lands from the various owners. Fortunately, the state already owned a small amount, and some that was still in federal ownership was conveyed by Congressional act the following year; but the majority was held by private railroads and lumber companies.

Although Brower was replaced as park commissioner in 1895—the victim of a change of administrations—he still continued his strenuous efforts on behalf of the park until his death ten years later. More than sixteen thousand acres had been acquired by that time, but about half of the proposed park was still in private ownership. Apparently Brower had been encouraged by the progress during his lifetime, though, leading him to comment: "The park will soon contain the only tract of standing pine within the borders of the state and this forest reservation will become easily accessible and of great value as a public resort." The thriving

An early-twentieth-century postcard shows off some of the typical facilities at Minnesota's famed Itasca State Park, established in 1891, which preserves the headwaters of the Mississippi River. MINNESOTA DEPARTMENT OF NATURAL RESOURCES

33,000-acre Itasca State Park is today ample testimony to the accuracy of Brower's prediction. Fortunately, Brower's vision had been kept alive by other Itasca champions, including Mary Gibbs, who was appointed superintendent of the park in 1903—the first woman to hold such a position in either a state or a national park.

It is not surprising that the idea of preserving open space would take hold early in America's populous and rapidly industrializing Northeast. With the possible exception of northern New England, most of this region was rapidly feeling the pinch of continuing growth and development well before the turn of the twentieth century. The leadership position assumed by the state of New York in both urban and rural park development has already been noted, but other states in the area were also stirring.

New Hampshire, for example, had become so concerned about the rapid depletion of its forestlands that it created a state forestry commission in 1881 to deal with the problem. In its first report, issued in 1885, the commission acknowledged that "Our mountains and hills, our lakes and streams, our pure air and clear waters, our green hills and waving forests, are a constant attraction which grows stronger and extends farther year after year," and went on to describe and deplore the grave threat the state's growing tourism industry faced from the degradation of its countrysides.[15] The farsighted work of this commission essentially established the justification for and started the state thinking about the need for state parks. A modest beginning was made in 1891 with acceptance of a small parcel of donated land atop Pack Monadnock, a scenic mountain vantage point. That modest acquisition, now Miller State Park, paved the way for more spectacular projects soon to follow.

Forest preservation, and not recreation per se, proved to be the impetus for state park initiatives in a number of states. Pennsylvania provides another classic example. There, concern over deplorable forestry practices and disappearing woodlands had prompted the organization of the Pennsylvania Forestry Association in 1886, and the legislature followed with creation of a state forestry commission in 1893. Interest in preserving forests for economic reasons inevitably sparked a collateral interest in saving natural areas just for their scenic qualities alone. Proposals for "state parks" soon began to surface.

Reacting to one such proposal, a Philadelphia newspaper commented, also in 1893, that "while the establishment of a state park would only indirectly advance the [forestry] movement, it is a timely plan, and, sooner or later, its success will

15. Martha Carlson, "Born of Fire and Trespass," 2.

be considered by all of our states where settlement is rapidly and surely leveling the forests and doing away with scenes of natural beauty."[16] The "state park" site in question was Valley Forge, the site of the Continental army's storied encampment during the bitter winter of 1777-1778. Happily, the legislature passed the bill under consideration in 1893, authorizing the acquisition of 250 acres at Valley Forge at a cost not to exceed twenty-five thousand dollars. Thus was born Pennsylvania's first state park, but after many years of state management it was transferred to the National Park Service on July 4, 1976, to become the nucleus of the newly authorized Valley Forge National Historic Park.

However, Valley Forge was only a small part of a much grander success story that made the state of Pennsylvania a national leader in forestland preservation. By 1900, the state had acquired some 110,000 acres for this purpose, much of it already-abused forestland purchased for as little as fifty cents per acre. Even so, the potential benefits of all of the land—properly rehabilitated and managed— were already foreseen. The governor himself was quoted as saying in 1900 that "These reservations are to be the parks and the outing grounds of the people forever." Not long afterward, Pennsylvania's commissioner of forestry, J. T. Rothrock (who also happened to be a medical doctor), added his own views:

There is still another aspect of the forestry question in this country. Sedate and busy citizens, especially those past middle age are apt to think lightly of the uses of the woods as a source of recreation. For one moment only, attention may be called to the sanitary value of the forests, and especially the forests of our high grounds. The time will come shortly when a recognized function of the reservations which the state is now acquiring will be to restore to health and usefulness men who otherwise would have ended their lives prematurely by disease, after having become charges upon the bounty of the Commonwealth. Surely, if it is worth the while of the state to lavish its money on hospitals and asylums for the restoration to health of those who are already ailing, it would be a wise and nobler thing to prevent invalidism by providing rest amid healthful surroundings, and restoration to usefulness of those who might be saved or could be saved.[17]

Dr. Rothrock had astutely put his finger on a major purpose of parks—and recreation in general—long before it was commonly acknowledged.

While northeastern states concerned themselves with forest preservation—

16. William C. Forrey, *History of Pennsylvania State Parks*, 4.
17. Ibid., 5.

A combination of historical significance and natural scenery led Pennsylvania to acquire the site of the Continental Army's winter encampment at Valley Forge as its first state park. Shown here in the 1920s, it continued to be a popular destination site and was eventually incorporated into a much larger Valley Forge National Historical Park. PENNSYLVANIA DEPARTMENT OF CONSERVATION AND NATURAL RESOURCES

and, consequently, with forest parks—Michigan was taking another look at Mackinac Island. Since 1875, the War Department had been nominally administering the property for the "health, comfort, pleasure, benefit, and enjoyment of the people." In 1895, though, Congress passed an amendment authorizing the secretary of war to convey the island to the state "for a state park, but for no other purpose." By that time, unfortunately, a choice piece of the island had been developed as an upscale summer resort, catering principally to the very wealthy. Even so, the state received some 1,700 acres of the 2,100-acre island, including the historic Fort Mackinac, and placed it under a specially created Mackinac Island State Park Commission. Although properly regarded as Michigan's first state park, the island and another nearby property (Fort Michilimackinac, acquired by gift in 1909) are still managed today by a separate commission rather than as part of the regular state park system.

Meanwhile, back out West, the brand-new (1890) *state* of Wyoming was making another venture into the park business. Although its brief tenure as the nominal custodian of Yellowstone National Park a few years earlier had not proved altogether successful, in 1898 Wyoming accepted a piece of land of its own for public recreational use. This property, known originally as the Big Horn Hot Springs Reserve, was a gift from the Shoshone and Arapaho Tribes, which had received it in 1867 as part of the Wind River Reservation. Reminiscent of the Indian Springs episode in Georgia many years before, the Hot Springs property was ceded to Wyoming because of the wide popularity of the springs' waters for therapeutic purposes. Under the terms of the gift agreement, the springs were to remain available to visitors for free "soaking" throughout the year.

Lacking a more suitable management agency, the young state placed the Hot Springs property under the control of its Board of Charities and Reform. Little is known of its management and use during the early years, but the Hot Springs property obviously turned out to be a real boon for the state of Wyoming. Located on the banks of the Bighorn River and with a major railroad line running right through it, the site eventually became the third most popular attraction in the state (behind only Yellowstone and Grand Teton National Parks). In 1984, the Hot Springs site, now over a thousand acres in size, was transferred by the Board of Charities and Reform to a full-time state parks agency.

One of the last major "state park" initiatives of the nineteenth century was in Massachusetts, and it involved the state's highest peak, Mount Greylock. Although forest conservation was again a significant factor in this effort, it came with a different twist: The concern of Mount Greylock's champions was not nearly so much over loss of the forests' economic potential as it was over the desecration of the mountain's scenic grandeur. Mount Greylock to them was not just a wooded hillside; it was instead a natural shrine fully deserving of the reverence in which it had been held for generations.

As is true in so many cases, the effort to save Mount Greylock came almost too late. Increasing industrialization in New England created new demands on the area's natural resources, among them lime, metal ores, and wood for lumber and charcoal. New scars on Mount Greylock—from timbering, fires, and landslides—were observed regularly with great dismay by those who had long cherished the splendid panorama of the Berkshires. Galvanized by the urgent need for action, citizens in the area formed a Greylock Park Association in 1885 and proceeded immediately to purchase four hundred acres around the mountain's summit. The association also saw an opportunity to get some return on its investment by capitalizing on the recreational potential of the site. Over the next decade, it erected an observation tower, built roads, and collected fees for the use of its facilities.

Business was erratic, however, and mounting losses soon persuaded the association to offer the property to the state.

With intense lobbying by a number of environmental groups, the Massachusetts legislature passed a bill in 1898 to acquire the summit from the Greylock Park Association, appropriating twenty-five thousand dollars for purchase of an additional 3,324 acres as well. The new law also provided for the county to appoint a three-member commission to administer the "state reservation," and it put up funds for operation and for construction of new improvements. Two years later, the county was authorized to extend a road all the way to the top of the mountain, opening up the site for vehicular access and a consequent boom in recreational use. Ultimately, the county-appointed board of commissioners was superseded by direct state management, but it is interesting that the project—now exceeding 12,500 acres in size—is still called by its original designation: Mount Greylock State Reservation.

A Reflective View

As the nineteenth century came to an end, there still was no indication that a state park "movement" was forming, either nationally or in any given state. No state, for instance, as yet had more than a single true park (as opposed to historic and commemorative sites). But the body of experience that was being accumulated from the various individual projects around the country was impressive. Three of those projects, especially, stand out as precedent-setting milestones: Yosemite Valley, Niagara Falls, and Itasca.

California's noble undertaking in the Yosemite Valley, although not ultimately successful as a *state* park, was truly ahead of its time. Conceived almost a decade before even the first national park, it had no precedents to guide it. Consequently, a lot of mistakes were made, but from those mistakes valuable experience was gained. Probably the most important lesson learned from that experience was that a park, as a public enterprise, should not be expected to sustain itself financially—especially in a remote wilderness setting.

In taking on Niagara Falls as its first state park project, New York sought not to exploit or to rely on the site's obvious commercial potential, but rather to reduce the negative effects of the excessive commercialism that already existed. In doing so, it established another important state park precept: The act of preserving public spaces can be justified on its own merit, even if the cost must be borne by the public at large.

Itasca—Minnesota's farsighted effort to preserve a large, unspoiled natural area for public use, without undue consideration for inherent commercial potential or broader economic ramifications—is important because it succeeded where Yosemite had failed. In view of its broad scope and the diversity of preservation and recreation purposes it was intended to serve, Itasca, more than any other single project, probably deserves recognition as the real prototype of a classic state park.

After years of experimentation, marked by far more successes than failures, the random state park ventures of the nineteenth century may not as yet be regarded as a *movement,* but all in all they constituted a very promising beginning.

4

The Momentum Builds
State Parks Expansion in the Early Twentieth Century

The Tenor of the Times

After a half-century of trial and error, the state park idea at the dawn of the twentieth century at least had something of a track record. True, a mere handful of states had actually tested the concept, and several of those efforts had been less than impressive—some even outright failures. But the undeniable success of such high-profile projects as Niagara Falls, Itasca, and Valley Forge surely must have caught the attention of park advocates elsewhere around the country, sparking interest where there had been none and offering encouragement for preservation efforts already underway.

Whether it was itself a natural side effect of societal change or a purely seren-dipitous occurrence, the increased public awareness of state parks could not have been more timely. The turn of the century was generally a time of prosperity and optimism in the United States—a period of enlightenment that produced a number of progressive causes and campaigns, including what some have called a "back-to-nature" movement. Especially in the Northeast and the Midwest, many of the intelligentsia and the civic-minded leadership (the "do-gooders," if you will) were seeking out places to save and the means to save them. One possibility of course was to promote their pet project as a new national park—an increas-ingly popular idea at the time—but that would require congressional action, a lengthy and uncertain process at best. So, what about a more homegrown alter-native—like a state park? It was a novel, but intriguing, idea.

Although a standard concept of a "state park" still had not gelled—nor was the term itself yet in general use—the growing number of successful projects nonetheless offered useful precedents for a variety of new land preservation proposals. State parks had already been created to protect watersheds, prevent overexploitation of forests, and maintain and enhance tourism opportunities; some had been created even for purposes that seemed at the time to have no immediate practical value, such as the preservation of historic sites and natural scenery. Increasingly, new park advocates could look to these precedents to help justify and generate support for their own efforts, and the number and diversity of state park projects began to multiply.

Concurrently with the increase in individual projects, however, a fundamental change was taking place in the evolution of the state park concept. While many of the new projects were conceived, promoted, and pursued in virtual isolation by highly motivated citizen groups, state governments themselves were taking a more comprehensive look at the whole issue of state parks: If one park was good, would more be better? And, if so, how should they be selected, acquired, and managed? This awakening interest by a few states in the early years of the twentieth century laid the groundwork for a systematic approach to state park planning and represented the first real tremors of a state park "movement."

Of the several factors that contributed to the newfound appreciation for state parks at the time, probably the most important have already been mentioned. First, of course, was the legacy created and passed on by the state park pioneers of the previous century, providing helpful examples of what could be accomplished— as well as what should be avoided. Similarly, the concurrent rise of a national park consciousness was important. Although fewer in number than the state projects, the national parks received more widespread publicity and succeeded in exciting the public imagination and stimulating interest in parks generally. The ever-increasing industrialization and urbanization of America, especially in the East, was causing people to turn more to the outdoors for relief and restoration, and, because times were good, the people were generally disposed to support programs to acquire and protect open spaces for their diversion and play. These factors combined to create a highly conducive climate for furthering park causes. For good measure, the times were graced by still another favorable circumstance: a genuine champion of parks and conservation in the White House.

Theodore Roosevelt was the true standard-bearer of the Progressive Era in America. His personal interests were wide and varied, to be sure, but one of the principal recurrent themes of his tenure as president of the United States was the conservation of America's natural resources. He left an incomparable legacy in this field, and he took particular pride in the establishment of five national parks and numerous national forests and wildlife refuges during his presidency. Scant mention of state parks may be found among Roosevelt's voluminous writings, but he may well have given them a major boost indirectly, and perhaps inadvertently.

In October 1907, during an excursion on the Mississippi River with his Inland Waterways Commission, Roosevelt was approached about the possibility of convening a national conference on the conservation of natural resources. He readily agreed, and the conference was held the following spring. Later, he reflected on the importance of the event:

> In the November following I wrote to each of the governors of the several States and to the presidents of various important national societies concerned with natural resources, inviting them to attend the conference, which took place May 13 to 15, 1908, in the East Room of the White House. It is doubtful whether, except in time of war, any new idea of like importance has ever been presented to a nation and accepted by it with such effectiveness and rapidity, as was the case with this conservation movement when it was introduced to the American people by the conference of governors.[1]

In that distinguished group, which Roosevelt himself addressed for a full fifty minutes, were the governors of thirty-eight states and territories, many of whom undoubtedly had had little prior exposure to the purposes or principles of natural resources conservation. Referring to the impact of that opening speech, Roosevelt biographer William H. Harbaugh wrote: "Probably no event of Roosevelt's turbulent career evoked a more spontaneous and universally favorable reaction than the three-day conference he had then opened."[2] The conference covered a lot of ground, and there is no record that state parks were specifically addressed; but clearly the overall experience had a quick and dramatic effect on the nation's governors. Within hardly more than a year, some type of conservation agency had been established in at least forty-one states. Teddy Roosevelt's larger-than-life personality surely permeated all of these proceedings and helped influence a conservation consciousness at the state level that opened the door for a variety of follow-up programs. A golden opportunity was now at hand for major progress on the state parks front.

1. William H. Harbaugh, ed., *The Writings of Theodore Roosevelt*, 150–51.
2. William Henry Harbaugh, *Power and Responsibility: The Life and Times of Theodore Roosevelt*, 335.

Interstate Initiatives: The Palisades and the Dalles

That golden opportunity was not lost. Several of the states that had already tested the water were now moving ahead with additional park projects, while an increasing number of other states were also getting involved. Some even, in a move unprecedented for the times, were working cooperatively to preserve outstanding natural areas that spanned state boundaries.

As early as 1895, New York and New Jersey had begun a joint effort to protect a highly scenic stretch along the Hudson River, known as the Palisades, from further quarrying operations. Most of the affected area lay in New Jersey, but it provided cherished views to the people on the other side of the river in New York. The New Jersey Federation of Women's Clubs seized the initiative and succeeded in convincing the legislature in that state to enact protective measures. New York soon joined in the effort, in 1900, creating the Commissioners of the Palisades Interstate Park and appropriating a modest amount of money for land acquisition.

As welcome as they were, these initial governmental measures were still considered inadequate by many of the project's supporters. Not to be denied, they then undertook a vigorous campaign to raise additional funds. In New York especially, highly motivated and well-connected civic leaders—led by George W. Perkins, the Palisades Commission's first chairman—were able to secure large donations of both funds and lands. The legendary financier J. P. Morgan himself put up the first $122,500 to buy out the quarrying operation, and this was followed by substantial contributions from other prominent individuals with recognizable names like Harriman, Gould, Vanderbilt, and Rockefeller. Soon afterward, the State of New York reentered the picture, floating bond issues in 1910 and 1916 for acquisition of parklands at the Palisades and elsewhere.

The Palisades Interstate Park stands out as another classic example of early preservation projects being accomplished largely through citizen—rather than government—initiative, and even today it retains a special management status apart from the regular state park program of either state. Whether it fit the state park mold or not, the Palisades clearly had a positive influence on other park projects soon to follow. In the opinion of Raymond Torrey, writing for the National Conference on State Parks in 1926: "No other park development in the country has done more to stimulate the state park movement."[3]

3. Raymond H. Torrey, "State Parks and Recreational Uses of State Forests in the United States." In *A Report Epitomizing the Results of Major Fact-Finding Surveys and Projects Which Have Been*

At the same time New Jersey and New York were taking steps to preserve the Palisades of the Hudson, a similar joint project was underway farther west. Concerned interests in both Wisconsin and Minnesota had recognized the need to protect the "dalles" of the St. Croix, the river that separates the two states. Long appreciated for its spectacular scenery, this rugged river gorge was being increasingly degraded by wanton vandalism, and it would take action by both states to remedy the problem. As it happened, two of the individuals who first stepped forth to provide help had already proven their interest in state parks by earlier legislative exploits.

In Minnesota, state representative John Sanborn, the sponsor of the legislation that created Itasca State Park in 1891, now produced a bill in 1895 authorizing land acquisition at the dalles and further providing for cooperation with the state of Wisconsin to ensure that both sides of the river were protected. Funds were appropriated that same year, and land acquisition proceeded almost at once. The establishment of the "Inter-State Park" was immediately hailed as the "rescue of the Dalles of the St. Croix from neglect and vandalism," although it would be many more years before actual on-site management would succeed in accomplishing that worthy goal.

Meanwhile, Wisconsin was on a parallel track. State representative William Baker, who had sponsored the bill that created that state's short-lived "state park" in 1878, again took the lead in securing legislation in 1895 to appoint a commission to investigate the purchase of land at the dalles for a state park. Four years later, funds were appropriated for this purpose, and the following year, 1900, Interstate Park was formally established as Wisconsin's first.

Although the two states proceeded in a somewhat coordinated fashion to protect their respective sides of the St. Croix, no formal joint management mechanism was instituted, as in the case of the Palisades. Both states used the same designation, "Interstate Park," and each continued to administer its area independently as part of its own state park system. Years later, in 1988, the two states would enter into a reciprocity agreement honoring each other's entrance permits for weekday use, believed to be the only such arrangement in the country.

Undertaken under the Auspices of the National Conference on Outdoor Recreation, 70th Cong., 1st sess., 1928, S. Doc. 158, 47.

New York and Pennsylvania: Leading the Way

With its great diversity of scenic treasures and its growing concern for preservation, it is not surprising that America's Northeast would be in the vanguard of the state park movement. By the early 1900s, most of the states in the region had already jumped on the bandwagon, but two of these clearly stand out as pacesetters: New York and Pennsylvania.

New York, especially, was blessed with an enlightened and caring citizenry, and—just as important—an affluent one. Citizen interest had already prompted the state government to act on behalf of Niagara Falls and the Adirondack and Catskill Mountains, and in the wake of those landmark successes a number of civic-minded individuals now started to come forth with generous donations of private property worthy of preservation. One of the first and certainly most notable of these was in the gorge of the Genesee River, an area often referred to as the "Grand Canyon of the East." The nucleus of what was to become one of New York's most spectacular state parks was given to the state in 1906 by William Pryor Letchworth, who was concerned that the burgeoning demand for hydroelectric power in the area would surely pose a serious threat to the Genesee. As New York still had no suitable state parks agency to accept such a gift, Letchworth stipulated that the land be placed under the control of the American Scenic and Historic Preservation Society. This body, despite its name, was essentially a New York–based organization created in 1895 to recommend and promote a variety of preservation endeavors. It first achieved prominence in connection with the Palisades project, and it continued to play an influential part in New York's preservation efforts for the next several decades.

Letchworth's donation set a valuable precedent and was soon followed by others. By 1920, New York had acquired—either directly by donation or by citizen-initiated legislative action—at least another half-dozen park properties not already mentioned, including Thatcher, Clark, Enfield Glen (later, Robert H. Treman), St. Lawrence, and Saratoga Springs.

By the time of the Saratoga Springs acquisition, in 1909, New York seems to have settled upon a fairly consistent approach for administering its parks. Still without a central state parks agency, the state would create a special commission of interested citizens to pursue acquisition—with either donated or appropriated funds—and oversee subsequent operations. The procedure appears to have worked remarkably well until the sheer number of individual commissions and similar administrative bodies became unwieldy a few years later.

In 1924, the State Council of Parks was created in an effort to pull all of the diverse groups together under a single umbrella agency with a uniform state parks policy. In taking this important step, however, New York was careful to avoid a purely bureaucratic approach that almost certainly would have undermined the strong tradition of citizen involvement that had been responsible for so much of its prior success. Instead, under a system designed largely by the brilliant planner and civic leader Robert Moses, it simply brought the heads of the various commissions (which by now had been regionalized) together as members of the new Council of State Parks. This heavy reliance on citizen participation would continue to be a significant factor in the success of the New York state parks program.

Pennsylvania, meanwhile, was continuing aggressively to pursue its program of state forest reservations—which by the early 1900s had expanded to more than three hundred thousand acres. Given the sometimes subtle distinctions between the two concepts, it was inevitable that the same concern for forest preservation would produce a corollary interest in state parks. This happened quickly in Pennsylvania. A department of forestry was created in 1901, and Dr. J. T. Rothrock was appointed as its first commissioner. Dr. Rothrock's enthusiasm for therapeutic outdoor recreation was already well known, and in this he was joined by other foresters who recognized the benefits to be derived from public recreational use of the state forests. The governor, too, endorsed the idea wholeheartedly. In addressing the legislature in early 1903, he noted the vast sums of money being spent to develop city parks around the state and commented: "These reservations [the state forests] are nature's parks, belonging to the people, far preferable in my judgment to artificial parks."[4]

This interest from the top was manifested first in the establishment of a series of camps in the state forests to cater to the recuperative needs of patients suffering from tuberculosis and similar ailments. As it happened, the initial site chosen for one of these camps was at the Mont Alto Forest Reservation, which had been partially developed as a resort when it was still in private ownership. Many of the resort's recreational facilities were still functional when the property was acquired by the state in 1902, and these were simply converted to public use. Thus, Mont Alto became Pennsylvania's first "state forest park." A similar situation occurred a year later when another previously developed tract was acquired and opened to the public as the Caledonia State Forest Park. A pattern was thus

4. Forrey, *Pennsylvania State Parks*, 7.

established not just for active recreational use of state forestlands, but also for the identification of a part of those lands as "state parks."

Interest in "public outing grounds" continued to grow in Pennsylvania. Dr. Rothrock was a tireless advocate for further recreational use of the forest reserves, calling for measures to designate certain areas specifically for that purpose. Other voices aided the cause, and in 1911 the legislature responded by creating a commission to examine a number of properties that had been proposed for new state parks. It would be several more years, however, before any concrete action resulted. In 1917, the legislature authorized new parks at Fort Washington and Washington Crossing (on the Delaware River) to augment Valley Forge in commemorating Pennsylvania's Revolutionary War history. During this time the state also accepted several private donations of land for park purposes, bringing its total of both recreational and historical parks to at least nine by 1920.

Minnesota and Wisconsin: The Momentum Continues

The interstate park on the St. Croix had been a success, but neither Minnesota nor Wisconsin was content to rest on those laurels. Minnesota—although it proceeded sporadically, on a one-at-a-time basis—continued deliberately to acquire park properties as the opportunities arose. Its next acquisition was in 1905, and by 1920 it had added five more properties to its inventory. As the state had no central agency to administer its parks at the time, this function was nominally assigned to the state auditor. In practice, however, new acquisitions were typically placed under the custodianship of a local superintendent with a great deal of autonomy for day-to-day management. To make policy decisions and provide general oversight, an advisory body was established for each park, with its members usually selected from among the project's proven champions and supporters. Although it was not without its problems, this system seemed to work fairly well until it was replaced by a central state parks agency in the 1930s.

Wisconsin, too, had other parks in mind. In 1903, the legislature authorized the governor to appoint a special commission to take a look at Devil's Lake for state park purposes, and two years later it expanded the investigation to include the famous Dells of Wisconsin as well. The commission reported its findings in 1907, recommending that the Devil's Lake site be acquired and that the Dells be studied further. Unfortunately, despite an outpouring of support from the locality, the bill to authorize Devil's Lake failed by a single vote. Recognizing the growing public interest in state parks, however, the same legislature decided to address the subject on a more comprehensive front. Instead of pursuing projects independently of each other, it established a three-member state park board to consider the whole field and "make recommendations regarding the acquirement of any new parks." The word "any" may suggest a lack of total commitment at the time, but in any case the legislature had issued a farsighted directive that would within a few years help set a steady course for the rapid growth of Wisconsin's state parks program.

The new Wisconsin state park board, to its credit, recognized the need for professional guidance in carrying out its task and hired a landscape architect from Massachusetts named John Nolen. It proved to be an excellent choice. It is unclear just how much actual experience Nolen had had in state park work, but in his report—which really was the substance of the state park board's report as well—he demonstrated a classic mastery of the subject. After making important references to all of the recent developments in the parks field generally—including

Wisconsin was well ahead of the times when, in 1908, it hired Boston landscape architect John Nolen to help develop a comprehensive plan for state park acquisition. Nolen later did similar work for Illinois, and both states benefited greatly from his farsighted recommendations. WISCONSIN DEPARTMENT OF NATURAL RESOURCES

Roosevelt's White House conference that had been held just the year before—he went on to outline a highly cogent rationale for a system of state parks and recommended immediate action on four specific projects. "Who questions nowadays that simple recreation in the open air amid beautiful surroundings contributes to physical and moral health, to a saner and happier life?" he asked rhetorically. Who would dare question such an obvious truism? Certainly not the state park board; it incorporated Nolen's entire commentary in its report to the governor in 1909, with the notation that the members "heartily concur in his report and recommendations."

Wisconsin followed up aggressively. Three of the four park properties that Nolen had recommended were acquired within the next eight years: Peninsula in 1910, Devil's Lake (which had failed earlier) in 1911, and Wyalusing in 1917. Only the Dells, which was heavily developed by commercial interests by this time, proved elusive—but even it would eventually come under state park control when it was transferred to the state as a "natural area" in 1999.

In 1915, the legislature replaced the state park board—along with similar agencies dealing with forestry and wildlife—with a new professional state conservation commission. Although this reorganization instituted a means for central control and direction of the several programs, in the process state parks were administratively combined with forestry. This move, which some observers considered a "shotgun marriage" that would weaken the parks' identity and influence, actually prefigured a trend that would be followed by a number of states in later years.

California Bounces Back: Big Basin Redwoods

New York and Pennsylvania, Minnesota, and Wisconsin were not the only states reprising their earlier state park performances. At the turn of the century, California came roaring back with a new state park campaign that, like Yosemite, carried far greater than just statewide significance. This time it centered on *Sequoia sempervirens,* the mighty coast redwood trees, the likes of which were found nowhere else in the world. As before, it was a long and difficult battle against formidable adversaries, but because the goal was seen as such a clear imperative the proponents persevered and ultimately prevailed.

California's redwood forests had long been a source of awe and wonderment for those who beheld them, and for decades various preservation proposals had been put forth at both the state and federal levels. The federal government had, in fact, taken steps to preserve samples of the related species *Sequoiadendron*

California's big trees had long captured the public imagination, and in 1902 the state acquired a significant stand as the first part of its Big Basin Redwoods State Park. Here depicted in the 1930s is the park "Warden's Office" (administration building), a fine example of classic state park architecture. © CALIFORNIA STATE PARKS, 2003

giganteum, the Sierra redwoods, in several national parks created a decade before. But in spite of a heroic effort in the late 1800s by Ralph Sidney Smith, an area newspaper editor, it was not until 1902 that any real success was achieved on behalf of the coast redwoods. That momentous achievement was embodied in the establishment of California's first true state park: the California Redwood Park, later renamed Big Basin Redwoods State Park.

Credit for sparking the renewed campaign to save some of the coast redwoods is generally given to Andrew P. Hill, a professional photographer who became passionately involved and helped form the Sempervirens Club in 1900 to lobby on behalf of preservation. Many other influential persons, particularly writers and educators, were enlisted in the cause. After briefly considering the possibility of a national park, the group decided to pursue the idea of a state park instead. A bill for this purpose was introduced in the 1901 state assembly and, after more than the usual legislative twists and turns, eventually was passed into law. The bill provided for appointment of a Redwood Park Commission to oversee the project and a sizeable appropriation for initial land acquisition. Continuing machinations by various park opponents, however, stalled actual implementation of the new law until late 1902, when the first twenty-five hundred acres were purchased.

A small, but important, part of the spectacular coast redwood forests had finally been saved—and California at last had a real state park.

Although it would be more than two decades before other recreational parks were added to its system, California in the meantime turned its attention to the preservation of its historical resources. Continuing deterioration and loss of important landmarks had, in the eyes of many, reached a crisis by 1902, and this led to the creation of a coalition of preservation groups called the California Historical Landmark League. Through the efforts first of the Landmark League and later of the various organizations that succeeded it, many of the state's most significant historical treasures were saved for posterity and deeded to the state of California. Eventually, in 1928, these sites would be pulled together and incorporated as an important component of California's new and rapidly expanding state park system.

A Succession of Successes

It is significant to note that some of the earliest state park projects involved properties, either natural or historic, that merited nationwide attention: Niagara Falls, the San Jacinto Battleground, the coast redwood forests, to mention a few. Some of them even rivaled the national parks of the time in public interest and acclaim. Unfortunately, such spectacular natural features and nationally significant historic sites were not equally distributed around the country—but this did not prevent the growing fervor for preservation from spreading across the land. If the varying quality of available resources had any dampening effect on local enthusiasm for new parks, it was not apparent. The number of states pursuing preservation projects of some kind continued to escalate.

Ohio already had a long history of public recreational use of its state-operated canals and reservoirs, dating back to the mid-nineteenth century; so it was not surprising that one of these popular areas, the Licking Reservoir, was formally dedicated as a public park in 1894. Two years later, the name was changed to Buckeye Lake, now regarded as Ohio's first state park. It would not officially be accorded state park status, however, until many years later, in 1949, when Buckeye Lake and eighteen other variously administered public recreation areas would be pulled together and placed under the newly established Division of Parks.

Illinois also joined in early. In 1903, it acquired its first state park, Fort Massac, a pre-Revolution military outpost on the Ohio River. A few years later, in 1909, the legislature created an Illinois Park Commission to "investigate and report on the preservation of certain lands for public parks." The new commission hired Boston landscape architect John Nolen (who was finishing up his similar work in neighboring Wisconsin) and went to work on a state parks plan. Acting on the commission's recommendation, the state acquired its first natural area park, Starved Rock, in 1911, which was then combined with Fort Massac and several other small properties to form the nucleus of a state park *system*—one of the earliest steps in this direction.

It should not be surprising after the interest generated by the Palisades Park campaign that New Jersey would be motivated to pursue other park-related projects. This it did in quick succession, first with establishment of its Bass River State Forest in 1905, followed by at least seven others before 1920, including the Mount Laurel *State Park* in 1908.

Maryland was not far behind. It had acquired a small state forest along the Patapsco River in 1907 and quickly recognized the recreational and other benefits to be derived from expanding the area. In its 1910–1911 biennial report, the State Board of Forestry called for establishing demonstration forests in each county of the state to provide timber, protect the watersheds, and preserve scenic beauty. Where Patapsco was concerned, however, it was more specific: "The Patapsco Reserve is located only a few miles from Baltimore in a picturesque region, where it can best serve as a State Park for recreation and pleasure. It is the desire of the Board to increase the area of the reserve and to develop it along park lines."[5] The following year, 1912, funds were appropriated for additional land acquisition, and Patapsco was established as the earliest component of Maryland's eventual state forest and park system. Interestingly, that same legislature also authorized the acquisition of Fort Frederick, one of the nation's best-preserved pre–Revolutionary War forts; and although its purchase was not consummated until 1922, it was the first such area to be officially designated a "state park."

In a coincidence of names, Rhode Island identified Lincoln Woods as its first state park property in 1907, while that same year, a half a continent away, North Dakota obtained Fort Abraham Lincoln for its first state park. Rhode Island, recognizing the need for more recreation areas around its growing cities, had created a Metropolitan Park Commission to look into the problem. Among the commission's recommendations was a proposal to acquire a number of desirable properties in suburban areas, one of which was a composite site known as Lincoln Woods, on the outskirts of Providence. Purchase of the numerous private

5. Maryland State Board of Forestry, *Report for 1910 and 1911*, 26.

holdings was undertaken the following year and continued incrementally until the entire 653-acre tract was eventually obtained.

In the North Dakota case, Fort Abraham Lincoln, a frontier military post near Mandan, is of interest as the home station of the U.S. Seventh Cavalry, commanded by the swaggering Colonel George A. Custer. It was from here that Custer led his command on the ill-fated expedition that ended with the famous battle at the Little Big Horn. President Theodore Roosevelt himself signed the instrument conveying the fort site to the state from the federal government, but the property remained in its deteriorated condition for many years before restoration could be undertaken.

It stands to reason that the western states with their huge expanses of public domain land would be slow to consider local land acquisition for park purposes. And indeed, with the obvious exception of California, this proved largely to be the case. It is somewhat surprising, therefore, that Idaho, which had become a state only as recently as 1890, would be appropriating funds to purchase its first state park as early as 1911. In this case, though, it came about more as a consolation prize in lieu of a national park proposal that failed.

As documented by Thomas R. Cox in *The Park Builders,* Idaho's U.S. Senator Weldon B. Heyburn, a vehement states'-righter with a fiery temper, first proposed the idea of a national park in the area of Lake Chatcolet in legislation submitted in 1907.[6] For various reasons—one of which was the growing concern in Congress about the number (and their prospective costs) of national park proposals coming before that body—Heyburn's bill never made it through both houses. As a compromise, the wording was changed to instead allow the state of Idaho to purchase the land for a *state* park. After some internal controversy over the means of funding, the property was purchased and the park named in honor of Senator Heyburn. It was a signal accomplishment (Cox deemed the result "one of the finest state parks anywhere"), but perhaps somewhat ahead of its time: Idaho would not establish another state park for forty-four more years.

By the second decade of the twentieth century, it seemed that state park initiatives were under way just about everywhere. Interest remained particularly strong in the Northeast, where New York and Pennsylvania were leading the way. Connecticut accepted its first property, at Mount Tom, in 1911, but really got its program going in 1914—and it was already thinking in terms of a park system instead of just individual projects. A temporary state park commission had been

6. Thomas R. Cox, *The Park Builders,* 14–31.

Not long before his infamous "last stand," George Armstrong Custer (third from left, without hat) poses with staff and family members on the steps of his quarters at Fort Abraham Lincoln in the Dakota Territory. This historic structure has now been reconstructed as part of a North Dakota state park. NORTH DAKOTA PARKS AND RECREATION DEPARTMENT

created by the 1909 legislature, "with the charge to prepare a plan for acquiring and organizing park lands." Acting on that group's recommendation four years later, the general assembly replaced the ad hoc commission with a permanent one, and Connecticut was in the park business for good. As its first employee, the commission hired Albert M. Turner, an able and experienced park professional. Under Turner's leadership, the state undertook an aggressive park acquisition program, mostly through donations, accumulating an impressive inventory of nineteen properties by the end of the decade.

The ball was now really beginning to roll. On the other side of the continent, Washington State also had taken steps in anticipation of creating a state park system. In 1913, the legislature established the State Board of Park Commissioners, apparently to facilitate acceptance of a substantial donation of private property on Orcas Island. That donation (now a part of Moran State Park) was not accepted until 1921, after new legislation had revamped the park commission, but the original commission did accept two smaller donations in 1915 as Washington's first state parks. Many others were to follow in short order.

Take Your Next Summer's Outing at

BEAUTIFUL HEYBURN PARK

The Coming Playground of the Northwest

Boating, Bathing and the Best Bass and Trout Fishing in Idaho. Reached via
Red Collar Steamship Line, O. W. R. & N., and Chicago, Milwaukee & Puget
Sound Railways. For Further Particulars Address George D. Wright, Supt.

Establishing a state park was one thing, promoting its use was another. Fliers or handbills
such as this early one for Idaho's Heyburn State Park were one means. IDAHO DEPARTMENT OF
PARKS AND RECREATION

South Dakota splashed onto the state parks scene in a big way (literally) in
1919, with the formal establishment of its Custer State Park. This sprawling,
sixty-thousand-acre chunk of the Black Hills was acquired by the state in 1910
through an exchange of scattered "school lands" for a consolidated tract of public domain land.[7] The property was originally designated a state forest rather
than a park—possibly to avoid confusion with the Wind Cave National Park,
which had been established on immediately adjacent property in 1903. In 1913,
though, a substantial part was declared a state game reserve, and funds were

---

7. "School lands" were tracts from the public domain (initially section 16—but later, section
36 also—from each township) granted by the United States to the states to be used in support
of public schools.

appropriated to enclose the area with a forty-mile-long, eight-foot-high, "game-tight" fence. The fencing project proved difficult, however, as did certain other aspects of its management as a game preserve. Not long afterward, in 1919, the legislature redesignated the property a state park.

Instrumental in this chain of events was Governor Peter Norbeck (later a U.S. senator), who had been smitten by the scenic beauty of the area as a young man many years earlier. Norbeck also took a deep personal interest in the operation and management of the new park, serving on the first Custer State Park Board along with two other members of his choosing. This board—which would in time evolve into a broader-based state park board under the Department of Game, Fish and Parks—was responsible for setting the standard of tasteful design and development that serves the park well unto this day. In its scope, character, and management direction, however, Custer did not start out as a typical state park, nor does it fit that description today. In fact, it is still managed as a one-of-a-kind park under a separate division from the rest of the South Dakota state park system. Clearly, Custer State Park was conceived and implemented as a self-contained, stand-alone unit, and it would be at least another quarter-century before South Dakota would expand its horizons to embrace other state parks. Along the way, through additional land exchanges and acquisitions, Custer State Park was expanded to its present-day size of seventy-three thousand acres.

Indiana: Enter Richard Lieber

Indiana, another aggressive leader in state park development, embarked on its program in a similar manner and at about the same time as had Washington. Citizen interest in preserving prized tracts of scenic property threatened by private development led the governor to appoint a state park commission in 1915, even before it had any parks to administer. It didn't have long to wait, however. Determined efforts were simultaneously under way to raise private funds for the acquisition of two separate sites in the western part of the state.

One of these, the McCormick's Creek Canyon, had been used for a sanitarium for wealthy patrons since 1880, as well as for casual recreation by the local people. So it was that when the sanitarium closed in 1914 the idea of preserving the scenic site for public enjoyment received wide popular support. The property was held by an estate at that time, however, and was subject to imminent sale. With the county taking the lead, the land was purchased jointly by Owen County and the state and accepted by the park commission in 1916 as Indiana's first state park. Meanwhile, the other citizen park initiative was facing a more difficult challenge.

Turkey Run—Indiana's second state park, also acquired in 1916—has added significance for state park lore because of the first appearance of Richard Lieber, one of the true giants of the field. Lieber, a German patrician who had emigrated to this country as a young adult, was a man of many interests and talents. Fortunately for both Indiana and the nation, one of his most passionate civic endeavors would involve the creation of state parks. In 1915, Lieber led a movement to raise private funding for the purchase of the Turkey Run property, which he hoped could be presented as the first state park the following year during Indiana's centennial celebration. This property also was held in an estate and was scheduled for auction the following spring. Although Lieber's group had succeeded in raising twenty thousand dollars by the time of the sale, it lost the bid to a lumber company that wanted to cut the standing timber. Not ready to give up, the group persuaded the successful bidder to sell them the property, intact, for a substantial down payment and the balance at a later date. They then set about finding additional funds.

Impressed with both the beauty of the property and the commitment of Lieber's group to saving it, several prominent Indianapolis citizens made generous donations to the cause. One of these donors was Carl Fisher (who was soon to gain fame in Florida as the flamboyant developer and promoter of Miami Beach), a member of the board of directors of the Indianapolis Speedway. In addition to his personal gift, Fisher also employed his legendary powers of salesmanship to persuade the Speedway board to pledge 10 percent of the proceeds from the next Memorial Day race—surely an unprecedented coup in the annals of private fund raising! With financial solvency thus assured, Lieber and his colleagues cut their deal with the lumber company and closed on the first 288 acres of Turkey Run in November of 1916—regrettably to become the second, rather than first, Indiana state park.

From these early successes—which, in this instance once again, were due more to citizen than government initiative—Indiana moved deliberately to consolidate its state parks program. In 1919, the legislature took the next step by creating a department of conservation and an appointive conservation commission. Colonel (an honorary rank conferred on him by the governor, who named Lieber as his "military secretary" in 1917) Richard Lieber was appointed as the department's first director and served ably in that position until his retirement from

One of the true giants in the state park movement in the first half of the twentieth century was Indiana's Richard Lieber. Here, circa 1920, he surveys the scenic grandeur of one of his state parks. INDIANA DEPARTMENT OF NATURAL RESOURCES

government in 1932. In another fortunate selection, Stanley Coulter, dean of the Purdue University School of Science, was appointed a member of the new conservation commission. Both Coulter and Lieber went on to distinguish themselves in national conservation circles and to render outstanding service to the state of Indiana in the process. We will hear more about them, especially Lieber, in pages to come.

The South Awakens

By 1916 the war in Europe was becoming a major preoccupation on this side of the Atlantic as well, but still not so much as to deter interest in civic improvements generally or in park programs specifically—whether local, state, or national. On the contrary, parks seemed to be as popular as ever, with an ever-increasing number of states entering the field. As noted, most of the northeastern states were already beyond the dabbling stage, and the state park idea had hopscotched

Sites with grand vistas are always likely candidates for new state parks. When North Carolina acquired Mount Mitchell—the highest point in the eastern United States—in 1916, this lookout tower was one of the first structures erected. NORTH CAROLINA DIVISION OF PARKS AND RECREATION

all around the country as well—with one major exception. Where were the southern states?

For all its natural diversity and vast outdoor recreational potential, the South still had not made any significant move to preserve its scenic treasures or to provide for public breathing room. Thomas Cox, in contrasting park motivations in the Pacific Northwest with those of the rest of the country, attributed this generally to a lack of progressivism: "In the South, poverty, traditions of limited government, the weakness of transcendentalism (thanks in part to its ties to abolition), and the pastoral-plantation ideal that extolled the country estate rather than unsullied nature, combined to discourage participation in the state parks movement."[8] Whatever the reasons, the region continued to lag behind most of the country for another two decades—but the situation was already beginning to change.

In North Carolina, for example, concern over the effects of poor timbering practices had begun to surface well before the turn of the century and had caused the legislature to address the problem as early as 1891. It was this concern over deteriorating forests that prompted the governor in 1915 to propose the establishment of a state park on Mount Mitchell (a full decade, incidentally, before creation of the national park in the nearby Great Smokies). In appropriating twenty thousand dollars for the purpose that year, the legislature took note of the fact that Mount Mitchell was important not only as the highest peak east of the Mississippi River but also for watershed protection, forest management, and scenery preservation. The next year, 1916, some 795 acres was acquired, and Mount Mitchell became North Carolina's first state park.

To be sure, Florida at the turn of the twentieth century was still very much a frontier state. The government was too small and poor to deal effectively with its more pressing problems, let alone seriously consider the matter of state parks. Even so, there were some among the growing citizenry of the state that held a deep appreciation for the peninsula's semitropical beauty and a fervent desire to see it protected. The vast freshwater marsh system south of Lake Okeechobee, commonly known as the Florida Everglades, became an area of special concern almost from the time of the first white settlement. The concern intensified as increased visitation and development in the area threatened to destroy some of the most scenic spots—one of the most celebrated of which was Paradise Key, a small area of high ground covered with towering royal palms. It could not have been

8. Cox, *Park Builders*, 12.

known at the time, but Paradise Key became a rallying point that started the long and still-active crusade to save the Everglades.

Repeated calls for legislative intervention to save Paradise Key unfortunately fell on deaf ears. As it happened, however, among those asked to join in the call for state action was the Florida Federation of Women's Clubs. Instead of simply adding its voice, the Federation decided to take on the project of creating and operating a park itself. Under the determined leadership of its president, May Mann Jennings, the wife of a former governor, the federation persuaded the legislature to convey 960 acres of state-owned land to the federation for park purposes in 1915, and this was matched by a like amount from private railroad interests. A year later, the park was formally dedicated with great fanfare under its new name: Royal Palm State Park.

Although it was never operated by the state, the mere existence of a Royal Palm State Park could not help but contribute to the awareness of the state park concept among those Florida officials who were involved in its establishment. The legislature, especially, had a lot of firsthand exposure, as it was called on at almost every one of its biennial sessions to help out with additional land or financial support—sometimes given, sometimes not. It would be another ten years before that body would take up the question of creating its own state parks program, but at least by that time certain of its members would have been well indoctrinated in the practical aspects of public park operation.

As for the fate of the "state park that wasn't," after more than a quarter-century of largely hand-to-mouth operation by the Florida Federation of Women's Clubs, the Royal Palm State Park was conveyed to the U.S. Department of the Interior in 1947 to become part of the Everglades National Park. Fittingly, Paradise Key, the heart and soul of the project from the start, was selected as the site for the new national park's primary visitor center, where its beauty can still be appreciated by all who enter.

Iowa: A Case Study in Park Motivations

There is no clear pattern, either geographical or typal, discernible from the state park initiatives in the United States in the early twentieth century. Although communications were still primitive by today's standards, most of the states probably would have been aware of major developments—such as the Palisades and the Big Basin Redwoods—through the mainstream press. Smaller projects, especially if they were innovative or distinctive, may well have been noted in newsletters or symposia of the emerging professional organizations. Still, each state seemed to be adapting in its own way to the various social, economic, and demographic undercurrents driving the incipient state park movement. The difficulty in analyzing the matter in depth and trying to draw any meaningful conclusions stems from the fact that too little research and documentation has been done in individual state cases. Thomas Cox, in his groundbreaking work *The Park Builders,* sheds some helpful light on three states—Idaho, Oregon, and Washington—but there apparently have been few scholarly, in-depth examinations of a single state's park program. Rebecca Conard's treatment of Iowa in *Places of Quiet Beauty* is probably the most recent.[9] Iowa may not be a typical case, but its experience leading up to its entry into the state park field makes an interesting story. Unfortunately, we have room here only for a quick review. Probably few people outside Iowa would think of that largely agricultural prairie state as fertile ground for a dynamic state parks program. Yet, when the state officially took up the cause in 1917, its inventory of park properties expanded so quickly that the governor obviously felt fully comfortable in inviting the first National Conference on Parks to meet in Des Moines only four years later (more about that in the next chapter). But unlike most of the states that had preceded it in either formulating a program or acquiring properties, Iowa was not primarily responding to a public clamor for parks and recreation areas or simply taking advantage of serendipitous opportunities to acquire public lands. Rather, the architects of its program saw state parks—or at least the term *state park*—as a means to accomplish much broader conservation goals. As Conard put it: "Iowa's state park system was born from a hope of centralizing control over resource use. Scenic preservation and outdoor recreation were among the motives, to be sure, but they were not the driving force."[10] The explanation for Iowa's different slant on state park programming lies in the story of the men who influenced it.

Iowa, of course, is famous more for its corn and hogs than for its natural attractions, so it is not especially surprising that there was no early groundswell of public sentiment for preservation. But the state has a legacy of progressivism that has produced a host of leaders and scholars in many fields. One of those fields, in the broadest sense, was the natural sciences, and it was the disciples of those sciences, especially botany, that really shaped Iowa's early park movement. Conard credits two men in particular with major contributions: Thomas McBride and Louis Pammel.

---

9. Rebecca Conard, *Places of Quiet Beauty.*
10. Ibid., 4.

Although the efforts of the two men were largely intertwined, they each played important individual roles as well as their collaborative one. McBride, who became known as the "father of conservation in Iowa," began his advocacy of parks at least as early as 1895 as a member of the Iowa Academy of Science. In 1901, he and Pammel organized the Iowa Park and Forestry Association, made up largely of like-minded scientists who subscribed to the broad, comprehensive approach to resource management and use. The group's mission statement was sweeping in its scope, but it specifically provided for "the creation of one or more state parks in the vicinity of our lakes and streams." By 1917, the group, under a new name—the Iowa Conservation Association—was poised to play an influential part in the passage that year of Iowa's first state parks legislation.

The 1917 act set up the rudiments of a state parks program under the state game and fish warden, but it also provided for the appointment of a board of conservation with broad investigative and advisory authority. By this time, Pammel, who was a good bit younger than McBride, was taking a more active role in promoting the association's agenda. When the governor finally got around to appointing the board of conservation more than a year later, after a spate of start-up controversies had been resolved, Pammel was asked to serve. His fellow members then elected him as the board's first chairman, and in that capacity Pammel would exert a powerful influence on the development of Iowa's new state parks program until his retirement from the board in 1927.

With the machinery for implementation of its new state park act finally in place, Iowa lost no time in selecting and acquiring its first state parks. At the time, though, it was still unclear as to what form those parks would take. Although there was some difference of opinion on the board about such policy matters as purposes to be served, selection criteria, and so forth, Pammel's strong bias in favor of serving primarily scientific interests apparently prevailed. When he sensed that there might be a move to give greater consideration to recreational needs, he preemptively steered the board in another direction. Instead, they would select parklands from an initial list compiled of properties already determined to be "suitable"—virtually all of which had been identified previously by Pammel's colleagues in the scientific community. It apparently was through this process that Iowa's first park, Backbone, and a number of others were selected. Acquisition began almost at once, and Backbone State Park was formally dedicated in early 1920.

From its beginning in 1917, Iowa's state parks program quickly evolved and solidified. Just two years later, the law was amended to remove the state fish and game warden from the decision-making process and concentrate state park responsibilities in the board of conservation. The legislature that year also provided a direct appropriation to the board for park acquisition. In 1923, the board membership was increased from three to five and given staggered terms, thus providing for more stability and a broader range of opinions. Clearly, though, the board of conservation was steadily becoming more than just a state parks agency, and its ever-broadening scope in a way made it more difficult to deal with specifically state park issues. Over time, however, the board seemed to hit upon a workable formula for success, because it moved rapidly and effectively to produce one of the most prolific state park systems of the early twentieth century.

Summing Up

In the two decades between 1900 and 1920, America's state park movement started to come of age—if not yet mature, it certainly was enjoying a robust adolescence. The period had seen rapid growth and progressive change, but not just in the numbers and types of individual projects. Building on the mixed experience of the late nineteenth century, state park programs by 1920 were not only more numerous but noticeably more focused and better organized. They had no choice; rapid, consequential changes were taking place in almost every aspect of society. Interest in pure preservation was as strong as ever, and demand for outdoor recreation as an antidote for the ill effects of an increasingly stressful workplace was burgeoning. To top it off, the travel boom triggered by the availability of affordable automobiles and the concomitant expansion of road and highway systems brought parks of all kinds into the spotlight as logical destination areas. Thus, out of necessity, states were beginning to think in terms of planned, coordinated programs designed to create a *system* of parks, recognizing important differences both in the park properties themselves and in the purposes the parks were intended to serve.

Great strides had been made in just about every aspect of state park philosophy and practice, but obviously the level of progress was not consistent across the board. A few states were already way out in front, others were following the leaders, but almost half were still largely oblivious to the whole idea of state parks. Of those that had taken some initiative, most could point to only one or two, usually isolated accomplishments. But there were at least a half-dozen that already had extended their horizons and embarked on more systematic programs, not only for state park acquisition but for park development as well. In several instances, states were even working together for mutual benefit, and the feasibility of the "interstate" park had been emphatically demonstrated.

Clearly, motivations, techniques, and results varied greatly from state to state—and often even from park to park—but there were a growing number of unifying points emerging as well. For one thing, the term *state park* was now in general use, although still without a standard definition. A distinction was being made between the state's responsibility for parks and that of the other levels of government, and also between the respective functions of state parks and state forests. Probably most important, though, was the growing acceptance of a fundamental state park *rationale*—that state parks in all of their many variations were a good thing, and that every state should have them. These were rudiments of a state park movement in the making. The momentum was steadily building, and there would be no turning back.

What was now needed was a catalyst of some kind to bring the movement together and give it definite form as well as substance. That was about to happen.

5

Coalescence
The First National Conference on Parks

The Rise of the National Parks

If the state parks by about 1920 seemed to be making real progress, they still were being greatly overshadowed by the increasing popularity of the national parks. A number of new national park proposals had been put forth soon after the establishment of Yellowstone in 1872, but Congress had not yet accepted the notion that the country really needed a whole bunch of parks, and consequently it had been slow to act. By 1900, for instance, only five such parks had been created, and three of those were in the "big trees" area of central California. The idea was rapidly catching on, however, and the situation was about to change.

In September 1901, Theodore Roosevelt suddenly assumed the presidency upon the assassination of William McKinley and brought with him a genuine interest in just about everything wild and natural. While parks per se may not yet have been among his highest priorities, his deep personal concern for natural resources conservation—especially forests and wildlife—immediately created a receptive attitude in the federal government for establishing more parks. He himself fully recognized the value of national parks for *preservation*—rather than less-restrictive *conservation*—purposes. Referring to his tenure as president, he later wrote: "more was accomplished for the protection of wild life in the United States [between 1901 and 1909] than during all the previous years, *excepting only the creation of the Yellowstone National Park.*"[1]

National forests and wildlife refuges constitute the preponderance of Roosevelt's impressive conservation legacy, but he also took particular pride in the establish-

---

1. Harbaugh, *Writings of Theodore Roosevelt*, 156; emphasis mine.

ment of five new national parks during his presidency—doubling the number he had inherited. Even more important, perhaps, was his active role in securing passage of the federal Antiquities Act in 1906, which authorized the president unilaterally to designate a variety of places of "historic or scientific interest" as national monuments. Roosevelt lost no time in putting the new law to use. Over the next two years he established sixteen such "national monuments," most of which eventually were incorporated into the national park system; several, such as Grand Canyon and Mount Olympus (Olympic), were later upgraded to "national parks."

Roosevelt's dynamic leadership was certainly a major factor in energizing the national parks movement of the early twentieth century, but in this effort he also had some very potent allies. Some of these of course were influential individuals who shared Roosevelt's idealism and love of the outdoors: John Muir, George Horace Lorimer, and George Bird Grinnell, to mention but a few. And at the other end of the spectrum were those who saw primarily the practical economic value of national parks as major tourist attractions. A variety of entrepreneurs, and especially the western railroad companies, actively promoted the creation and development of new parks to further enhance their lucrative tourism enterprises. With the almost immediate commercial success of developments at Yellowstone, Grand Canyon, and other high-profile parks, economic potential quickly rivaled—perhaps for a time even eclipsed—pure preservation as an incentive for establishing more national parks. Whatever the motivations, they were powerful—and the clamor for new parks continued to grow.

It was now becoming obvious that the situation involving America's national parks was getting out of hand. Not only was the number of parks and monuments constantly increasing, but critical differences of opinion about their purpose and how they should be managed were beginning to surface. These differences came to a head in 1913 with the famous—or infamous—Hetch Hetchy dam controversy, when Congress rejected the arguments of the preservation interests and authorized a reservoir in Yosemite National Park to provide water for the city of San Francisco. This serious setback was attributed in large part to the lack of effective park advocacy. As National Park Service historian Barry Mackintosh put it: "Hetch Hetchy highlighted the institutional weakness of the park movement. While utilitarian conservation had become well represented in government by the U.S. Geological Survey and the Forest and Reclamation services, no comparable bureau spoke for park preservation in Washington."[2] Fortunately, relief was just around the corner.

2. Barry Mackintosh, "The National Park Service," 2.

Relief came unexpectedly in the form of a champion named Stephen Tyng Mather. Mather was a successful Chicago businessman born in California of New England parents. From boyhood he had been an ardent lover of the outdoors, and as a young man he had learned to appreciate, firsthand, the scenic wonders of the new national parks. Some of the things he saw, though, concerned him. In 1914, he wrote to Secretary of the Interior Franklin K. Lane, an acquaintance from their days at the University of California together, to complain about conditions in some of the parks. As paraphrased by Horace Albright, Lane replied: "Dear Steve: If you don't like the way the parks are being run, come down and run them yourself."[3] Apparently the offer was taken seriously, because Mather lost little time in moving to Washington and signing on as Lane's assistant.

Placed in charge of the national parks, but with no budget or staff to speak of, Mather financed much of his early work out of his own pocket. He took on a young Horace Albright—who had been lured from California a year or so earlier by another of Lane's assistants—as his legal aide, and together they set about renewing efforts to get a separate agency in the Interior Department to manage the expanding national park system. Such efforts, led primarily by J. Horace McFarland, president of the American Civic Association, had been under way for several years but had not succeeded in convincing Congress to act. Mather made the difference. He helped draft a bill to his liking, and after a year and a half of his nonstop lobbying, a National Park Service organic act was finally passed, becoming law on August 25, 1916. Some months later, Mather was appointed as the new agency's first director, and Albright as his assistant. The team was now in place and ready to go to work.

Steve Mather's Dilemma

When National Parks director Stephen T. Mather took over his daunting new responsibilities in early 1917, there were fifteen national parks and as many as twenty-nine national monuments (although some not yet under Park Service jurisdiction). Because of their lesser status, the monuments for the most part were not a matter of much concern at the time, but those areas with the designation of "national park" were looked upon as something really special. The problem was that all of the national parks were not of even quality or equally deserving of that lofty status. In fact, many of the monuments were arguably superior to some of

3. Horace M. Albright, "Stephen Tyng Mather," 16.

the parks. These inequities and inconsistencies bothered Mather—and, while he might rationalize "grandfathering" all fifteen of the parks he had inherited, he was nonetheless concerned about the increasing number of questionable park proposals still coming before Congress. As his biographer, Robert Shankland, put it: "Mather knew what a national park ought to be, and much as he wanted every suitable site brought into the system, he wanted every unsuitable site left out."[4] He had already been fighting these battles for two years and was now fully convinced that being a watchdog, the arbiter of national park quality, would always be a necessary part of his new job.

Mather's great concern was understandable. He had brought into the job the instincts of a sensitive outdoorsman and the discriminating judgment of a connoisseur that made him want to preserve only the best; but now he also had a strong proprietary interest in the program he had helped create and didn't want to see that program callously manipulated by those who did not understand it. He had helped shape the philosophy and direction of the national parks program by his input into the 1916 organic act, which charged the new agency with the seemingly impossible task of conserving park resources while also providing for their use in such a way as would leave the parks "unimpaired for the enjoyment of future generations." In placing all of the then-existing parks under the newly created National Park Service, the law also provided for future additions: "such other national parks and reservations *of like character* (my emphasis) as may be hereafter created by Congress." The dubious inference could easily be drawn that Congress was establishing a quality standard based on the character of the parks already on hand. If so, that could be viewed as either good or bad, depending on who would make the determination and which existing parks would be used for comparison.

The situation concerning the evaluation and selection of new national parks obviously was a sticky one, and Mather had realized this almost from the start. As Shankland noted, there had been sixteen proposals for new national parks introduced in Congress in 1916 alone—the year the organic act was passed. If they had all been approved it would have doubled the total number on hand; and the fact that only two of them were actually authorized strongly suggests that the quality of the proposals overall was not that impressive. If left uncontrolled, a bad situation could only get worse.

Mather continued to fret over this delicate problem, seeking on the one hand

4. Robert Shankland, *Steve Mather of the National Parks*, 184.

to discourage and quash questionable park proposals and on the other to avoid ruffling any Congressional feathers. In time, he succeeded in more or less clarifying his own thinking on national park standards and had this played back to him in the form of a 1918 letter from his boss, Interior Secretary Lane. This secretarial directive seemed forthright and to the point: "In studying new park projects, you should seek to find scenery of supreme and distinctive quality or some natural feature so extraordinary or unique as to be of national interest and importance. . . . The national park system as now constituted should not be lowered in standard, dignity, and prestige by the inclusion of areas which express in less than the highest terms the particular class or kind of exhibit which they represent."[5]

It would seem that such a clear-cut policy, assiduously applied, would be sufficient to maintain the standards and uphold the dignity of a constantly expanding national park system. The problem, though, was that Congress was not in the least bound by Mather's views, even if articulated in a secretarial directive. Proposals for new parks of varying quality kept coming. While Mather was generally successful in warding off the most atrocious of these, the never-ending effort still required an inordinate amount of his time and attention that was sorely needed elsewhere.

Ironically, Mather himself was partly responsible for this spate of new park proposals. Knowing that he was dependent on Congress for appropriations, he pragmatically campaigned for more development in the parks in order to draw more visitors, generate public acclaim, and thereby help justify his annual appeal for more funds. The effect of such active promotion in most cases was to enhance the popularity of the parks and stimulate economic growth in the area. As noted earlier, entrepreneurial opportunities created a powerful stimulant for new park development, and Congress was bombarded with bills to make a national park out of this or that piece of available real estate.

Mather had done his best. He had personally weighed the merits of each park proposal, had clarified and codified the standards and criteria for park selection, had worked one-on-one with many members of Congress to upgrade questionable projects—but still something was not quite right. The growing public desire to create new parks, whatever the incentive, could only be regarded as commendable. Even if most of the proposed sites were not suitable for national parks, many of them were still worthy of preservation for the public good. Clearly, what was now needed was another front—a second filter to catch those desirable national

5. Mackintosh, "National Park Service," 2–3.

park "rejects" and thereby relieve the pressure on the national park system to compromise its quality standards. Who better to take on this important responsibility than the state governments, where interest in state parks was already steadily spreading?

Steve Mather's Solution

It was a great idea: get the states to acquire and preserve many of the would-be national parks as state parks, and leave the federal government free to consider only the very best—those with true national significance—for the national park system. Mather had found the perfect solution, a "win-win" approach that would admirably serve the purposes of park interests at every level. With his objective clearly in mind, he then turned his attention to implementation. Would the idea work? Was there really enough interest in parks at the state level to develop and sustain the federal-state partnership that would be required? He had to find out.

Mather was no stranger to state park related activities. He personally had worked closely with Californians in efforts to save the coast redwoods, and he had come into contact with other projects, such as the Palisades of the Hudson, during his extensive travels as national parks director. According to Horace Albright, though, Mather quickly undertook to assess the state park situation nationwide: "He began checking on what the states were doing about parks and found very little action throughout the country."[6] Whether Mather's assessment was accurate or not is immaterial—the fact is that it convinced him that he had to do something to "build a fire" under the states if his plan was to succeed.

It was sometime in late 1920 that Mather came up with the idea of calling a nationwide conference on parks. If he could get the key movers and shakers together in one place, it would be infinitely easier to make his pitch and, hopefully, spark the interest and enthusiasm that would set his plan in motion. He first tried the idea on his new boss, Secretary of the Interior John Barton Payne, who had succeeded Franklin Lane in that position earlier in the year. Payne, a man of substantial means and influence, had long been involved in park work in the Chicago area and would prove to be a valuable ally in Mather's crusade. He immediately gave the idea of the national conference his enthusiastic support.

In October 1920, Mather called an impromptu meeting in Chicago to take up the matter of the national conference with a wider circle of advisors. It is not

6. Barry S. Tindall, "An Interview with Horace Marden Albright," 47.

clear who all was invited to or attended the meeting, but according to one source they were "key men, apparently old friends, who were active in civic undertakings."[7] The group may well have included some of the individuals Mather is otherwise known to have consulted in the matter, such as H. C. Cowles of the University of Chicago, Richard Lieber of Indiana, Louis Pammel of Iowa, J. Horace McFarland of the American Civic Association, William Welch of the Palisades Interstate Park, Mrs. F. C. Farwell of the Garden Club of America, Herbert Evison of the National Parks Association of Seattle, and Jens Jenson of the Friends of Our Native Landscape. At any rate, the group was influential enough and supportive enough to give Mather the confidence he needed, and the decision was made to proceed at once with a national conference on parks.

Mather obviously had made a persuasive case. He pointed out that the really exceptional sites such as Yellowstone and Grand Canyon would be protected as part of a national park system, but that there were countless other sites of lesser quality that should be preserved, especially in areas of the country that were not likely to have a national park. He was especially concerned about providing park accessibility to families that could not afford a trip to the far western United States. He reportedly made a statement to the effect that there were "no sites in the East or South deserving of national park status," leaving a huge geographical void which he felt should be filled by the creation of state parks.[8] Mather's eloquence brought immediate results: Not only did his audience accept his rationale and endorse the proposed conference, but also they each pledged financial support to help get the initiative underway. Mather could hardly have asked for more.

One person who attended the Chicago meeting at Mather's specific request was a young man named Oze Van Wyck. The two had met earlier in the year at Yellowstone National Park, where Van Wyck, a journalist by profession, had served as a publicist for the concession operations there and later as a seasonal park employee. Mather obviously was impressed with Van Wyck and hired him to promote another National Park Service project known as the National Park-to-Park Highway. His talents were soon diverted, however, when Mather assigned him as the point man for the proposed national conference on parks. In this capacity— as a staff of one—Oze Van Wyck would render tireless, effective service and prove himself to be a real miracle worker.

7. Herbert S. Evison, "The Birth of State Parks," 6.
8. Ibid.

The Groundwork Is Laid

Des Moines, Iowa, was selected as the site of the proposed national conference on parks. It apparently was Mather's own choice (although he credited it to a suggestion by Secretary Payne), influenced by the considerable progress Iowa was making with its state parks program. Iowa governor W. L. Harding, recognizing the potential significance of the event, agreed to host the conference at his capital city. Immediately following the Chicago meeting in October, Oze Van Wyck left for Des Moines to start on the advance preparations. The second week in January 1921—barely two months away—had been selected as the time frame for the conference, and there was no time to lose.

Van Wyck set up shop in the offices of the Iowa State Historical Department, where he worked very closely with the department's curator, Edgar R. Harlan, in addressing the formidable logistical issues that confronted them. The two proved to be an effective team and would later be named as joint secretaries of the conference. Their first big task was to compile a list of all of the organizations and individuals to be invited. The conference organizers wanted a diverse representation, and just about everybody they could think of was included: government officials, outdoor clubs, sportsmen's groups, garden clubs, academics, chambers of commerce, and on and on. In the end, the list grew to some fifteen hundred names, and each one was extended a formal invitation by Governor Harding. President Woodrow Wilson, on his sickbed suffering from a recent stroke, was persuaded to sign a letter endorsing the conference and encouraging attendance. Stephen Mather's personal prestige and popularity as national parks director was made a central issue in all of the promotional efforts, hoping that it would carry appropriate weight with the targeted audience. In an effort to solicit maximum participation by state governments, both Iowa's Governor Harding and Mather made personal appeals at the annual conference of governors in Pennsylvania that December.

Every reasonable effort had been made within the limited time available to publicize the conference and promote a good turnout. A diverse, chock-full three-day program, with Mather himself as the featured speaker, had been hastily put together. Now, all that was left to do was sit back and wait for January 10. It was the first event of its kind, and no one really knew what to expect.

The Conference Convenes

Some two hundred people showed up at the Fort Des Moines Hotel on Monday, January 10, 1921, for the first-ever National Conference on Parks. They represented a wide variety of interests from at least twenty-four states and the nation's capital. As might be expected, the host state of Iowa accounted for a substantial part of the attendance—something over fifty percent, in fact. Invited speakers made up about a third of those from other states. It was still an impressive assemblage, to be sure, containing a number of distinguished politicians, leaders of state and national organizations, and respected members of various relevant professional fields. In numbers, diversity, and quality, the group certainly fulfilled every expectation. The big question now, though, was whether those in attendance really knew why they were there, and whether they would accomplish anything worthwhile.

The opinions varied. Mather himself seemed to be pleased, and Horace Albright went so far as to assert: "The conference was much more successful than we had anticipated, and, in fact, was so successful that Mather thought we ought to keep it going." Some detached observers praised it as "an inspiring and auspicious event." Still others were not so sure. Harlan himself, as quoted by Rebecca Conard, later confessed that "I have never yet caught the fundamental purpose nor the source of inspiration of the enterprise."[9] His confusion apparently was shared by some of the other conferees at the time, as well as by later analysts seeking to assess the continuing legacy of the conference.

As a matter of fact, there was confusion from the start. Mather, the driving force behind the whole affair, no doubt had a pretty good idea of what he wanted the conference to accomplish: in essence, to recommend and support measures to encourage and facilitate the creation of "a large number of state parks." But planning for the conference proceeded so quickly and with such minimal formal organization that much of the original purpose and focus may well have been lost in the process. Even the title of the conference was misleading. It was publicized and generally referred to as the "First National Parks Conference," strongly implying that it was to deal not with state parks but with national parks. Even in its published proceedings it was called the "National Conference on *Parks*," not *state* parks.

9. Tindall, "Interview with Albright," 47; Rebecca Conard, "The National Conference on State Parks: The Early Years," 2.

ENTRANCE TO THE LEDGES, BOONE COUNTY

PROGRAMME

National Conference on
PARKS

BALL ROOM, HOTEL FORT DES MOINES
DES MOINES, IOWA

Janaury 10-11-12, 1921

Auspices of the Department of the Interior
and the State of Iowa

ANCIENT GAME PATH, BACKBONE PARK, DELAWARE COUNTY

Although hurriedly planned, the first "National Conference on Parks" offered a full three-day program, with dozens of nationally prominent speakers. COURTESY OF REBECCA CONARD

The program that was put together was broad and varied, but relatively little of it actually dealt with the primary subject of state parks. Part of this undoubtedly was due to the fact that the emerging concept of state parks was still rather fuzzy and not well understood. Even so, of the several dozen presenters, no more than a fifth could be said to have any direct connection with state parks administration. Oddly, the preponderance of the program dealt not with the mechanics of creating new state parks, as Mather had intended, but with peripheral subjects such as biological and historical resources, landscape architecture, beautification, city planning, and so forth. These discussions were all well and good, some of them probably even inspiring, but they offered little in the way of specific, practical advice or guidance for would-be state park promoters. In the final analysis, it was Mather's detailed presentation alone that defined the purpose and provided the substance of the conference.

Steve Mather's Agenda

Stephen Mather obviously had handpicked many of the presenters for the First National Parks Conference in order to ensure that certain important aspects of the subject matter were emphasized—and possibly also to provide an "amen chorus" for his own presentation. But, as he preceded the others at the rostrum, he went to some length to lay out his personal agenda up front in the hope of setting the tone he wanted. This he did at the opening session of the conference with a wide-ranging speech that, by itself, provided sufficient justification for the entire event. In fact, it would be fair to say that it provided the launching pad from which the National Conference on State Parks, as an organization, subsequently took rise. At any rate, he left no doubt as to what he wanted and what he hoped the conference would accomplish.

Mather acknowledged right off the bat that he had never given much thought to state parks until after he had become national parks director. It was only then that he had seen the importance of promoting both national and state parks as complementary programs. He cited several instances in which he had found it necessary to discourage someone's fond hopes of creating a national park on an inferior tract of land, repeatedly making the point that these properties would have made dandy state parks if only the states in question had acted. Although surely not intended, he may even have revealed something of a personal bias by referring to such cases as "problems" for him. Obviously, having to explain that the subject properties were not of national park caliber and maybe should be referred to the states was, if anything, a distraction from his primary mission and a nuisance he would just as soon avoid. On the whole, though, his pitch was one of cooperation and partnership, recognizing that each level of government had an important role to play. "We heartily believe in municipal parks, county parks and state parks," he said; "We believe in parks of every kind because they are good for the people."[10]

But the principal focus throughout his talk was on state parks. Mather noted that the National Park Service had been gathering data on state parks for the previous two years, and "it has been brought home to us how much has been done by relative few states and how little has been done by the majority of states."[11] He wanted more action at the state level and felt that the place to start was for each state government to set up the machinery for accepting donations of property and creating state parks. "Every state in the Union should have a park commission," he said, pointing to the Iowa Board of Conservation as a fitting example. He also pushed the idea that each state's program should be structured in a similar, if not identical, fashion, to facilitate interstate cooperation and provide "a common basis for discussion in a national convention of park commissioners that might well be held every year." To drive his point home, he then tossed out a challenge of sorts: "I offer the thought that one of the great needs of the movement for state parks is a model form of law, creating the machinery by which each state can proceed to the creation of a park system. I hope this conference . . . can evolve a statute [for this purpose] that we can recommend to the legislatures."[12]

Mather had laid out rather specifically what he thought the conference should do and what he hoped the individual states then would do, but he also was prepared to offer help. One can argue Mather's motives—whether he simply wanted to provide a safety valve for his beloved national parks, or wanted instead to make sure that no good opportunity for preserving *any* desirable park property was lost. But he appeared to be genuinely interested in seeing the state park movement succeed, and undoubtedly he had given the matter of assistance a lot of thought. He proposed seven areas in which the National Park Service might be of direct help to the states in furthering their state park programs:

1. acting as a clearinghouse for state park information and compiling and publishing pertinent data itself;

10. Stephen T. Mather, "The United States of America and Its Parks," 11.
11. Ibid., 11, 12.
12. Ibid., 12.

2. providing supportive publicity for fund-raising efforts for parkland acquisition;

3. including state park locations and information on national park maps;

4. providing planning advice on park projects in which both the state and the federal governments share an interest;

5. providing game animals from Yellowstone and other national park areas for stocking state parks;

6. supporting state efforts to obtain federal lands for state parks;

7. preserving roadside timber to enhance scenery along state roads traversing federal lands.

Mather may have lectured at length about what the states still had to do to meet their state park responsibilities, but he had also demonstrated that he was prepared—figuratively, anyway—to "put his money where his mouth was."

What Was Accomplished?

After three days of what must have been a nonstop talk-fest, the first National Conference on Parks came to an end. Whatever else it did, it certainly generated enough excitement to elicit a consensus call for a second one, and that may well have been its most important single accomplishment. The conference resolutions committee, chaired by Mather's friend Henry Cowles of the University of Chicago, drafted the formal language: "That, as a means of cementing all park interests into a harmonious whole and to provide for further conference and exchange of ideas, this body recommends the adoption of a policy of an annual meeting of this character, and recommends in particular the organization of a second conference on parks in 1922."[13] A committee was appointed for the purpose, with Interior Secretary Payne (soon to be leaving that post) as chairman both of the committee and of the future conference.

In addition to perpetuating itself, the conference did take up several issues of substance and adopted a few other resolutions. Most of these pronouncements fall into the "God and Motherhood" category, but a couple are worthy of specific mention. One was in direct response to Mather's call for standardizing state park legislation. The preamble stated: "That it is incumbent upon our governments, local, county, state and national, to continue to acquire sites suitable for recreation and the preservation of wild life, until eventually there shall be public parks within

13. National Conference of Parks, "Proceedings of the First National Conference on Parks, Des Moines, Iowa, January 10–12, 1921," 24.

That the first "National Conference on Parks" was well-attended is evidenced by the large crowd at the formal banquet, at which the national parks director Stephen T. Mather was the featured speaker. COURTESY OF REBECCA CONARD

easy access of all the people of our nation." The premise was thus laid for action at every level of government, but then the resolution seemed to narrow its focus to state implementation only: "To facilitate such acquirement we recommend the appointment of a special committee to study the park laws of the several states and to confer with the Executive Committee of the National Conference of Commissioners on Uniform State Laws, with a view to the preparation and presentation of model drafts."[14] A committee was appointed to pursue this recommendation also, with Everett Millard (another Chicagoan) as chairman. The committee's eventual findings will be discussed in the next chapter.

One other resolution is of interest, not particularly for what it says but for what motivated it: a fundamental and long-standing controversy over sometimes conflicting, sometimes competing, purposes of public parks and public forests. The language itself is innocuous enough: "That this Conference recognizing the fundamental value of forest recreation recommends the establishment of further National, State, County and Municipal forests and that the recreational use of such areas be correlated with similar activities in other publicly owned areas."[15] That the issue was even considered, though, came about purely by accident.

14. Ibid.
15. Ibid.

A man named Arthur Carhart was at the conference representing the U.S. Forest Service, but he was not scheduled to be on the program. During a lull in one of the sessions, Herbert Evison suggested to the moderator that he call on Carhart for a report on recreational use of the national forests. Following Carhart's impromptu remarks, Mather reportedly jumped to his feet and severely criticized the Forest Service for even venturing into the recreation field, which he felt was the exclusive province of parks. Cooler heads prevailed after a brief but heated discussion, but the subsequent adoption of a resolution clearly favoring the Forest Service position is somewhat surprising in view of Mather's dominant presence at the conference.[16] This episode is of only passing interest but is cited here primarily as further evidence that the conference ranged widely, and at times haphazardly, over the entire field of parks and recreation.

There was still another area in which the conference—or at least some of the participants—sought to carve out a legitimate niche, and that had to do with the tourism, or commercial, aspect of prospective state parks. The vast majority of the conferees were there representing academic interests, particularly the natural sciences, preservation and beautification interests, and park-related professions like landscape architecture. But there were a few from the commercial sector, representing transportation and other tourism interests, who were less concerned with creating parks than with promoting their recreational use and reaping the anticipated economic benefits. There is no record that this latter group caused much of a stir at the conference, but Mather played right into their hands with some of his comments about the importance of travel opportunities and overnight camps. "I believe we should have comfortable camps all over the country, so that the motorist could camp each night in a good scenic spot, preferably a state park," he said.[17] Somehow, this is supposed to have generated an unofficial conference slogan: "A state park every hundred miles," presumably on the assumption that that was a reasonable one-day's travel distance for a touring family at the time. While the slogan—or even the concept on which it was based—was not acted on by the conference, it took root and would reappear as a controversial, if not totally unwanted, specter again and again in later years.

So the first National Conference on Parks was now history. As noted earlier, it was generally proclaimed a success; but in terms of Mather's original intent to stimulate more state park activity, its effectiveness is not at all clear. For one thing,

16. Evison, "Birth of State Parks," 7.
17. Shankland, *Steve Mather,* 187.

it was pretty much a case of the clergy preaching to the choir. Much of the audience Mather wanted to reach was conspicuous by its absence (only nine of the twenty-nine states that had no parks to speak of at that time were represented, and not all of those by official state delegates). Moreover, except for Mather's presentation, there was no clear focus on state parks at all, nor especially on their role vis-à-vis the national parks. Judged as a single, isolated event, it would be difficult to call the conference an unqualified success. As part of the catalyst that precipitated much serious philosophizing about state parks over the following two decades, however, it probably deserves the recognition it has been accorded as one of the milestones in the evolution of the state park movement.

6

"A State Park Every Hundred Miles"

The National Conference on State Parks Goes to Work

Getting Organized

Stephen Mather's evangelistic zeal had carried the day. Not only had the first-ever National Conference on Parks provided a forum for timely discourse, it also had laid the groundwork for its perpetuation as the National Conference on *State* Parks (hereinafter, also *the Conference* or *NCSP*). The question now was how to capitalize on the momentum and channel the interest that had been generated into a suitable course of action. Success in that endeavor would require Mather's continuing close involvement, but even with his prodigious energy and drive he could not do it alone. He would have to look to others for help.

The Conference had selected Judge John Barton Payne as its chairman, of course, but he had resigned as secretary of the interior to accept appointment as head of the American Red Cross and could not be looked to for more than nominal leadership. Probably anticipating that circumstance, Mather had wisely positioned himself as vice chairman, so he could keep a sharp eye and a firm hand on the situation. The business of the Conference was to be conducted by an executive committee, consisting of the chairman, the vice chairman, and eight other individuals: Miss Beatrice M. Ward as secretary, Dr. Henry C. Cowles of Illinois, Herbert Evison of Washington, Dr. L. H. Pammel of Iowa, W. H. Stinchcomb of Ohio, Major William A. Welch of New York, Theodore Wirth of Minnesota, and Albert M. Turner of Connecticut.

It was an excellent group, well balanced in talents and interests, if not by geographical distribution. Beatrice Ward, then an employee of the National Park Service, was to become the Conference's first staff person under a loan arrangement worked out by Mather. Of the others, two—Cowles and Pammel—were academics, while all the rest were engaged in some aspect of park-related work. Most had actively participated in the Des Moines conference, but two were newcomers specifically recruited for the committee. Not surprisingly, both of these additions were park professionals, but they were drawn from distinctly different backgrounds. One was William Stinchcomb, director of the Cleveland Metropolitan Park System; the other was Albert Turner, a state park man through and through. As the first chief of the Connecticut state parks, Turner was widely recognized and admired for his sound philosophy and farsighted innovations in the field. In its judicious make-up, the executive committee of the new National Conference on State Parks clearly bore the mark of Steve Mather's discriminating hand.

Although without a means of financial support and with only a single "borrowed" employee, the Conference was now organized and ostensibly ready to go to work. Its name had been altered by the deliberate inclusion of the word *state*, but the intended import of that change was still unclear. Was it supposed to narrow the scope of the Conference's agenda specifically to state-operated parks; or was it simply meant to differentiate between the *national parks* on the one hand and all lower-level parks on the other? The resolutions adopted at the Des Moines conference offered little guidance, as they could easily allow either interpretation. In due course, however, a composite "object statement" was cobbled together:

> To urge upon our governments, local, county, state and national, the acquisition of additional land and water areas suitable for recreation, for the study of natural history and its scientific aspects, until there shall be public parks, forests, and preserves within easy access of all the citizens of every state and territory of the United States; and also to encourage the interest of non-governmental agencies and individuals in acquiring, maintaining and dedicating for public uses similar areas; and in educating the citizens of the United States in the values and uses of recreational areas.

Obviously designed to provide a little something for everybody, the statement was so broad and widely ranging as to be almost useless, and it would continue to be massaged and revised over the years to come.

Initially, anyway, the Conference had at least two clear mandates: first, to attempt the preparation of model legislation for establishment and operation of state park programs, which Mather had specifically requested and the Conference had resolved to do; and second, to plan another conference for 1922. Committees had already been appointed for each of these two undertakings, and it was now incumbent on the Conference leadership only to see that the committees did their jobs. The committee on model legislation was chaired by Everett L. Millard, who was active in art and beautification programs in the Chicago area. Chairing the committee on the 1922 conference was none other than the redoubtable Judge Payne himself, doing double duty along with his chairmanship of the permanent Conference.

Chairman Millard and his committee clearly had a daunting task in trying to devise a "one size fits all" legislative act for establishing a state parks program. After looking at the laws creating many of the state park programs already in existence, the committee quickly came to the conclusion that attempting to synthesize their better features into a single uniform model law would be inadvisable. The states were just too different, especially politically, to suggest that one approach to state park development would be adaptable to very many of them, certainly not all. The committee further consulted with the Commission on Uniform State Laws and found that body in complete agreement that the idea was unworkable.

In reporting his concerns to Mather in February 1922, Millard concluded, "Under these circumstances, anything that we could prepare would be merely educational, without a present prospect of securing general adoption." Mather seemed to understand, but he replied, "I can easily see how it would be impossible to have an entirely uniform bill on State parks, but I do think that their method of creation, development, and administration to a certain extent, should be similar."[1] As something of a compromise, Millard's committee submitted a report to the 1922 conference offering a number of suggestions for features to be included in prospective state parks legislation. Foremost among these was a recommendation that the state parks program be administered by an appointed citizen board of commissioners with complete rule-making and executive authority. How much influence the committee's recommendations might have had on subsequent state park legislation is impossible to say and is probably immaterial, anyway. Still, this whole exercise is of interest primarily for the lesson it should have taught (but apparently didn't), that most of the state park programs are too dissimilar to address them all in generalities as one homogeneous group.

1. Everett L. Millard to Mather, February 10, 1922; Mather to Millard, February 14, 1922; both in National Conference on State Parks Board of Directors Papers, series 3, box 1, NRPA Library.

Judge Payne's committee presumably had a much easier time with its assignment. One of Payne's colleagues on the National Conference on State Parks executive committee was Major W. A. Welch, the highly respected general manager of the Palisades Interstate Park in New York and New Jersey. Thus it was that when the 1922 conference committee went looking for a host site, Welch was close at hand. The conference was held in May of that year at Bear Mountain in the Palisades Park—a spot so popular that the conference returned there several times in later years.

In 1923, a third national conference was held, this time hosted by Colonel Richard Lieber at Indiana's Turkey Run State Park. It is significant that both the 1922 and 1923 meetings were conducted in state park properties, as this choice of venue seemed to accentuate the state park connection and suggest a pattern for future conference locations. Now, with three successful, well-attended meetings under its belt, the Conference seemed to have gained a measure of stability and maturity. While that alone must have provided some welcome comfort to the leadership, in other areas of its program it had yet to make much of a splash.

Not only was he the driving force behind creation of the National Conference on State Parks, Stephen Mather's energy and enthusiasm kept the organization motivated and focused throughout its formative years. Here, in 1926, he addresses the sixth national conference, at Hot Springs, Arkansas. NATIONAL PARK SERVICE

For the first three or four years, in fact, the NCSP existed as hardly more than a name. Judge Payne continued as its chairman, with Mather as the power behind the throne. The indispensable Beatrice Ward, now with the loftier title of "executive secretary," capably handled the day-to-day office duties. The Conference's limited operations were at that time supported entirely with voluntary donations, the erratic nature of which made it all but impossible to plan any kind of systematic program. Still, Mather and company persevered and the organization managed to survive. The year 1924, however, brought about a completely unanticipated development that would give the National Conference on State Parks new purpose and enable it to expand its program into areas previously beyond its reach.

The National Conference on Outdoor Recreation

The obvious corollary to parks is outdoor recreation (see Chapter 2), so it seemed reasonable that if park interests could have a national convocation so, too, could the advocates of outdoor recreation. This, in effect, was the case presented to President Calvin Coolidge by some of his advisors in early 1924, convincing the president to call a "National Conference on Outdoor Recreation" for May of that year. Although the titles used were identical in structure, there is no clear evidence that the outdoor recreation initiative was influenced by the successful National Conference on Parks of three years earlier. Still, the broad overlap between the two interests was obvious, and there was no way that outdoor recreation was going to be deliberated in any depth without due consideration of parks as well.

In his first formal statement on the subject, Coolidge went so far as to put outdoor recreation on a par with education as a government priority, and accepted for the "National Government" the lead role in formulating a "definite and clearly prescribed national policy" for providing outdoor recreation opportunities for the "rank and file of our people."[2] He then assigned the task of coordinating the effort to the secretaries of war, the interior, agriculture, and commerce, and to the assistant secretary of the navy. Later, the secretary of labor was added. Coolidge's proposal reportedly received such an enthusiastic response that he followed up soon afterward with a specific call for a national conference to be held in Washington, D.C. He appointed the assistant secretary of the navy, Colonel Theodore Roosevelt (son of the late president), as chairman of the event, with the other

2. Calvin Coolidge, "Statement of Need of a National Outdoor Recreation Policy," in National Conference on Outdoor Recreation, *Proceedings of the National Conference on Outdoor Recreation,* 2.

secretaries as honorary chairmen. Roosevelt's selection was pretty much preordained, as he apparently had been one of the principal advocates of the conference idea in the first place.

Coolidge had laid out a fairly detailed agenda for the proposed conference, with a good bit of emphasis on areas for federal involvement. However, he was careful to point out that "this is not an effort to federalize recreation at the expense of State, municipal, local, or private interest therein."[3] Rather, he stressed the importance of enlisting the whole gamut of potential players in both the conference itself and in the coordinated programs he hoped would deliver to "the average American outdoor recreation, with all that it implies." Roosevelt lost no time (he had none to lose) in extending an invitation on the president's behalf. On May 5, he sent out notices to a wide range of organizations that might be interested, urging them to send one or more delegates: "The success of the endeavor depends mainly upon the whole-hearted cooperation of such as you. I therefore most earnestly bespeak your real interest in this important matter."[4]

Although the notice was short, the response it elicited was impressive. Over three hundred people showed up, representing 128 national organizations. Probably anticipating a madhouse upon their arrival, Roosevelt had wisely appointed committees in advance to deal with nine specific subjects on the conference agenda. Of these, only one—"A survey and classification of recreational resources"—made room directly for consideration of state parks. Fortunately, however, the scope of the conference broadened and diversified somewhat as its work progressed, and state parks received much greater attention in the end than was probably originally contemplated.

Like its state parks predecessor, the National Conference on Outdoor Recreation quickly took on a life of its own, setting up a hundred-member "general council" to oversee its activities. Of this august group, there were at least a dozen or so who were no strangers to state parks—including Herbert Evison, Richard Lieber, John Barton Payne, Theodore Wirth, and, specifically representing the National Conference on State Parks, William A. Welch. The conference also established a number of committees, including one on "State Parks and Forests,"

3. Calvin Coolidge, "Statement of the President Calling a National Conference on Outdoor Recreation," in National Conference on Outdoor Recreation, *Proceedings of the National Conference on Outdoor Recreation*, 4.

4. Theodore Roosevelt [Jr.], "Invitation to Organizations to Participate in Conference," in National Conference on Outdoor Recreation, *Proceedings of the National Conference on Outdoor Recreation*, 6.

chaired by Charles Lathrop Pack of the American Nature Association. That committee served as the primary vehicle for consideration of state park issues over the five-year life of the conference, and its work deserves at least some passing comment.

In its formal report, Pack's committee identified its job as one of "summarizing present conditions with respect to State parks and forests, analyzing present and future needs and making constructive recommendations for meeting these needs." After first noting that "The function of national parks is obviously the preservation of such areas as have outstanding scenic beauty of interest to the Nation as a whole," the report continued: "State parks should be created for these three principal purposes: To preserve additional scenic areas of outstanding or typical qualities which *are not deserving of national park or monument status;* to provide a system of unspoiled natural areas so distributed as to furnish outdoor recreational opportunities to all the population; and to retain in public ownership areas of historic interest and value." I call attention to the italicized phrase because it seems to reflect a common sentiment at the time that state parks could not (or perhaps *should not*) aspire to the same quality standards set for the national parks. However, the report pursued this line of thought a step further: "County parks and park systems properly occupy a place in this series of graduations down from the national park to the city park. Areas not suitable for State parks and specially adapted for local recreational purposes may be properly utilized as county parks and administered by county government."[5]

The committee's purview included both state parks and forests, of course, and, although a fairly clear distinction was made between the two for discussion and analysis, the report's recommendations seemed designed to fit both categories equally. Recognizing that available information on the important subjects of inventory and financing was sorely inadequate, the committee offered two main "suggestions":

> That data be gathered from the appropriate sources bearing on the extent, nature, administration, and present service of all parks and forests now set aside for administration by the individual States and counties.

> That data be gathered from the appropriate sources bearing upon funds and appropriations now available or in prospect in the several States for the acquisition of State parks and forests.

5. Charles Lathrop Pack, chairman, "Report of the Committee on State Parks and Forests," in National Conference on Outdoor Recreation, *Proceedings of the National Conference on Outdoor Recreation,* 192 (emphasis mine), 193.

The report then concluded with a general exhortation, which was also later adopted as a resolution by the full conference:

> We urge upon our Governments, local, county, State, and National, the acquisition of land and water areas suitable for recreation, and preservation of wild life, as a form of the conservation of our natural resources, until eventually there shall be public parks, forests, and preserves within easy access of all the people of our Nation, and also to encourage the interest of nongovernmental agencies and individuals in acquiring, maintaining, and dedicating for public use similar areas.[6]

The close similarity of that passage and the "object statement" of the National Conference on State Parks (quoted earlier) leaves no doubt about the influence the state park proponents were able to exert in the deliberations of the conference.

The need for more and better information on just about everything proved to be one of the dominant themes of the National Conference on Outdoor Recreation, and steps were taken to initiate studies and surveys in several specific areas. One of these was state parks. In discussing plans for follow-up actions, Chauncey J. Hamlin of New York, who was chairing the session, offered his idea on exactly how a state park survey should be conducted:

> We have an organization known as the National Conference on State Parks, of which Judge Payne is chairman, represented at this meeting by Major Welch and others, and we desire to have the organization conduct a survey of the State park situation throughout the United States. The practical way in which we hope that will be done is this: Some able man will be employed and given his salary, his railroad fare, a pat on the back, and started out for a year's trip to spend a week in each of the 48 states to determine the present park situation; to call on the governors and forestry people, and others interested in the State parks and to carry to each State that he visits the story of what is being done in the other States . . . and he will describe the methods. I cannot think of any more practical way of conducting a State park survey and of arousing interest in State parks.[7]

The chairman may have been indulging in a frivolous bit of micromanagement, but the modus operandi he suggested was ultimately followed almost to a

6. Ibid., 193.

7. Chauncey J. Hamlin, Remarks to the National Conference on Outdoor Recreation, Washington, D.C., December 11[?], 1924, in National Conference on Outdoor Recreation, *Proceedings of the National Conference on Outdoor Recreation*, 9[?].

tee. A grant of $12,500 was put up by the Laura Spelman Rockefeller Memorial to finance the work, and the National Conference on State Parks happily accepted the assignment. The "able man" hired for the job was Raymond H. Torrey, a journalist by profession, who signed on as "field secretary" in 1925 and remained for several years, later becoming secretary of the American Scenic and Historic Society. Further financial support from the Rockefeller Memorial enabled the state park survey work to continue through 1926 and half-time in 1927. The results were published first in 1926, in book form by the National Conference on State Parks, and later, in 1928, as part of the final report of the National Conference on Outdoor Recreation.

With the submittal of Torrey's report, the National Conference on State Parks creditably satisfied its obligation to the National Conference on Outdoor Recreation, and there is no evidence of further direct involvement by the former in the latter. However, the collateral benefits to the NCSP from that relatively brief collaboration were substantial. In effect, the funding from the Rockefeller Memorial, the creation of a full-time staff field position, and the broad national exposure from the survey project itself were largely responsible for putting the National Conference on State Parks, as an organization, "on the map." The resulting surge of interest stimulated by that newfound credibility is discussed in the following section.

As a footnote, the National Conference on Outdoor Recreation continued its work only until 1929, when it officially went out of business. It did hold a second general conference in 1926 and published a number of reports, but it apparently succumbed from declining interest and a lack of funding—or perhaps the lack of a Stephen Mather.

Stumping for State Parks

The events of 1924–1925 growing out of the National Conference on Outdoor Recreation did indeed pump new life into a languishing National Conference on State Parks. An important new assignment and, especially, the funds with which to carry it out proved to be a potent elixir. Moreover, a separate grant from the Laura Spelman Rockefeller Memorial was made to the Conference in 1925 through the Federated Societies on Planning and Parks—a newly formed federation consisting of the American Civic Association, the American Institute of Park Executives, the American Park Society, the National Conference on City Planning, and the National Conference on State Parks. (The stated purpose of this group was "to render to communities and individuals more convenient and effective service, and to do so with a minimum expenditure of effort and money." In fact, though, its principal initial concern seems to have been the distribution of the Rockefeller funds on some kind of a pro rata matching basis.) In short order, the Conference was able to double its staff (from one position to two), move into separate quarters of its own (in Washington's Union Trust Building), build stronger ties with allied interest groups, and embark on a nationwide survey of considerable magnitude and import. Clearly, a reinvigorated organization was now on the move.

It is significant that, as its first program-related employee, the Conference hired a newspaperman. Probably the organization's greatest weakness had been its lack of publicity and outreach—outside its immediate circles, it was virtually unknown. Charles Lathrop Pack, in his committee report to the National Conference on Outdoor Recreation, had observed, "The movement leading up to the creation of a state park is generally of necessity preceded by the awakening of public sentiment."[8] If the National Conference on State Parks wanted to awaken enough public sentiment to get a whole state park movement energized, it would darn well have to start making some noise.

The national survey of state parks and forests was a perfect vehicle for making contacts across the country and spreading the gospel of state parks—just as Hamlin had envisioned. Such a golden opportunity did not escape the astute Mather's notice, and he made the most of it. Over the next year or so, Raymond Torrey was constantly on the go, visiting forty-six of the forty-eight states, some more than once, gathering data and generating interest. Mather also kept himself and Beatrice Ward busy, getting in a plug wherever they could. Although others were undoubtedly called on to assist from time to time, these three—Mather, Torrey and Ward—became the principal "voices" for state parks throughout the 1920s.

The message those voices delivered was essentially twofold: first, even though there was still a long way to go, a lot of encouraging progress was being made on the state parks front; and, second, the National Conference on State Parks was responsible for much of that progress. Through radio talks, personal appearances, and a variety of print media, the basic message—or some major aspect of it— was hammered home. Interestingly, each of the three principal spokesmen seemed to concentrate on a different area of emphasis, although they varied their pitch freely as the occasion or purpose required. Mather was very generous in his praise of individual state accomplishments, and waxed eloquently about exciting

8. Pack, "Report of Committee on State Parks," 192.

opportunities that still awaited. Torrey drew on his research for the national survey to talk about the history of state parks and to assess their current status in facts and figures. Ward, as might be expected of the "office manager," was most likely to discuss the organization and inner workings of the Conference itself. All together, though, they painted a fairly complete and balanced picture of what was going on with America's state parks.

A great deal was going on with America's state parks during that time. For sure, a number of previously inactive states climbed on the state parks bandwagon and many new parks were acquired and developed. What is not so certain is just how much the NCSP contributed to those results. Mather was a master at public relations, though, and was not above putting everything in the best possible light. About the Des Moines conference, he said: "It was the first of a series of remarkably inspirational meetings and the State park idea began to grow like a snowball." Later on, he referred to the Conference as "the national organization of State recreation progress." Speaking of recent growth in state parks, he commented: "The past six years [1921–1927] has seen the greatest progress[,] and we believe one of the greatest factors in this steady progress has been the work of the National Conference on State Parks."[9]

Considering his honest passion for the cause he had set in motion, however, Mather can readily be forgiven for indulging in a little innocuous horn-tooting. The important point is that, while most of the states might have continued to make significant progress individually on their own, it was the National Conference on State Parks that provided a medium for communication, exchange of ideas, and mutual encouragement among the states, and it thereby created the opportunity for a cohesive nationwide movement in state parks.

The Expanding Fold

Between 1921 and 1930, nine—possibly ten—more states established their first state parks, as compared with seven for the period of 1911 to 1920. This modest increment from one decade to the next would appear to be simply the normal progression of an ascending trend. Still, the increase was impressive by any measure, and its timing was such that it had to be attributed at least in part to the good work of the National Conference. Nebraska, which in 1913 had made a tentative effort at forest land preservation, joined the ranks in 1921 by setting aside a

9. Stephen T. Mather, unpublished texts for speeches and radio talks, 1925–1928, in Board of Directors Papers, series 3, box 1, NRPA Library.

section of "school land" for its Chadron State Park. That same year, the legislature created a state park board to administer Chadron along with other parks that might later be acquired. The board was initially placed in the department of public works, but in 1929, after several more parks had been acquired, it was combined with the game and forestry functions in a new agency.

Oregon came next. The state had dabbled in the park business as early as 1890, when it accepted nominal responsibility for a public use area at the Sodaville Mineral Springs, but it was not until 1921 that a serious program was begun—primarily to preserve the roadside beauty of Oregon's highways. The program was set up under the state highway commission, which established a small tract of donated land as the Sara Helmick State Park in 1922. A new law passed in 1925 expanded the program and allowed the state to seek out larger properties that were not necessarily tied to the highway system.

In 1927, Charles G. Sauers of Indiana came to Oregon as part of a west coast tour for the NCSP. His object apparently was to push the Conference's recommendation for a single, independent agency to administer state park programs. Oregon would have none of that "fool idea," however. While the state highway commission may not have viewed parks as a high enough priority to please some advocates, the assured funding source it provided was deemed more important than a separate, parks-exclusive agency. In 1929, though, the highway commission did consent to hire a full-time state parks superintendent—but it would be many more decades before Oregon's state parks would gain independent agency status.

Although its famous "hot springs" had ended up as a national rather than a state park unit, Arkansas reentered the picture in 1923 with another park proposal that had determined advocates pulling hard in both directions. This time, the property was a scenic section of the Ouachita Mountains, a part of which had already been donated to further a local campaign for establishment of a national park. The National Park Service opposed the idea, however (a position in which it would be strongly supported later by the NCSP), and eventually the 1923 state legislature authorized acceptance of the property to become the Petit Jean State Park. Four years later, the legislature created a state parks commission to select, acquire, and manage additional properties, and the Arkansas state park system was under way.

The year 1924 brought two more states into the state parks fold—Vermont and Missouri—but in both cases, as with many others, seeds of interest had been planted years before. Vermont lagged somewhat behind its neighboring states of

Oregon's entry into the state parks field was motivated by the desire to preserve its scenic highway corridors, which led to the establishment of numerous roadside parks called "waysides." They proved to be popular stopping points for motorists, as evidenced by this scene at the Bradley Wayside in the 1920s. OREGON PARKS AND RECREATION DEPARTMENT

New Hampshire, Massachusetts, and New York, but concern for its forest resources had led to the establishment of a state forest service as early as 1909. A tract of land donated in 1924 was designated the Mt. Philo State Forest Park, and this was followed by an act of the legislature in 1929 that provided specific authority for acquisition and operation of state parks and for charging fees to generate revenue for their support.

Missouri citizens had been agitating for a state parks program at least since 1907, when they convinced the legislature to consider a bill for that purpose. Although that attempt failed, it was followed in 1914 by the creation of a senate committee to inspect potential park properties, and in 1917 by passage of a bill to set up a fund under the fish and game department for the acquisition of state parks. The first such property to be acquired with this fund was Big Spring, in 1924 (now part of the Ozark National Scenic Riverways)—although a historic site, Arrow Rock Tavern, had been acquired the year before by other means. The state moved aggressively after that, accumulating six park areas by 1925, and fourteen by 1928.

Georgia was another reentry into the state parks arena. The Indian Springs property that it had received from the Creek Indians in 1825 had been leased out to private interests for almost a century when, in 1925, the legislature passed the "Forestry Administrative Act," providing funds for work by the state board of forestry. Under that authority, Indian Springs and another property (Vogel) in the north Georgia mountains were established as "state forest parks." They remained under the jurisdiction of the board of forestry until 1931, when a "state park" system was established with Indian Springs and Vogel as its first two units.

A continent away, Nevada also was thinking "parks." An enlightened leadership had recognized that modern improvements in transportation and other facilities would increase tourism and create a demand for access to the state's scenic areas. Although most of its territory was owned by the federal government, the state took the initiative in 1923 to set aside choice areas on its own. At the governor's recommendation, the legislature passed an act that year authorizing the establishment of "state recreational grounds and game refuges." Within two years, fifteen such areas had been designated by gubernatorial proclamation. All but one of these apparently fell under the "game refuge" classification and were placed under the state fish and game commission for management. As there was no appropriate state agency to take the remaining one, Cathedral Gorge, it was entrusted to a private group called the Cathedral Gorge Pageant Association. Although it would be several years before Cathedral Gorge—along with other sundry properties—would be subsumed by a state-operated park system, it is commonly regarded as Nevada's "first state park" by virtue of its 1925 designation.

The neighboring Appalachian states of Kentucky and West Virginia also entered the field about that time. Responding to growing citizen interest, the Kentucky legislature passed a bill in 1924 creating a state park commission. Among its duties, amplified in 1926, the commission was to examine and recommend suitable park sites and propose methods of acquisition, either by donation or by "popular subscription." Heroic promotional efforts by the commission's first chairman, Willard Rouse Jillson, soon paid off, as four new park properties were acquired by the end of the year. Others soon followed, including Cumberland Falls in 1931. This acquisition was especially significant because it culminated a long rough-and-tumble battle with hydropower interests in which the NCSP actively joined on behalf of the state (more about that later).

In West Virginia, park interest was coming to a head by 1925. That year, the state's Game, Fish and Forestry Commission purchased a large tract of land as a wildlife and timber reserve that would later, in 1937, be redesignated the Watoga State Park. Of more direct importance, though, was the creation in 1925 of a State Forest, Park, and Conservation Commission to make recommendations for properties to comprise a state park system. The commission presented a list of desirable properties to the 1927 legislature, along with a cogent appeal for an expeditious acquisition program. The legislature apparently got the message. The first of the recommended properties was acquired the following year and became the Droop Mountain Battlefield State Park.

Texas was not counted as a "new" state park state with the above group, but it probably should be. It had, at least unofficially, considered itself in the park business with the purchase of the San Jacinto Battleground site in 1883. Since that time, though, it had been virtually inactive until 1923, when Governor Pat Neff convinced the legislature to create a state parks board. The board's immediate primary task was to solicit donations of land for "parks and camping places" throughout the state, and in this effort it proved remarkably successful. By 1927, it had lined up donations of some twenty-four sites, totaling almost two thousand acres. This was one case where the promotional campaign of the National Conference on State Parks seems to have been a particularly persuasive factor, and Stephen Mather was quick to give (and take) credit. In a 1925 radio address, he heaped on the praise:

> [T]he last year has been the most spectacular of all,—when Pat M. Neff, then Governor of Texas, closed his executive desk and went out to talk State parks for weeks to the people of his own state. Up to that time Michigan held the record by having 25 State parks to their credit but Governor Neff's whirlwind campaign, concentrated entirely on the State park idea, brought the State by actual gift 51 areas for State parks. Not a cent had been appropriated for their purchase.[10]

The Emergence of System Planning

While these nine or ten "new" states were making their first serious ventures into the state parks field, many of the states with older, more established pro-

10. Stephen T. Mather, "State Parks and Forests," [1928?] manuscript prepared for public delivery, in Board of Directors Papers, series 3, box 1, NRPA Library, 1. Mather apparently was relying on preliminary data when he used an obviously inflated figure of fifty-one donated sites.

grams also were expanding and, in some cases, plowing new ground. It was at about this time that the state park idea really began to take on a consistent shape nationally, and a state park profession—embodying standard elements of philosophy, mission, terminology, and so on—was beginning to emerge. Up to now, most of the states had been more or less designing their programs as they went, and each such program bore distinct influences of the determinant factors prevailing in its own area, including physical, cultural, economic, and, especially, political. Thus, park programs of particular states—and sometimes of entire regions of the country—often reflected a certain tradition characteristic of their area.

The park programs of the northeastern states, and later those in the south, evolved largely from a "forestry" tradition, while in many of the plains and western states, it was a "game and fish" tradition. Tourism and the desire to stimulate commerce, especially in rural and undeveloped areas, provided still another important tradition that helped direct the course of many state park programs. But now, in the 1920s, with greatly enhanced communication among the states and the inevitable cross-fertilization of ideas, those traditional distinctions were steadily being erased by an unplanned, yet very real, move toward standardization.

As might be expected, the growing number of states that had committed themselves to a state parks program were now turning their attention more toward procedural issues. It was one thing to establish a few parks, but something else entirely to plan, develop, and operate them effectively. One important consideration was to think of parks in terms of a *system,* rather than as just a bunch of separate, unrelated properties. Albert Turner had made an excellent case for the system approach as early as 1914, in a report to the Connecticut general assembly—stressing such factors as natural suitability, distribution, size, accessibility, and level of development of park properties.

Others built on Turner's ideas or came up with their own. In 1920, Pennsylvania instituted a classification system in an effort to match each park property with its most beneficial recreational use; and in 1930, thanks to a newly formed Pennsylvania Parks Association, it received its first state parks master plan, entitled "An Outline of a Balanced State Park System for Fifteen Million People."[11] Minnesota, New York, and California were also among the earliest to recognize the need for overall system planning. In reporting to the legislature in 1923, the Minnesota state auditor commented on the haphazard acquisition process and resulting uneven quality of that state's parks—a situation he deemed "thoroughly

11. Forrey, *Pennsylvania State Parks,* 21.

bad."[12] His insightful analysis got immediate results—legislation was adopted that same year to address the cited problems in what has been called the probable beginning of the Minnesota state park *system*.

New York and California, both with growing numbers of parks, were confronted with complex issues of administrative organization as well as with system planning—and each found an effective approach for addressing its particular situation. As noted earlier, New York's parks had evolved largely through a series of independent citizen-led projects, each with its own autonomous governing council. This had created a chaotic situation that frustrated any hope of overall coordination and control. New York's solution, masterminded by the inimitable "power broker" Robert Moses, was to obtain legislation in 1924 to create an umbrella agency called the State Council of Parks, with powers to oversee and regulate the numerous individual councils. Moses was named chairman of the state council (a post he retained, for all practical purposes, until 1963), and he proceeded to guide the state through one of the most ambitious and successful park expansion programs of all time.

On the opposite coast, California was facing up to the deficiencies in its own state parks program, still in its infancy. Although California had, in effect, started the ball rolling with its pioneering efforts to establish a state park in the Yosemite Valley over a half-century earlier, by 1925 it had accumulated only five state park properties and a number of historic monuments. Seizing the initiative, the Save-the-Redwoods League proceeded to set up its own state parks committee to look at the situation. What the state needed, the committee concluded, was a plan to guide its state parks program, a commission or similar structure for administration, and a source of funds for implementation.

An effort was made to secure legislation for the purpose in 1925, but, despite personal lobbying by Stephen Mather and other notables, the governor refused to sign the bill into law. A second attempt was made in the following legislative session, in 1927, with a new governor in office. It succeeded, and in relatively short order, California got its first state park commission, a new state parks chief, and an already jump-started program. And it surely was not a coincidence that the 1928 meeting of the National Conference on State Parks was held in California soon afterward, helping to boost the passage of a $6 million bond issue for state park acquisition, which set a precedent for effusive citizen support of park causes that continues to this day.

12. Meyer, *Everyone's Country Estate*, 81.

Connecticut's Albert Turner, "an outstanding interpreter of the spirit of state parks," was one of the first to adopt a system approach to state park planning and development. CONNECTICUT DEPARTMENT OF ENVIRONMENTAL PROTECTION

The California experience provided a number of useful lessons for other states to ponder, but probably its most valuable contribution at the time turned out to be the state park survey that the new commission almost immediately contracted with Frederick Law Olmsted to make. Olmsted—the son of the famous Central Park designer of the same name—submitted his report in 1929, and it is still regarded as one of the classics of state parks literature.

Many other states were making progress in various aspects of their state parks programs, of course, but they are far too numerous to receive mention here. The important point is that the period of the 1920s was one of much innovation and refinement—and some of it undoubtedly was due to the promotional efforts of the National Conference on State Parks.

A Look at the Numbers

As noted earlier, Mather and others were quick to claim a share of the credit for state park advances, and they repeatedly pointed to comparative figures to make their case. The "pre–Des Moines" number of states with state parks was almost always given as twenty (sometimes nineteen), but in due course Conference spokesmen were citing numbers as high as forty-three (1925), forty-six (1926), and forty-two (1927). The figure fluctuated depending on the speaker and exactly what indicator of new state park activity he was purporting to measure (actual parks, legislation introduced, official expressions of interest, and so forth).

The problem with this numbers game is that—even after the completion of Torrey's survey in 1926—available statistics simply were not that reliable. There were no standard definitions in use at the time to prevent the inevitable "apples and oranges" comparisons, and some of the states obviously did not know what to report. Moreover, there was much confusion between programs—state parks, forests, wildlife preserves, historic memorials, and others. Consequently, a certain property might be included for one count and excluded for another, depending on how it was regarded at the time. As discussed in an earlier chapter, these problems constitute a nightmare for park statisticians and taxonomists, but because of the nature of the beast the resulting discrepancies will never be satisfactorily reconciled. Fortunately, the problem is more of an academic than a practical concern.

It is interesting, though, that prior to the convening of the National Conference on State Parks, no effort had been made to inventory state park progress in a systematic way. Apparently, an informal tally was made at the Conference that, as reported by Freeman Tilden, revealed that twenty-nine states were still without state parks at the time.[13] That figure provided a benchmark of sorts, and following the Conference interest in counting parks greatly intensified, presumably as a means of measuring subsequent acquisition progress. Torrey's 1925 survey found that thirty-six states were reporting one or more parks, and three of the other states had state forests supporting recreational use—leaving nine states with neither. All together, Torrey reported a total of 578 state parks with 2,663,271 acres, and 156 state forests with 1,699,900 acres. He also included a third category of "other lands, unorganized for recreation," but these were too varied and unspecific to deal with in numerical terms.[14] Notwithstanding the deficiencies discussed above, Torrey's report is of value as the first comprehensive inventory of state park accomplishments in the country.

At about the same time that Torrey's survey was released, the American Tree Association published its own state parks inventory in the 1926 edition of the *Forestry Almanac.* The article, entitled "State Parks and Forestry," stated, "Closely allied with the development of State Forests, the creation of State Parks has gained marked popularity within the past few years. Many of these areas combine with scenic beauty, historic significance or other notable character, forest value." Although this count produced totals of only 272 state parks in twenty-eight states, it is of particular interest because it not only identified every park by name but also marked their approximate locations on an outline map. Thus, while it may not have been as complete as Torrey's, it left no doubt as to which specific properties were included.[15]

In 1928, the National Conference on State Parks published a second comprehensive assessment of America's state parks, this one prepared by Beatrice Ward Nelson (she had married fellow executive committee member Wilbur Nelson, of Virginia), entitled *State Recreation: Parks, Forests, and Game Preserves.*[16] Although the focus of this report was somewhat different from Torrey's, Nelson did include her own real estate count, identifying twenty-five states with state parks and an additional ten with state forests only. Her unit totals were 347 parks with 2,722,550 acres, and 212 forests with 2,750,195 acres. That these figures, just two years later, differed so drastically from Torrey's had to be due largely to the methodologies used.

Regrettably, because all of these early counts—understandably enough—were

13. Freeman Tilden, *The State Parks: Their Meaning in American Life*, 5.
14. Torrey, "State Parks and Recreational Uses," 16–17.
15. "State Parks and Forestry," 193–96.
16. Beatrice Ward Nelson, *State Recreation: Parks, Forests, and Game Preserves*, 430–31.

at such variance, their reliability and comparability are greatly diminished. Still, much useful information can be gleaned about individual states by selective use of the data. For what it's worth, by my "reconstructive" count there were probably thirty states that, by 1930, had formally designated at least one property that might reasonably be called a state park. If this 50 percent increase in state park activity did not constitute the "snowball" effect Mather had claimed, it at least indicated substantial progress toward realization of the NCSP's putative goal of "a state park every hundred miles."

7

Dubious Progress

Assessing the Relevance of the National Conference on State Parks

Looking for Direction

Almost from the start, the precise purpose of the National Conference on State Parks had been unclear. In calling the first conference in 1921, Stephen Mather himself seemed to know exactly what he wanted to accomplish, but others, such as Iowa's Edgar Harlan, were not so sure. Reports of that first meeting hint at apparent misconceptions, differences of opinion, conflicting motives, and, at times, possibly even general confusion about what was going on. Given the hasty preparations for the Des Moines conference, however, and the limited understanding of the subject matter by most of the participants, one might excuse some lack of unity and consensus on that occasion. But over the following decade or more the NCSP—even as it developed as a structured, permanent organization—was still seeking a coherent sense of purpose that would guide its program along a consistent path.

A large part of the problem no doubt lay in the patchwork "object statement" that obviously had been thrown together to placate, if not please, all of the diverse interests. For one thing, its stated purposes were far too ambitious for the infant organization to address with any hope of overall success. For another, possibly more troublesome, it also provided for actions in support of potentially competing interests: federal versus state (or county or city) government levels; recreational versus scientific uses; public versus private venues; and management programs for parks versus forests (or preserves)—and quite likely a few others merely implicit therein. Nowhere, however, either by word or implication, did it give any special recognition or status to state parks as a specific class. Trying to reconcile the many inherent conflicts in an overly broad and awkwardly worded mission statement soon became a major preoccupation for the NCSP.

Some specific areas of potential friction were becoming apparent even before adjournment at Des Moines. It was clear, for instance, that a philosophical dichotomy existed between those who saw parks primarily as a means of providing active recreation (especially to serve the expanding automobile travel market) and those who advocated maximum preservation of natural scenery. Moreover, the second group was split further according to the reasons for preservation: to provide aesthetic and spiritual gratification, or to serve purely scientific interests. While one participant was defending "auto camps" as a public necessity, others were touting natural parks as "social safety valves" and places to "restore the soul of man," or as "laboratories of natural science." Even the landscape architects present injected a note of potential discord by seeking, however subtly, to stake a claim for their profession as the logical planners of state parks. Then, of course, Mather himself had provided fuel for latent controversy with his call for a uniform approach to state park administration and his combative assertion that forest managers should stay out of the park and recreation business altogether. And this was just the beginning.

These and similar philosophical and procedural issues continued to command the NCSP's attention for years to come, as the organization sought—with questionable success—to define its purview and sharpen its focus on its core objectives. The NCSP had no authority, of course, and certainly did not represent the collective state park systems of the country; still, as it became better known and respected as a professional clearinghouse of sorts, more state park administrators started to participate—or at least to keep abreast of its activities. From a practical standpoint, this gave the organization more legitimacy and helped to strengthen its nominal association with the state park movement that was plowing ahead steadily on its own. In a very real sense, the NCSP was now drawing more vitality from the nation's state park programs than the other way around. Under these changing circumstances, the work of the NCSP would eventually be seen as less academic and of more practical value to the state park administrators, and this in turn enhanced the organization's image with those practitioners that should have been its principal constituency from the start.

But effective communication in those early years was a problem, and the NCSP was still a small, insulated organization with limited outreach. The obvious highlight of its program of course was the annual meeting, which provided a forum for both formal presentations and informal discussions. In time, several regional conferences were established as well, helping to carry the NCSP's message closer to the field. As noted earlier, Mather and other principals also spread the word through occasional speeches and radio talks as the opportunities arose, and in 1927 the organization initiated a monthly bulletin in an effort to provide more timely news updates. Still, all of these measures combined probably did not reach a very wide audience, and certainly not on a regular basis.

The Conference's official business, meanwhile, was conducted by a handpicked executive committee, with little apparent input from the outside. Consequently, the whole conduct of the National Conference on State Parks was really determined by a relatively small clique, and it may or may not have reflected the mainstream interests of the national constituency it purported to represent. While this circumstance in itself was not necessarily a fault, it is something that needs to be kept in mind when considering how sometimes questionable policy was made and tangential program activities pursued for this supposed "state parks" organization.

Issues Raised, If Not Resolved

In spite of the fact that its "object statement" failed to make any specific mention of state parks, the NCSP did, over time, devote a good bit of its agenda to issues related to state parks. Lacking the organizational flexibility, staff capabilities, and authority to deal directly with such matters itself, it attempted at least to facilitate some kind of public airing for a variety of issues it deemed to be of general interest. In the early years, this seems to have been done by having one of its leaders or some other respected speaker expound his or her views in a speech or written article. Sometimes it was accomplished simply by providing the forum for such presentations.

Many individuals participated in this discourse, but the views of a select few seem to have been given special credence. In addition to Stephen Mather, Beatrice Ward Nelson, and Raymond Torrey, of course, these included prominent professionals and scholars such as Harold Caparn, Stanley Coulter, Laurie Cox, Herbert Evison, James Greenleaf, Richard Lieber, Charles Sauers, and Albert Turner—to mention some of the stalwarts. Initially, most of the contributed opinion pieces came not from state park personnel (of which there were still relatively few), but from related professions, notably landscape architecture, and from academics. In time, however, as the state parks profession continued to grow, representatives of that field began to dominate the discourse and the subject matter took a decided turn from the theoretical to the practical. In 1930, the NCSP published a collection of pertinent essays and articles—including contributions by most of the individuals listed above—entitled *A State Park Anthology*.[1] This volume continues to serve as a useful reference for state park scholars, but only a few of its authors were actually from the state parks profession.

The issues dealt with in these and other monographs of the time ranged from the mundane to the momentous, but they were essentially the same issues as those still vexing state park administrators today. Learned park professionals can (and did) argue opposing points of view till the cows come home, but they are not likely to change each other's minds on such subjective issues as setting standards for site selection, determining whether and how to classify park units, deciding what types of activities to permit and what types and degrees of park development to provide, setting fees and raising revenue, selecting the type of parks administrative structure that works best—or even defining the term "state park" itself. Because there is rarely any one solution that works best in every state, unanimous agreement on such matters is all but impossible. By providing a forum for discussion of such important topics, however, the NCSP served a useful purpose in exposing its ever-expanding audience to new information and ideas—even if its modest efforts in this regard never really led to much in the way of demonstrable results.

There was one important issue at the time that properly belonged squarely in the lap of the NCSP, because it was the one that helped give rise to the Conference idea in the first place: defining a proper relationship between state parks and national parks. Mather had left no doubt that he viewed state parks primarily as a line of defense for the national parks—a means of diverting pressure to create national parks on what he considered unsuitable properties. He regarded such pressures as his "problem," and his solution in these cases was to offer a state park instead. Although he certainly did not say so explicitly, it is easy to infer from his statements that he felt the national parks should have "dibs" on the most spectacular landscapes in the country, leaving the state parks to pick from the "leftovers." By extension, then, it might be assumed that Mather considered the quality of the resources involved to be the distinguishing difference between the two levels of parks.

1. Herbert Evison, ed., *A State Park Anthology*.

Mather, of course, readily acknowledged the importance of having state parks in their own right, regardless of any relationship they might have to the national parks. This interest was no doubt genuine, but the record strongly suggests that his primary concern was to buffer the national parks and maintain their high quality standards. Herbert Evison, however, drawing on his personal acquaintance with Mather, held the opposite opinion, arguing instead that protecting the national parks was merely a "secondary consideration." Horace Albright, who succeeded Mather as national parks director and was a close associate from the beginning, essentially agreed with Evison. However, Albright held an even broader view—expressed years later—of the role of state parks, going so far as to say that "state parks are, in many ways, more important than the national parks." For practical and political reasons, the national park system would peak out at some finite point, he reasoned, and it would then fall to the state parks to carry on the work alone.[2]

Still, in the formative years of the NCSP, there seemed to be a general view within the National Park Service that state parks would always be a "backup" system to deal with properties that did not meet the high quality standards set for national parks. Arno Cammerer, who also would later become national parks director, held this view but saw the interlevel relationship as more comprehensive than that. In addressing the NCSP in 1930, he commented, "The relationship between the two classes of reservations [parks] is so close that we want to follow every development in the State park line and to give you the moral support of the National Park Service, as well as the benefit of our own experience, when your problems touch upon ours, or ours upon yours, as the case may be."[3] This may well be seen as a generous (if just slightly condescending) acknowledgment of a legitimate role for state parks.

But then Cammerer went on to make a distinction: "I believe I am not far wrong in stating that one of the outstanding differences between the State parks and national parks is that the former are primarily scenic areas susceptible of detailed development for public use but chiefly of local interest, while the supreme scenic values of national parks have been founded upon their national and international reputation."[4] Sorting out that labored syntax, it appears that Cammerer

2. Evison, "Birth of State Parks," 5; Tindall, "Interview with Albright," 47.
3. Arno B. Cammerer, "The Relationship between National and State Parks," address to the National Conference on State Parks, Linville, N.C., January 17–20, 1930, in Board of Directors Papers, series 3, box 1, NRPA Library, 2.
4. Ibid.

was citing not one but two additional conditions for distinguishing between state and national parks: in addition to resource quality, he would include the degree of public use (presumably recreational) and the geographical sphere of interest (although in this case *regional* might have been a more appropriate term than *local*).

Cammerer made one further point of interest in a quote he attributed to Ray Lyman Wilbur, who was then the secretary of the interior (who, incidentally, had served as one of the original members of California's state park commission): "State parks . . . are the natural complement to the national parks in providing Americans with a fully rounded out system of scenic areas and of open spaces devoted to outdoor recreation."[5] This statement is useful because it offered a description of the state/national park relationship that a majority at both levels could accept. State park proponents for the most part acknowledged the differences between state and national parks (although probably more in terms of scale than of purpose) and were readily willing to look to the national parks for advice and guidance. Some, in fact, cited national parks as an inspiration, if not as a model, for their own state park initiatives. However, they also saw certain advantages that state parks had over their larger, more remote national counterparts, and did not want their programs dismissed as simply lower-level—and certainly not *inferior*—versions of the national parks.

Differing as they did (and do), the state park programs could reach no clear consensus on the issue of how they should relate to the older, better-established national parks program. Indiana's Sauers, for one, felt that the national parks "should serve in many ways as models and guides for the establishment and control of the park systems of the individual States,"[6] but others obviously saw little similarity and nothing to emulate. Meanwhile, the NCSP made no more effort to referee or broker a consensus position on this issue than it had on any others, but the subject was about to take on a whole new dimension with the implementation of the Emergency Conservation Work program, discussed in the next chapter.

Selective Advocacy

Where specific park proposals were concerned, the NCSP seemed ready enough to take a definite position and lobby for the outcome it desired. Some analysis of these cases is instructive, because it provides an insight into what was motivating

5. Ibid., 3.
6. Charles G. Sauers, "Some Principles of State Park Management," 130.

the NCSP's policy makers at the time. Judging from the battles it elected to join and the sides it took on the issues, it is sometimes difficult to tell whether the organization was concerned more with promoting state parks or protecting national parks.

In Arkansas, efforts had been underway for several years to promote establishment of a 163,000-acre Mena National Park in the Ouachita Mountains. When earlier attempts had failed, a part of the area had been designated as the Petit Jean State Park, and another, much larger part was already in federal ownership as the Ouachita National Forest. Members of the NCSP executive committee had visited the area in 1926 and found it lacking. It would "unquestionably lower the standard of the National Parks," wrote Executive Secretary Beatrice Ward.[7] It probably helped a lot that both the National Park Service and the U.S. Forest Service also opposed the idea, but when bills to create a park were introduced in Congress in 1928, the NCSP led a successful campaign to defeat the measure. The motive here was clearly to defend the quality of the national park system.

An interesting sidelight to the Mena controversy was the concern the NCSP expressed over a ploy some of its allies were proposing as a means of protecting national park standards. Simply put, the idea was to create another system of federally managed areas that would fall somewhere between the national parks and the state parks in quality. Thus, properties that didn't measure up to national park standards would not have to be rejected outright (often a politically unpopular move), but could instead be referred to the new category for consideration. The concept itself is a valid one and provides the basis for the modern distinction between a park and a recreation area. Still, the NCSP was fearful that if it should be implemented it would seriously undermine many of the country's less-committed state park programs, which presumably would then simply defer to the new federal program to meet their park needs. From a practical standpoint, the concern was largely unfounded because—as Judge Payne observed at the time—such a new program would be so expensive that Congress wouldn't pass it anyway.

In the late 1920s and early 1930s, the NCSP went to bat for new state parks in North Dakota and Montana in order to counteract national park proposals of dubious quality. One of these involved a portion of the Badlands in North Dakota being promoted as a Roosevelt National Park. At first, it appeared that opposition efforts had succeeded, when at least part of the area was designated for a

---

7. Beatrice M. Ward to J. Barton Payne, March 6, 1928, in Board of Directors Papers, series 3, box 1, NRPA Library, 2.

time as Roosevelt State Park. That status was short-lived, though; the national park idea again gained momentum, and the area was eventually established as the Theodore Roosevelt National Memorial Park some years later. In the Montana case, however, the scenario was reversed. A largely ignored Lewis and Clark National Monument, created in 1908, was finally deeded to the state in 1937 to become the site of Montana's first park. Score: one win for state parks and one loss for national park purity.

Probably the most celebrated, and hard-fought, project the NCSP got embroiled in, though, involved the scenic Cumberland Falls of Kentucky. In the 1920s, the Cumberland River was yet another of the country's waterways being eyed covetously by big private power developers. When it appeared that a plan to dam the river and impound the area around the falls was gathering momentum, preservationists quickly countered with a park proposal instead. In 1926, the NCSP resolved to join the fight to save the falls—but it would not be easy. With the governor and the Federal Power Commission already looking favorably on the dam project, it appeared to be almost a "done deal."

In the meantime, though, Senator T. Coleman du Pont of Delaware, a former Kentuckian, offered to put up the $230,000 needed to buy the five hundred acres surrounding the falls if the state would establish it as a park. Timely intervention by the NCSP and the American Civic Association managed to delay issuance of a license by the Federal Power Commission, but it was not until 1930 that the state legislature finally acted decisively on the park proposal—overriding vetoes by the governor of separate bills to accept du Pont's offer and to condemn lands for a state park. Regrettably, Senator du Pont died before the park deal was consummated, but his family not only honored his original pledge but put up an additional $170,000 for land acquisition. The Cumberland Falls State Park that came into being the following year is now one of Kentucky's prized scenic attractions.

This was a decisive—and no doubt highly satisfying—victory for the NCSP's state parks agenda, proving that the organization could indeed wield considerable influence when it really tried. In the process, it also managed to recruit some powerful new allies for its cause. Among them was a tenacious newspaper editor named Tom Wallace, who campaigned relentlessly in the *Louisville Times* on behalf of the state park. Wallace joined the NCSP board of directors in 1930 and served as its chairman from 1945 until 1958. During this long tenure, his became a highly respected and influential voice for state parks everywhere.

While certainly no attempt has been made to examine every instance of the NCSP's involvement in a direct advocacy role, on the basis of the few above examples it appears that its track record was pretty good overall. It proved to be a formidable adversary when it considered the issue worthwhile—and this raises an interesting question of why the NCSP did not actively pursue a more aggressive advocacy on behalf of state parks as its contemporary organization, the National Parks Association, was doing for the national parks.

Into the Sunset

The National Conference on State Parks continued under that confusing name for many years, of course, but its path took many twists and turns, and its relevance to the state park movement became tenuous at times. It went through its first leadership change in 1927, when Judge Payne stepped down and was succeeded by Stephen Mather as chairman—although Payne remained on the board for another five years. By 1928, the organization apparently decided it was time to take itself seriously and formally incorporate. In doing so, it promulgated a slightly different version of its "object statement," adding as a purpose for acquiring land and water areas "the preservation of wild life, as a form of the conservation of our natural resources." The state parks agenda was getting broader all the time.

Due to failing health, Mather relinquished his position as National Parks Director to Horace Albright in 1929, but he continued serving as chairman of the NCSP board until his death in early 1930. During his tenure, he was fortunate to have very competent help in the position of executive secretary. The ever-dependable Beatrice Ward served until 1929, when she left to marry Wilbur Nelson. Herbert Evison then took over the position, bringing with him a wealth of experience in state park and related work. After four years, though, Evison also left—in his case, to help the National Park Service get cranked up for administering the new Depression-era conservation work programs. Beatrice Ward Nelson was lured back to fill the void on a pro tempore basis until some other arrangement could be made. That other arrangement finally came in 1935.

It was the middle of the Great Depression, and just about every aspect of American life was feeling the economic pinch. The NCSP, without any material means of support, was struggling to exist. Its solution was to join with another organization of compatible interest in order to share facilities and reduce the overhead costs for both. The choice of partners was the American Planning and Civic Association, itself recently formed through a merger of the American Civic Association (long an NCSP supporter) and the National Conference on City

Many of the most eloquent and effective supporters of the state park movement came from outside the parks profession. One of the most ardent was Kentucky newspaperman Tom Wallace, shown here in front of the magnificent Cumberland Falls, which he helped save from development. © LOUISVILLE COURIER-JOURNAL

Planning. It was a marriage of convenience—intended for a three-year trial run— but it proved to be a harmonious one. In return for assuming a modest share of expenses, the NCSP got office space, clerical support, and an information outlet through the APCA's quarterly publication, *Planning and Civic Comment*. Possibly most important of all, it also got Miss Harlean James as its new executive secretary.

Harlean James was another one of those wonder-workers with which the NCSP seems to have been blessed throughout its existence. She took on the job with little or no previous exposure to state parks, but with superb organizational skills and prodigious energy, and she managed to hold the NCSP together through thick and thin for twenty-three years. When she retired as executive secretary in 1958, the Conference showed its appreciation by making her an honorary life member and an ex officio member of its board of directors. She died in 1970.

In the late 1930s, the NCSP changed its governing structure to provide for broader participation in the decision-making process. The old ten-member executive committee (which had no term limits) was replaced with a board of fifteen directors to be elected by the Conference membership for five-year staggered terms. In addition, the outgoing board would appoint ten "life members," who, as a body, would fill their own vacancies as they occurred. It was hoped that this new arrangement would make it easier to bring more actual state park practitioners into the inner circles of the Conference, while also providing for perpetuation of the patriarchal "brain trust" that had carried the ball thus far.

Also about this time, the board of directors approved a revised version of its "objectives":

> The object of the Conference is to inform the public through a central clearinghouse of information, publications, conferences, courses of training in schools and colleges, and by other educational means, of the value of state parks, historic sites, forests and preserves, suitable for recreation, study of natural history and science, preservation of wildlife and conservation of natural scenery, by development within the States of well balanced state park systems; to the end that every citizen of the United States shall have easy access to state recreation areas and appreciate their value as a recognized form of land use.

Although still something of a syntactical hodgepodge, this new declaration clearly narrowed the scope of the Conference's purpose and also suggested a definite change of emphasis. Instead of urging governments and other interests to acquire lands for multiple conservation purposes, the new, more modest intent was simply to inform the public of the value of those lands. In other words, it was now to serve primarily an educational rather than a lobbying purpose. And instead of trying to be so catholic in the scope of programs it addressed, the new version specifically, for the first time, highlighted state parks as a principal focus. True, it also included "historic sites, forests and preserves" along with "parks"; but by placing the modifier *state* before the whole series, it tended to imply that the reference was to state-level programs in each case. Moreover, the statement could easily be parsed in such a way as to assert that the "value" of these various areas was created "by development within the States of well balanced state park systems." At any rate, after two decades or so of existence, the National Conference on State Parks was at last formally recognizing state parks as a raison d'etre.

The makeover of the NCSP in such fundamental aspects as its organizational structure and mission statement reflects something of a cultural change at the organization. Undoubtedly, Mather's illness and consequent death had something to do with the turn of events; the loss of his charismatic presence indeed created a serious void. Although other strong personalities such as Richard Lieber and Tom Wallace would come along to provide able leadership, it could never be quite the same without Mather as the guiding spirit. Over the following decade, the changes in the organization—some deliberate, some accidental—would become more and more apparent.

Primarily, it was a matter of the people involved. In the early years, the organization was dominated by prominent, well-connected, civic-minded citizens who saw the NCSP as an opportunity to provide a specific public service and then probably move on to something else. Many of them were, like Mather, men and women of substance who could afford not only to pay their own way but also to help out with organizational expenses. It was, in a very real way, more of a dilettante than a professional involvement. Over time, largely by design, the leadership as well as the rank-and-file membership began to reflect less of the patrician and more of the plebeian attitude. The organization had moved on to a new phase of its work, and as more down-to-earth state park professionals became involved, the more directly state parks became its focus.

As hard as it tried to promote more active involvement by state park people, though (no doubt to help legitimize its name and ostensible purpose), the NCSP just couldn't shake the de facto dominance of certain entrenched factions, most particularly the National Park Service. In 1937, for instance, the organization still had only fourteen of the state park directors among its membership of several hundred, but a full sixty professional staffers from the National Parks. This disproportionate representation continued to be a concern for some in the NCSP—both among its leadership and its rank and file—and a few institutional changes were made in the hope of rectifying the situation.

Harlean James, after only a few years with NCSP, began to notice a shift in the organization's character. Commenting on the matter in 1938, she said, "In the beginning it was natural that the membership would be largely a general citizen membership of those who 'hoped.' As time has gone on, we have now a very large number of state park officials actually concerned with the administration of state parks as going concerns. . . . With the increase in state park activities, a large number of new people have been brought into the field. The character and service of the National Conference on State Parks are changing somewhat to meet new needs." She went on, "During the early days it was hard to interest members to the extent of taking very much responsibility. Therefore, the Conference . . . was set up with a self-perpetuating Board in order to insure continued service. . . . [In the opinion of the board] the time has come to bring into the direction of the organization more of those who are working in the field of state parks."[8]

In achieving one thing, though, the NCSP had lost something else of possibly greater value. True, it was evolving into an organization of state park professionals with a state parks agenda; but it seemed to be losing (if it had not already lost) that aura of lofty purpose with which it was born. Much of the spirit, vitality, and excitement of the Mather years was gone. For all of the good work that the organization might yet continue to do, it is still a paradox that the NCSP, in seeking to cater to the operational needs of state parks *people,* sacrificed much of its value to the state park *movement.*

In the end, the National Conference on State Parks never did really "find itself." Because its purpose was never quite clear and its agenda never entirely consistent, it is difficult to find any reliable criteria for measuring its success. Stephen Mather should not be too disappointed, though. The national parks fared very well overall, and the minimal number of "losers" in the system to this day is certainly a tribute to his personal efforts if not those of the Conference he initiated. Where state parks are concerned, however, the jury on the NCSP's contributions is probably still hung. There is no question that the Conference served a useful purpose early on, focusing needed attention on the state parks movement and providing for the first time a means of bringing state park interests together for their common good. The Conference also claimed credit for stimulating much of the continuing expansion in the state parks field, but the actual extent of its influence is debatable. Beyond those several important accomplishments, the legacy of the National Conference on State Parks is a slippery subject better left to individual assessment.

What the NCSP may have failed to do in catapulting America's state park movement into general prominence, however, would soon be taken up in dynamic fashion through a totally different initiative—as we shall see.

8. Harlean James, report of the Executive Secretary to the National Conference on State Parks, Norris, Tenn., May 11, 1938, in Board of Directors Papers, series 3, box 1, NRPA Library, 1–3.

8

An Unexpected Boon
Economic Recovery and a New Deal for State Parks

America's state park movement had been at least temporarily energized by the work of the National Conference on State Parks, and the resulting growth had been steady if not phenomenal. But even at the dawn of the fourth decade of the twentieth century, no more than a handful of states could honestly claim to have a well-established system of parks. Some of the others had made a creditable start but had failed to follow through. And the rest—probably a dozen or more—had not caught the spark at all.

There were two obvious reasons for this apparent inertia: lack of interest and lack of money. Because—as history has amply demonstrated—the availability of money will quickly stimulate interest, the solution to the problem could be reduced to that one factor: a reliable funding source. Who would have thought, as the national economy seemed in a headlong free fall, that financial assistance for state parks on a scale previously undreamed of was just around the corner?

The Roosevelt Imperative

The nation had endured more than three years of steadily worsening economic depression by the time the new president, Franklin D. Roosevelt, took office in March 1933. People were desperate and looking for relief in some form, however unconventional it might be. Roosevelt had plenty of ideas along those lines, which the voters must have liked, because they catapulted him into office by a substantial majority over incumbent Herbert Hoover. He had promised a sweeping package of relief measures as a "New Deal" for America and lost no time in putting them into place. Most of them called for the creation of new agencies and new programs directed at specific economic recovery objectives, and the very first of these to be implemented was one he called Emergency Conservation Work. The program envisioned a wide range of resource rehabilitation measures, and it would prove to be a monumental boon to America's state parks.

Roosevelt got down to business in a hurry. In his inaugural address given on March 4, 1933—his first public words as president—he laid out his priorities. Among them:

> Our greatest primary task is to put people to work. This is no unsolvable problem if we face it wisely and courageously. It can be accomplished in part by direct recruiting by the Government itself, treating the task as we would treat the emergency of war, but at the same time, through this employment, accomplishing greatly needed projects to stimulate and reorganize the use of our natural resources.[1]

Many of the ideas he proposed to carry out had been formed and nurtured during his previous four years as governor of New York, wrestling with the same Depression-related problems at the state level—and he knew exactly what he wanted to do. He had identified as two of his major concerns the rampant unemployment among the nation's youth and the sad condition of many of the country's natural resources, and he proposed to attack both problems with a single offensive.

Within weeks of his inauguration, on March 21, he sent a message to Congress calling for action:

> I propose to create a civilian conservation corps to be used in simple work, not interfering with normal employment, and confining itself to forestry, the prevention of soil erosion, flood control, and similar projects. I call your attention to the fact that this type of work is of definite practical value, not only through the prevention of great present financial loss but also as a means of creating future national wealth. . . .
>
> I estimate that 250,000 men can be given temporary employment by early summer if you give me authority to proceed within two weeks.[2]

1. *Inaugural Addresses of the Presidents of the United States* (Washington, D.C.: U.S. G.P.O., 1989).

2. Franklin D. Roosevelt, "Three Essentials for Unemployment Relief," in *The Public Papers and Addresses of Franklin D. Roosevelt* (New York: Random House, 1938), 2:80.

Congressional response was just as swift. A bill was introduced on March 27, entitled "An Act for the Relief of Unemployment through the Performance of Useful Public Work, and for Other Purposes." By March 31, it had been passed by both houses of Congress and sent to the president for signature, which was quickly affixed. The act gave the president broad authority to hire unemployed men and put them to work on a variety of conservation projects on public (and, in certain exceptional cases, private) lands. To finance these operations, it authorized the use of an unlimited amount of unexpended funds from existing public works appropriations. Thus, for the two-year life of the authorization, the president was given virtually a free hand and a blank check.

Roosevelt lost no time in converting ideas into action. Just five days after passage of the act, he issued an executive order to implement it. The order named Robert Fechner, of Boston, as "director of emergency conservation work," and called on the secretaries of war, agriculture, the interior, and labor to each appoint a representative to an advisory council to assist Fechner. Horace Albright, then director of the National Park Service, served initially as the Department of the Interior's representative. At the time of his selection, Fechner, a transplanted Georgian (born in Tennessee), was general vice president of the International Association of Machinists. He was highly respected as a labor leader with great organizational skills, and these would soon be put to effective use. The almost absolute power given by the president to the director of emergency conservation work would make the appointee a veritable czar, and because such power carried with it fully as much potential for failure as for success, Fechner's selection for the job proved to be a happy one indeed.

Immediately after their appointments, Fechner and his advisory council met with Roosevelt to get their marching orders. In the course of the discussion, Roosevelt took a piece of cardboard that lay on his desk and proceeded to draw a rough diagram of the organizational structure he envisioned for the Emergency Conservation Work (ECW) program. That penciled sketch thus became the blueprint for the start-up of the program, and Fechner would comment later that "after three years we are still following, in practically every detail, the suggestions that the President made to us on the occasion of that first meeting."[3]

The basic plan was pretty straightforward. The Labor Department would handle recruitment of the "junior enrollees"—the young, unemployed men who were

3. Robert Fechner, Remarks at the C.C.C. Boys' Exposition, New York City, June 2, 1936, U.S. Department of the Interior Library (SD143 .A263 [D]), Washington, D.C., 3.

Robert Fechner, a highly regarded labor leader from Boston, was selected by President Franklin Roosevelt to head the innovative Emergency Conservation Work program in 1933. Under Fechner's competent guidance, the Civilian Conservation Corps built hundreds of new state parks during the 1930s. NATIONAL PARK SERVICE

the target group of the program—assisted by the public welfare agencies in each state. Later, when eligibility was extended to a limited number of World War I veterans, the Veterans Administration assumed responsibility for that group. The War Department, primarily through the U.S. Army, took on probably the most demanding task of all—physically examining, enrolling, clothing, equipping, housing, feeding, transporting, and otherwise caring for the millions of men who passed through the ranks of the Civilian Conservation Corps, as the field units, or camps, were collectively called. Finally, the responsibility for selecting, planning, coordinating, and supervising construction or performance of the thousands of diverse field projects was assigned primarily to the Departments of Agriculture and Interior. If there was any reluctance on the part of these departments to participate fully and enthusiastically in the ECW program, they knew better than to show it. Robert Fechner was ever present with his ironfisted authority to see that the president's wishes were understood and carried out. This was a personal priority with Roosevelt. He knew what he wanted, and he knew how to get it.

The Civilian Conservation Corps

The program on which the country was now embarked was called Emergency Conservation Work, but its instrument of implementation would be forever known as the Civilian Conservation Corps, the CCC. Actually, neither term was used in the act that authorized the program. Roosevelt presumably had coined the first when he used it in his executive order as part of Fechner's new title; and he had also referred to establishing a "civilian conservation corps" in communicating his intentions to Congress. At any rate, although "Emergency Conservation Work" continued to be used for most official purposes, it was the name "Civilian Conservation Corps" that caught the public's fancy and quickly emerged as the program's popular identity. It became so well established, in fact, that the Congress made it official several years later in a 1937 act giving it independent agency status. By whatever name, though, the program would prove to be a remarkable success.

Roosevelt meant it when he had proposed treating the task "as we would treat the emergency of war." When he had met on April 5 with Fechner and his advisory council, he asked how quickly the first field camp could be established. Fechner replied that it would probably take a month. Roosevelt gave him two weeks. Undaunted, Fechner went to work. On April 7, the first enrollees were signed up, and by April 17—barely two weeks after passage of the authorizing act—the first CCC camp was operating in the George Washington National Forest, in Virginia, under the supervision of the U.S. Forest Service. Roosevelt's deadline had been met with two days to spare, and the Civilian Conservation Corps was on its way.

It was originally contemplated that as many as 250,000 young men would be enrolled in the CCC program. To qualify, they had to be between the ages of eighteen and twenty-five (later extended to seventeen and twenty-eight), unmarried, and on public welfare (although certain exceptions were allowed). These men, after selection by the Department of Labor and medical screening by the army doctors, were enrolled for a six-month period and assigned to one of the numerous camps that were being set up around the country and in the various territorial possessions. The camps were designed for a maximum of two hundred men each, with the army in charge of all administrative and custodial functions. After they had had a good night's sleep and a hearty breakfast, though, the men "belonged" to the technical agencies for a full day of work in the field, and this is where the program proved its worth.

The work proposed for the Civilian Conservation Corps was to cover a broad spectrum. The authorizing act itself had laid out a pretty tall order: "forestation of [public] lands . . . prevention of forest fires, floods and soil erosion, plant pest and disease control, construction, maintenance or repair of paths, trails and fire-lanes in the national parks and forests," plus a few catch-all categories. Given the nature of the work, the vast majority of the camps were assigned to the Departments of Agriculture and Interior for technical supervision. Between them, they accounted for about 97 percent of the total, with Agriculture alone responsible for over 70 percent. On the average, there were about 1,700 CCC camps existing at any given time, and the only material difference in their operation was in the work programs they conducted. Almost all of the park-related work, for instance, was assigned to the National Park Service of the Department of the Interior, which supervised an average of 345 camps per year for the nine-year life of the program. It is this particular part of the CCC program with which the rest of this chapter is concerned.

The National Park Service Takes Charge

Although Horace Albright was director of the National Park Service at the time, it was Conrad Wirth who carried the ball for the agency in implementing its part of the CCC program. Wirth (who himself would become director some years later) was a real workhorse with a proven record of accomplishment, and he was ably assisted by Herbert Evison, who had left the National Conference on State Parks to join the NPS just for this purpose. Together they provided the thrust needed to quickly mobilize available forces and get an action program under way. By the end of September 1933, the National Park Service already had 175 CCC camps operating in national and state parks.

To provide effective supervision of the growing number of camps within an expanding geographical area, the NPS decided to set up a system of field offices to be closer to the scene. One of the main functions of these offices was to conduct periodic inspections of the camps within their jurisdictions, with one NPS inspector assigned to every four or five CCC camps. Each camp—which was authorized to use up to two hundred enrollees, but seldom had that many—was provided with a project superintendent, in charge of the camp's entire work program, and eight foremen. One foreman with the appropriate qualifications was assigned to oversee specific tasks in each area of specialization.

While this system looked good in theory, it apparently did not measure up in

Most of the responsibility for implementing the Civilian Conservation Corps's state parks program fell to the National Park Service. As chief of the NPS Bureau of Planning and State Parks, Conrad Wirth proved to be an outstanding overseer of this challenging task.
NATIONAL PARK SERVICE

practice. As work projects became more complex and sophisticated, the different skills required increased accordingly. One estimate put the number of different jobs performed in CCC work at over a hundred. To deal with the problem of providing adequate supervision in the more specialized types of work, the CCC authorized the hiring of "locally experienced men," or LEMs. These were supposedly qualified individuals living in the immediate area who were available and willing to work. While they were nominally enrolled in the CCC, eligibility requirements were waived where necessary. It was this type of flexibility and expediency that enabled the CCC program to function so efficiently and accomplish so much in its relatively brief life span.

The National Park Service was given responsibility for supervising CCC work not only in the national parks but in state (and later, local) parks as well. Although most of the procedures and practices it devised for efficient performance of CCC work were applicable in all situations, there were some distinct differences where the state park projects were concerned. For one thing, the NPS was already present in the national parks and ready to do business when the CCC camps came in; in the state parks, special supervisory arrangements involving NPS staff had to be made in every case. For another, planning and design work for state park CCC projects usually required major—sometimes total—assistance from NPS staff, necessitating special procedures for intergovernmental cooperation. Probably the biggest difference of all, though, was that there were already plenty of national parks to host CCC camps, whereas in many cases the states had to scurry around looking for suitable properties for that purpose.

To its everlasting credit, the National Park Service—only seventeen years old itself—proved to be a truly sympathetic and helpful "big brother" to the state park systems in the implementation of the CCC program. While that program fully deserves all of the acclaim it has received for making the means available for state park development, it was the advice, guidance, and supervision of the National Park Service that ensured the quality of the results.

The CCC Program and the State Parks

On May 5, 1933, Robert Fechner sent a lengthy telegram to the governors of the forty-eight states, describing the Civilian Conservation Corps program and how the states could benefit. As a condition for participation, he asked for a guarantee that the state would accept full responsibility for maintaining the fixed improvements provided by the federal program on state property. Coming just a month after the CCC was created, this telegram was probably the first word most of the governors had heard about the new program. But they must have liked what they heard, because Fechner was obviously pleased by the feedback: "The States responded favorably, guaranteeing that their State legislatures would enact the necessary legislation and that the State would assume its proper obligation."[4] He would soon have reason to doubt their sincerity.

It is easy to see how the states—in those dark days of the Great Depression— could get excited about the prospect of federally funded projects that would put a lot of people to work and create parks and other improvements in the process. But that excitement was no doubt just as quickly dampened in some cases by the

4. Robert Fechner, Remarks at the National Park Service Conference of State Park Authorities, Washington, D.C., February 25, 1935, U.S. Department of the Interior Library (SB482 .A463), Washington, D.C., 17.

realization that, in order to participate in the program, a state must have state-owned lands on which to conduct the work. For those states that had already acquired state park and similar properties, this was not a problem; they were ready to go. The others, though—probably at least half—that still had no parks, or too few to take full advantage, faced the unthinkable possibility of being bypassed entirely by this potential gravy train. That unhappy prospect, however, provided the stimulus for some of the most aggressive, expeditious, and innovative land acquisition efforts the country has ever seen, and therein lies probably the greatest contribution the CCC program made to America's state park movement.

As the states thus busied themselves with acquiring new or additional lands, the National Park Service moved in quickly to establish CCC camps in as many as possible. All project proposals were initiated by the state, but the actual selection of work projects, assignment of camps, and supervision of work on state parks was a cooperative process, involving the state's designated "park authority" and the National Park Service. Considering the newness of the program, its inherent complexities, and the deliberate speed with which it was being implemented, the whole operation went amazingly well. In the first six months of the program, 105 CCC camps were established in state parks in twenty-six states—not a bad start at all. For comparison, the National Park Service had allocated only 70 camps to its own properties during this period, although the actual number of enrollees involved was not reported for either national or state parks.

This initial momentum continued to build over the next two years before the program peaked in 1935 and then started slowly to decline. Every six months, the participating federal agencies would sit down with Fechner to assess their progress and allocate the allowable number of camps among themselves. The whole program had proven immensely successful, and its popularity increased accordingly. To hear Fechner tell it, "almost every Federal department and every Federal bureau has found some way in which they could be benefited by a C.C.C. camp."[5] Whereas there had actually been some opposition to having camps in certain areas at first, now there were far more requests than could be granted. Roosevelt was pleased, of course, and at times he considered seeking additional funds to expand the program, and even to make it permanent.

The states also had every reason to be pleased. They continued to receive the lion's share of the camps allocated to the National Park Service, as reflected by the following numbers:

5. Ibid., 16.

Fiscal Year	Number of States Participating	Number of Camps	
		State Parks	National Parks
1933	26	102	70
1934	39	263	102
1935	45	475	115
1936	47	393	92
1937	46	337	83
1938	45	245	77
1939	44	227	83
1940	42	201	109
1941	36	194	91
1942	?	20	19

Source: Adapted from Conrad L. Wirth, *Parks, Politics, and the People,* 127; "Number of States Participating" compiled from periodic reports of the Director of Emergency Conservation Work.

Typical of the hundreds of Civilian Conservation Corps camps developed throughout the country was this one at Douthat State Park in Virginia. VIRGINIA DIVISION OF STATE PARKS

Although the figures for "state parks" presumably include those for local government camps as well, they nevertheless reflect the heavy emphasis the National Park Service placed on state park development needs. Conrad Wirth, in his 1980 book, *Parks, Politics, and the People,* estimated that of the approximately $467 million spent on CCC camps under National Park Service supervision, some $335 million was for state and local parks. In terms of both the amount of money spent and the number of camps assigned, about 75 percent of the total effort was directed to state parks.

Although the CCC program of assistance to state parks was going great guns, there were intermittent signs of trouble on the horizon. The states had been all too eager to accept the federal help, but now apparently some of them were finding it difficult to honor the commitments they had made. Fechner, of course, was very sensitive to this problem and had begun to fret over it by the second year of the program. In February 1935, the National Park Service called all of the state park authorities to Washington for a four-day conference—the first of its kind—to discuss a variety of issues concerning administration of the CCC program, and Fechner was one of the speakers.

After a few disarming compliments about state participation in the program, Fechner lowered the boom. Because he personally had been the one to elicit the promises of continuing cooperation from the states, he obviously felt that he had been let down by those which had not kept their part of the bargain. His chagrin was evident in his comments: "The President feels very definitely about this matter. It is not a gesture. And I want . . . to impress upon each one of you State representatives that this 'Santa Claus' business is not going to continue indefinitely." He went on: "I know that some States are already suggesting that the Federal Government ought to take over the maintenance of those improvements. . . . [I]f any State does feel that way about it, or if any State officials feel that way, I want to warn you that you are undoubtedly due to a rude awakening."[6]

Fechner no doubt made his point, but all his audience could do was carry the message home. What the state governors and legislatures might then do was another matter entirely—and some of them probably still continued to drag their feet. Even so, this appears to have been the only major source of friction between the CCC program administrators and the states, and it was not serious enough to cause any revision or redirection of the program. That is not to say, however, that there were not other differences and misunderstandings that had to be resolved. There is ample evidence of disagreements between various states and the NPS supervisors over the types of work that could be done. New York, for example,

6. Fechner, Remarks at the NPS Conference of State Park Authorities, 1935, 17.

apparently ran afoul of program guidelines with the construction of a couple of golf courses, and new road proposals were rejected in many instances as being too intrusive on the landscape. Evison once commented that "I venture to assert that at least a thousand miles of proposed road have been turned down."[7] The National Park Service may have appeared arbitrary and procedure-bound at times, but by insisting on strict adherence to certain standards and guidelines it was able to maintain a generally uniform level of quality throughout the program.

A Look at the Results

By program's end, in 1942, the Civilian Conservation Corps had built or improved 405 state parks in forty-three states and had done similar work on local parks in four others. Only Delaware had no NPS-supervised CCC camp (although there was an Agriculture-supervised camp at Trap Pond, which would later become Delaware's first state park). This was indeed an impressive record, greatly increasing America's state parks inventory overall, and probably more than doubling the number of developed parks open to the public. As early as 1935, Arno Cammerer, who had succeeded Horace Albright as National Parks director in 1933, was already noting the significance of the program's impact: "During these last two years, I believe the progress in the recreational field through state park work has gone fifty years ahead of what we could have expected without the E.C.W. program."[8] And the program had only just begun.

The nature and scope of the CCC work in those 405 state parks varied considerably, of course, but in many cases the product was a brand new turnkey recreation area, ready for public use. Many of these involved major terrain alterations as well, such as the construction of dams to create recreational lakes, and various environmental measures to revegetate denuded areas, prevent wildfires, and control erosion or flooding. While prominent visitor-use structures such as lodges, cabins, and suspension bridges got most of the public attention, countless other less glamorous but equally essential support facilities also had to be provided: wells, pumps, telephone lines, footpaths, and so forth. Nor were all of the park improvements achieved through new installations; in many instances it was necessary to eliminate unsightly or unneeded structures or

7. Herbert Evison, "National and State Parks in the Conservation Field," 12.
8. Arno B. Cammerer, Remarks at the National Park Service Conference of State Park Authorities, Washington, D.C., February 25, 1935, U.S. Department of the Interior Library (SB482 .A463), Washington, D.C., 4.

A Civilian Conservation Corps work crew arrives on the job at Valley of Fire State Park, Nevada, in 1934. NEVADA DIVISION OF STATE PARKS

conditions to enhance the attractiveness of the site. These included thousands of undesirable buildings, hundreds of miles of previously existing roads and trails, plus a number of borrow pits, trash dumps, and the like.

The reporting methods used at the time make it difficult to compile statistics for work specifically on state park properties, but Wirth attempted something of the sort in *Parks, Politics, and the People*. To distinguish from the national parks, he used a category called "state parks and related areas," which obviously also includes figures for the forty-two county and seventy-five metropolitan parks on which the CCC worked, and possibly even some others of minor significance. Still, that breakdown gives a good idea of the magnitude of the improvements provided on these nonfederal park projects:

> 152 bathhouses
>
> 1,463 cabins
>
> 5,370 acres of picnic grounds
>
> 11,587 acres of developed campgrounds
>
> 197 large dams
>
> 5,246 miles of roads and trails.[9]

9. Wirth, *Parks, Politics, and the People,* 145.

No mention is made of the lodges and other group-use facilities that, through their distinctive architecture and use of local stone and timber, became a lasting signature of Civilian Conservation Corps construction.

As significant as it was, this impressive array of new park structures was still secondary to the most important consequence of the CCC involvement with state parks: park land acquisition. As noted earlier, having properties already available was prerequisite for a state's participation in the CCC program. Because its original thrust was to relieve unemployment rather than to provide public recreation, the program offered no financial assistance for land acquisition. The beneficial, if uncontemplated, result was the most vigorous and accelerated period of state park acquisition up to that time.

While just about every state in the country added new properties to its state parks inventory during the CCC era, at least eleven of them acquired their very first major state park—and in practically every case it was due at least in significant part to the impetus provided by the CCC program. Most of these new states were in the South, where the state park idea had been slow to take root. Alabama acquired Cheaha State Park in 1933, followed by Louisiana with Longfellow-Evangeline, Mississippi with LeRoy Percy, and South Carolina with Cheraw in 1934. Florida was next with Highlands Hammock in 1935, then Virginia with Douthat in 1936, and Tennessee with Harrison Bay in 1938. The other newcomers spanned the country: Oklahoma with Lake Murray in 1933, New Mexico with Bottomless Lakes in 1934, Montana with Lewis and Clark Caverns in 1937, and Maine with Aroostook in 1938. With these additions, only five of the forty-eight states now remained without at least the start of a formal state parks program: Arizona, Colorado, Delaware, Kansas, and Utah (and even in some of these, helpful precedents had already been established).

Overall, the expansion of state park holdings during the CCC decade was significant. At the beginning of the program, in 1933, it was estimated that those holdings comprised some 965,000 acres. By 1939, after six years under the program, the estimate had increased to about 1,919,000 acres, or almost double. There is no reliable or complete estimate of state park acreage available for 1942 when the CCC ended, but it is safe to say that the figure would have increased still more—even in spite of the steady downsizing of the program.

Cammerer may have been carried away by his enthusiasm when he credited the CCC program for advancing the cause of state parks by fifty years, but there is no question that it had a tremendous impact on every aspect of the state park movement. Not only were there more state parks with greatly expanded acreage, but also those parks were better planned, more fully and appropriately developed, more competently staffed, and much better known and understood by politicians, park administrators, and the general public alike. True, the CCC program ended after only nine years, leaving its many accomplishments as a temporary surge in an otherwise gradual trend. But during that brief time, it helped lay a permanent foundation on which the state park movement would continue to build for many years to come.

The Legacy

As the CCC program was nearing its end in 1941, it offered this opinion of itself: "The Civilian Conservation Corps is the greatest working force for conservation that the United States has ever known. In the field of public recreation the Corps is helping to give expression to the highest meaning of conservation."[10] While that statement might be a little overblown, there are probably not many people today that would take serious exception to it. The facts and figures speak for themselves about the overall success of that unique program.

Where the state park movement itself is concerned, though, the important legacy of the CCC is manifested in more than just new parks, quality development, and restored landscapes. That supercharged nine-year experience provided an unequalled opportunity for all state park programs—the older, established ones as well as the new—-to learn, progress, and mature as a body. Subject as they were to the same rules, requirements, and purposes of the CCC program, for the first—and possibly the only—time in history they had to think and act alike in dealing with state park concepts and issues.

Some will argue that such forced uniformity is counterproductive, that it stifles the ingenuity and creativity of the individual states. That is a valid argument, but it speaks to only one side of the coin; as such, it should be used merely to temper and balance, rather than supplant, the other side. In other words, for there to be true national *movement* in the field of state parks, it must have an appropriate degree of uniformity, along with its individuality, to keep it moving in the same direction. The CCC experience helped give shape to the state park movement as no other single factor has been able to do.

The practical personification of the CCC program as far as the state park agencies were concerned was, of course, the National Park Service. NPS personnel devised the standards and procedures for the programs they administered, and

10. Federal Security Agency, *Conservation and Recreation,* 3.

Civilian Conservation Corps work in state parks took many forms. This crew is constructing underground access facilities in Lewis and Clark Caverns State Park, Montana. MONTANA DEPARTMENT OF FISH, WILDLIFE AND PARKS

they provided the day-to-day supervision of the work. This close involvement provided an opportunity for frequent contact between counterparts of the two government levels, and presumably proved enlightening for both. The National Park Service noted with apparent pride in 1936 that "the Federal Government, for the first time in its history, is actively engaged in cooperating with the States and their subdivisions in the development of . . . parks and recreation areas."[11] A year earlier, it was extolling the CCC as an opportunity to "extend its [NPS's] standards and influence by cooperation with the States in development of a Nation-wide system of State parks."[12] These and similar comments from the time suggest that the NPS willingly accepted the responsibility for assisting in state park development, and by doing so "to create a system of smaller, more numerous and more quickly accessible recreation areas to supplement the magnificent national parks."[13]

11. U.S. Department of the Interior, National Park Service, "Emergency Conservation Work under National Park Service Supervision," 1936, unpublished paper in the Department of the Interior Library (JK870 .N3A26), Washington, D.C., 1.

12. "Fourth Report of the Director of Emergency Conservation Work, for the Period October 1, 1934, to March 31, 1935" (Washington: Government Printing Office, 1935), 33.

13. National Park Service, "Emergency Conservation Work under National Park Service Supervision," 1.

How state park people felt about the relationship with the NPS is not as clear, but it is safe to say that it varied. Most of the references are positive, though. Indiana's Richard Lieber, reporting as president of the National Conference on State Parks in 1938, offered both a compliment and a caution: "The great National Parks have blazed the way, the State Parks have followed; of late in such profusion that we must determinately address ourselves to their proper use and management." The following year, Harold Wagner of Ohio, who succeeded Lieber as NCSP president, was also pointing to the NPS as a desirable model for classifying state parks. It would seem that a closer, more cooperative relationship was forming, and that the state parks were looking more to the NPS as a mentor and a model. Wirth, for instance, noted that between 1936 and 1942 eighteen states requested the help of NPS in rewriting laws to strengthen their parks and recreation programs.[14] (This interest was no doubt due in part to the 1936 Park, Parkway, and Recreational Area Study Act, which will be discussed in the next chapter.)

As for the Civilian Conservation Corps, in spite of its immense popularity, it was steadily heading toward extinction. After reaching its zenith in the mid-1930s and achieving independent agency status in 1937, it became the unintended victim of unrelated political controversy and changing Congressional priorities. In 1939, Congress created the Federal Security Agency at Roosevelt's urging, and the CCC was one of the several functions transferred to the new agency. Fechner vehemently objected to the loss of his autonomy and tendered his resignation. He was persuaded to stay on, but he died a few months later of complications from a heart attack.

Fechner's longtime deputy, John McEntee, succeeded him, but from that point on everything was downhill. With the country gearing up for war, the economy was improving and it became difficult to hire and retain enrollees for the CCC. The National Park Service, and others inside government and out, tried valiantly to make a case for continuing the program, but to no avail. Congress withheld further funding, and the Civilian Conservation Corps died a natural death on June 30, 1942. Among the many mourners undoubtedly were the supporters of America's state parks.

14. Richard Lieber, Report of the President to the National Conference on State Parks, Norris, Tenn., May 11, 1938, in National Conference on State Parks Minutes of Policy Making Bodies, series 1 and 2, box 1, NRPA Library, 2; Harold S. Wagner, "Proper Classification of State Parks," 179–81; Conrad L. Wirth, "A Report to Harold L. Ickes, Secretary of the Interior, on the Department's Civilian Conservation Corps Program," January 1944, unpublished paper in the Department of the Interior Library (SD143 .A21 [D]), Washington, D.C., 43.

9

Recovery and Beyond

Depression-Era Initiatives Look to the Future

Franklin D. Roosevelt, America's New Deal president, had moved swiftly and decisively to make good on his promises of relief. One of his immediate concerns, of course, was to create meaningful work for the vast numbers of unemployed youth, and his very first response had taken the form of the hugely successful Civilian Conservation Corps. More than just a relief agency, though, the CCC had actually produced dramatic results through a variety of resource rehabilitation projects and the development of new parks and recreation facilities. Everyone—the president himself, Congress, the press, and the public at large—had been duly impressed.

Roosevelt might have been forgiven for simply taking a bow and calling it a day at that point, but he was not about to do so. He recognized that it was not enough just to address the problems of the moment—as demanding as they obviously were—without also trying to do something about the underlying causes of those problems. He had had his brain trust working on this matter for some time, and over the next several years it came forth with a number of programs—some almost radical—for the long-range amelioration of the nation's social and economic ills. So comprehensive were these programs that they touched on almost every aspect of public interest, including parks and recreation. In so doing, they set in motion a series of actions that would help shape America's state park movement—and these are well worth a quick review.

The National Resources Board and the
First State Recreation Plans

The need for coordinated, long-range planning of the country's public works had been recognized long before the Roosevelt administration, but it had been difficult to establish effective governmental machinery for the purpose. Nevertheless, Roosevelt decided to give it another try. In July 1933, a National Planning Board was set up in the new Public Works Administration, ostensibly to lay some kind of factual basis to guide the agency's massive spending program. The original three-member board was revamped a year later with the addition of six federal-agency heads as ex officio members, and it was given a new name: the National Resources Board. Under this incarnation (one of several during its eleven-year life), the board took on the formidable task of instituting comprehensive planning not only at the federal level but in each of the states as well.

Faced with the mandate for quick action that emanated from on high, the

As the National Park Service's Depression-era responsibilities in state and local park development became more demanding, a special staff was assembled to handle the work under Conrad Wirth's direction. Wirth is shown here (front row, third from left) with some of his key assistants. On Wirth's left (in light-colored suit) is Herbert Evison, who also played a prominent role in the early development of the state park movement. NATIONAL PARK SERVICE

board enlisted help from every source it could within the federal government and produced its first set of preliminary reports by December 1934. These consisted of five volumes, dealing with the categories of land, water, minerals, public works, and general national planning procedure. Recreation was treated as two sections of the land report: "recreational requirements" and "recreational procedures." This initial product was admittedly hurried and preliminary—it was acknowledged at the time that all it did was identify the need for a more thorough study. That the report was completed at all in such a short time, however, was due to the extensive involvement of the National Park Service. As part of the board's task organization, a special recreational section was set up under the leadership of the Park Service's George Wright. The active participation by other NPS high-level staff, including Assistant Director Conrad Wirth, attested to the high priority the project was given.

But the operating policy of the National Resources Board was to decentralize its work as much as possible, and this meant involving the states to the maximum degree. Just a few months after its creation, the board formally called on the states to set up their own planning boards to cooperate with the national effort—even if this had to be done on an interim basis until their legislatures could meet. The response from the states was quick and mostly favorable. With consultation assistance from the national board, forty-four state planning boards were established in just over a year. It was under these state planning boards—motivated significantly by the desire to enhance their state's chances for more federal aid projects—that state-level recreation planning received its first major impetus. State park authorities, which were already closely involved with the Civilian Conservation Corps and similar New Deal programs, would play an important role in making sure that recreation needs received appropriate attention in these early state planning efforts.

Recreational Demonstration Areas

Not all of the New Deal programs were equally admired. One of the most controversial was the experiment in population redistribution that was eventually formalized under the Resettlement Administration in 1935. The idea of moving people off of submarginal land and onto lands of higher agricultural quality actually took shape the year before, when Roosevelt appointed a high-level Land Planning Committee to look into the possibilities. It was an appealing concept: Not only would it help provide a new start for the relocated families, it also

Work on the new Recreation Development Areas was conducted by the Civilian Conservation Corps in the same manner as in state parks. Here, an enrollee hews beams for a structure in the Swift Creek RDA (later Pocahontas State Park), Virginia. VIRGINIA DIVISION OF STATE

would create opportunities for other, better-suited public uses of the abandoned lands. And the potential scope of the undertaking was enormous; it was estimated that there were as many as 650,000 families marginally subsisting on up to 100 million acres of unsuitable land. If funds could be provided to relocate the impoverished occupants as a humanitarian object, it would incidentally open up a world of possibilities for new parks and recreation areas.

At this point, though, no such funds were available. All of the New Deal programs had been designed to employ, build, and improve, but not to acquire vast areas of land. The Land Planning Committee fully recognized the dual benefits the resettlement program would provide, however, and managed to persuade the Public Works Administration to put up $25 million for land acquisition. A special Land Program was created in the Federal Emergency Relief Administration to administer the funds, and the opportunity to utilize some of the acquired lands was extended to the various federal agencies whose programs might be benefited. Thus, for the first time under the New Deal, it was now possible to acquire new parks as well as to develop them.

The National Park Service was ready with a proposal. It envisioned converting submarginal agricultural lands near population centers to a variety of public recreational uses. Large natural areas close to the cities were, in fact, according to Wirth, "the most needed links in the nation's park and recreation programs." Actually, the NPS had identified four categories of uses to which the lands might be put: (1) additions to units of the national park system, (2) wayside, or rest, areas along the highways, (3) additions to state "scenic areas," and (4) a new type of vacation, or recreation, area close to urban centers. This last category would become known as "recreational demonstration areas" (RDAs) and would provide the basis for an entirely new line of activity for the National Park Service.

The administrators of the Land Program obviously liked the recreational demonstration area concept and avidly supported the NPS in its implementation. Capitalizing on that fact—and to demonstrate the high level of importance assigned to the new undertaking—the NPS moved quickly to set up a special Recreational Demonstration Projects Division in its Branch of Planning. Within a year, it had investigated more than four hundred tracts of land as potential RDAs, and twenty-five of these were selected, approved, and placed under development.

Several types of recreational demonstration areas were considered, but neither the terminology nor the concept used in each case was consistent throughout the program. All of the lands acquired under the resettlement program had to be determined as submarginal for their present economic use, but their intended recreational reuse could vary within a wide range. The primary object of the National Park Service was to obtain large, attractive natural areas of from two thousand to ten thousand acres in size within fifty to seventy-five miles of a fairly large city. On these properties it undertook to construct standard-type, low-maintenance camping facilities to accommodate both individual families and organized groups. The camping program was aimed principally at lower- to middle-income urban residents, the group deemed to be most in need of such types of recreation.

Camps were developed at minimal cost by workers from the Civilian Conservation Corps and the Work Projects Administration, but the proposed management and administration was not always clear. The NPS intent was to involve state and local authorities throughout the process, with the thought that they would eventually be called on to assume responsibility for maintaining the completed facilities and conducting the user programs. There was at least one interesting alternative available, however. Because the whole purpose of the resettlement program was to improve the lot of the people occupying submarginal land, a determination was supposed to be made in each case as to whether those occupants would be better served by relocation or by being given the opportunity to remain on the property in some kind of entrepreneurial capacity with the RDA—possibly as a concessionaire or a contract service provider. There is no indication that any after-the-fact assessment was made to see how successful this novel approach might have been.

The RDA initiative had been under way just over a year when Roosevelt, by executive order, created the Resettlement Administration and handed it the Land Program—lock, stock, and barrel—along with a number of other related functions (including, incidentally, the state land planning consultants then working for the National Resources Board). The Resettlement Administration was thus occupied with a much bigger kettle of fish, but it still continued to support the RDA effort through a separate division for land utilization, working directly with the NPS. Providing liaison for the Park Service was the ubiquitous Connie Wirth, who also was handling similar responsibilities for the CCC program along with his regular duties as assistant director of the Park Service.

The Resettlement Administration lasted only a couple of years before it got crossed up with Congress, which abolished the agency in 1937 and transferred all of its functions to the Department of Agriculture. Agriculture created the Farm Security Administration to take over all of the resettlement projects already under way, but it was prohibited from making any further land purchases for that purpose. Fortunately, some months earlier, all of the work connected with the Recreational Demonstration Areas had been transferred by executive order to the National Park Service. This gave the Park Service virtually a free hand to administer the program as it saw fit, while continuing to bill the Resettlement Administration—and presumably its successor—for the costs involved.

In all, at least forty-six RDA projects were completed, involving some 450,000 acres in twenty-four states. It is clear that the National Park Service intended from the outset to turn over many of these projects to the states (and, if the states weren't interested, to local governments), although it had no specific authority to do so until 1942. But the heavy involvement by the National Park Service—through first the CCC and then the RDA programs—in what were obviously more state- and locally oriented recreation projects apparently was becoming something of a sore subject at times. Every spokesman, from the secretary of the interior on down, went to great lengths to assure the states that the National Park Service had no desire or intention to take over the operation of state parks. Finally, on June 6, 1942, Congress granted authority for lands purchased under the RDA program to be either deeded or leased to the appropriate states, with all improvements, provided that they be used for pubic parks for a minimum of twenty years.

More than 140,000 acres of these lands were retained by the Park Service to create two new national park units and to augment several others, but substantially more—over 250,000 acres—was eventually deeded to the states and locals. Many of these properties, of course, found their way into the state park systems, where they are known today by such names as Oak Mountain (in Alabama), Yankee Springs (in Michigan), St. Croix (in Minnesota), Lake Murray (in Oklahoma), Cheraw (in South Carolina), and Montgomery Bell (in Tennessee). The last RDA to be conveyed was the Catoctin property, in Maryland, transferred to the state in 1954. It is perhaps of some additional interest because a substantial part of it was first separated out for construction of a presidential retreat, known today as Camp David.

A limited effort was made also to test the feasibility of the "wayside" category as a suitable recreational use of lands purchased under the resettlement program. The typically small size of these projects, however, combined with their disproportionately high purchase price (due to their frontage on major highways) militated against any large-scale implementation effort. Instead, the NPS decided to test the concept through a small number of pilot projects. South Carolina and Virginia volunteered to participate, and thirteen wayside areas, averaging about thirty acres each, were purchased. Apparently, it was determined on the basis of this experiment not to pursue the idea further, but Wirth, for one, opined that this very modest start likely paved the way for the rest-stop programs on today's modern highways.

The resettlement experiment was certainly one of the most unorthodox programs of the New Deal era. In its vast scope as well as its "social engineering" purpose, it is hard to imagine that anything of its kind would even be thinkable today. Yet, in the unusual circumstances of the 1930s, it not only was proposed, but also was funded and aggressively implemented over a period of several years. Whether or not it accomplished its primary purpose is not relevant here, but the collateral benefits it produced as the one major recreational land acquisition program of the New Deal certainly must be regarded as another welcome boost for a state park movement still trying to get on its feet.

The Park, Parkway, and Recreational Area Study Act

Stephen Mather had planted the idea of direct assistance to state parks by the National Park Service at the first National Conference on [State] Parks in 1921, but it would be more than a decade later, with the New Deal programs of the 1930s, before it became a reality. First the Civilian Conservation Corps and then the Recreational Demonstration Areas had proved of inestimable value, not only for the numerous individual parks they served, but in furthering the cause of state parks generally. The whole state park movement had surged ahead dramatically in just a few short years. But in this larger sense, all of the good work of the CCC and the RDAs—plus a modest amount of effort in state parks by the Work Projects Administration and the National Youth Administration—was still mostly uncoordinated and lacking in any overall plan. The original object had been to put men to work as quickly as possible, and there had been no time to think beyond each individual project. The National Resources Board, for one, had recognized this problem and was doing its best to promote systematic public works planning at the state level as well as the federal—but it was not enough. If federal assistance to state and local park and recreation programs was to continue, a much more comprehensive and reliable information base would have to be established.

The obvious need for congressional action in this matter was quickly recognized. Everyone acknowledged the problem and wanted to get started on a program of federal planning assistance to the states, but there was no clear-cut statutory authority to do so. With the CCC program at the height of its popularity, however, the timing in 1936 could not have been more propitious. The Department of the Interior seized the opportunity and requested additional authority that would enable it to undertake such fact-finding and planning activities as might be required to produce a clear picture of the park and recreation needs of the country. Congress responded by passing a short but important bill entitled "An Act to Authorize a Study of the Park, Parkway, and Recreational Area Programs in the United States, and for Other Purposes." The act was approved on June 23, 1936, and became Public [law] No. 770½, 74th Congress.

There were several features of this new legislation that are worthy of note. First, in authorizing and directing the Department of the Interior to make a comprehensive study, it specifically exempted from that study the "lands under the jurisdiction of the Department of Agriculture." This would appear to be further evidence of the inability of Interior and Agriculture to get their acts together where recreational use of the public lands was concerned. The act also allowed individual states to opt out of any studies simply by withholding approval. In a separate section, however, the act authorized the National Park Service to aid the states and their political subdivisions in planning their recreation programs. Presumably, such aid would be slow in coming to any state that refused to participate in the study. With the above notable exceptions, the legislation generally gave the Department of the Interior—specifically through the National Park Service—all the latitude and authority it needed. It is also significant, though, that the act failed to appropriate any funds for the purpose.

The quick success in obtaining the recreation study act is generally attributed to the favorable climate created by the splendid work of the CCC program, and also to the need for planning and coordination made so evident by the random nature of many CCC projects. Fechner himself held such a view. Soon after passage of the study act, he commented: "Naturally, a program [the CCC] in which the Federal Government was a participant to such great degree had to have nation-wide coordination in order to be carried out effectively and economically." He continued: "So you see, the planning and development of park areas on a national scale, started under the Civilian Conservation Corps program, can continue in line with a definitely conceived national plan for conservation and recreation. It is gratifying to me to know that such a fine program for the future is being planned upon the foundation of the work which has been done by the Civilian Conservation Corps."[1]

Others clearly shared this view. In a 1937 publication on the CCC program, the Department of the Interior offered a similar assessment: "So effective has been the work of the CCC in demonstrating how present needs for public recreation can be met through State park development that, under [the 1936] act of Congress a Nation-wide survey will be made by the National Park Service to inventory existing recreational areas and facilities in the Nation. This survey will lead to the development of a national recreation plan relating to park and recreational areas, large and small, in every corner of the country."[2] The point being driven home was: If you think the CCC program so far has done great things, just wait till we get our new nationwide recreation plan!

There was still another slant on the impetus for the recreation study act. Even before the legislation was passed, the National Park Service was harking back to the work of the National Resources Board for its inspiration: "Encouraged by the Administration's call for the National Resources Board report of December 1934, the Department of the Interior, through pending legislation, offers to extend its State cooperation park and recreation program indefinitely. Through the National

---

1. Robert Fechner, "State Park Development under the Civilian Conservation Corps Program," 204–5.

2. U.S. Department of the Interior, National Park Service, "The CCC and Its Contribution to a Nation-Wide State Park Recreational Program" (Washington: Government Printing Office, 1937), 16.

Park Service it would cooperate with the States and their subdivisions in the planning and acquisition of parks and parkways just as the Bureau of Roads cooperates in the construction of Federal aid highways and the Forest Service cooperates in the protection of forests." It went on, in more of a philosophical vein: "Once this tie is bound[,] the way to regional and national planning will be open. State boundaries will be forgotten in the effort to put the resources of whole regions to their best use, and the Nation will at last have put into action its awakening to the fact that the time has come to take care of herself."[3] Whew!

By the time the act was passed and the Park Service was faced with its implementation, a more practical and realistic attitude apparently prevailed. Still, the link between the recreation study idea and the work of the National Resources Board was being fully acknowledged. Ben Thompson of the NPS staff made this clear enough in his remarks to the National Conference on State Parks in 1937: "when the National Park Service was asked by the National Resources Board to prepare a report upon the recreational use of land in the United States, it was evident, from our first considerations, that the requisite information was not available." Then, after months of study, "When we rendered our report . . . in November, 1934, it was with the feeling that we had compiled 600 pages leading toward that which was not known. The real study was yet to be made."[4]

Thompson also offered some different insights into the purpose and mechanics of the Park, Parkway, and Recreational Area Study: "It is possible that that Act is more significant than has been generally realized, that is, if all agencies that come within its purview will take advantage of it. It sets up for the first time a permanent and official clearinghouse for dealing with, what might be called, the local, state, and national species of recreational currency, which have developed independently and, heretofore, circulated in separate channels without regard for harmful duplication, needless divergence, or for the national welfare." He continued: "But most important, perhaps, it provides direct channels for the conveyance of local requirements and recommendations to national agencies so that the national program, instead of being promulgated paternalistically, will itself be shaped by the information and the recommendations from the communities and States."[5] High-sounding words, but it remained to be seen whether the National Park Service would put its money where its mouth was. Whatever the

3. National Park Service, "Emergency Conservation Work under National Park Service Supervision," 9–10.
4. Ben H. Thompson, "The Park, Parkway, and Recreational Area Study," 210.
5. Ibid., 210–11.

study act's derivation, the National Park Service was now fully in the driver's seat and determined to proceed as it saw fit. True, Congress had provided no funds at all for implementation, but the Park Service got around this little problem by hiring personnel with CCC funds to do the work. It then set up an internal committee of key branch and division chiefs to oversee the task, with Conrad Wirth as its chairman, and set about developing a manual of procedure for the proposed study. In November 1936, a letter was sent over Secretary Ickes's signature to all of the state governors, enclosing a copy of the study act and asking specifically if the states wished to participate. All of the states replied affirmatively, and the following January a detailed manual was sent out, providing background and outlining how the study was to be conducted. Then the work began in earnest.

To assist the states directly, the National Park Service set up a decentralized task organization, with supervisors and technicians assigned to each of its four regional offices. Each regional supervisor was in charge of a number of state supervisors and their assistants, who worked with the designated authorities in the individual states. It was made clear at the outset that these state contact personnel were not there to do the actual work for the states, but only to advise and assist as requested. As there was no federal money to be handed out for planning, the only leverage the Park Service had to encourage steady performance by the states was the threat, real or implied, that a laggard state might lose out in the assignment of new CCC camps. As Wirth put it: "for if a state park was not part of an overall state park system, in accordance with the study, there were grave questions raised as to whether that park could be allotted a camp."[6]

For the state-level work, the study was divided into two principal parts: an inventory phase to collect information on existing conditions, and a study phase in which the collected data would be analyzed and consequent recommendations formulated. To assist in standardizing the inventory of recreation areas throughout the country, a specially appointed subcommittee of the National Resources Committee (as the National Resources Board was renamed in 1935) produced a new four-category classification system just for the purpose: "primitive," "modified," "developed," and "scientific."

Meanwhile, the National Park Service busied itself establishing liaison with all of the various federal agencies and nongovernmental organizations that might need to be consulted in the study process, and also in conducting a number of related subordinate studies on its own. Most of these studies were general in nature

6. Wirth, *Parks, Politics, and the People,* 172.

or dealt largely with national park matters, but one of them was an analysis of existing state park legislation from around the country—a project that had been specifically requested by state park representatives several years before. This must have been a subject of some considerable interest, because during this same period, 1936–1942, at least eighteen states requested help from the NPS in rewriting their laws to strengthen park and recreation functions.

It is also significant that the Park Service during this time initiated the first-ever controlled inventory of state park assets and programs. The first of these surveys was conducted for the year 1939 and published in two reports: one for "facilities and activities" and the other for "fiscal data." Unfortunately, only thirty-seven states reported for that year, but the systematic inventories were continued on an annual basis through 1962, with increasing accuracy and completeness.

Everything considered, the nationwide Park, Parkway, and Recreational Area Study proved to be a monumental undertaking. As in so many such cases, the study and planning exercise itself no doubt served a more valuable purpose than the planning documents it produced. According to Wirth, thirty-four states had completed studies by 1941, while forty-six states developed comprehensive state park system plans—presumably as an adjunct of the larger study process. It is questionable that very many of these documents served much of a purpose, coming as they did on the eve of America's entry into World War II and the total distraction that attended it. Still, the four-year education in park and recreation planning that the experience provided helped to produce a crop of outstanding state park administrators that emerged after the war. And that in itself probably made the whole undertaking worthwhile.

Never satisfied with the hurried report it had prepared in 1934 for the National Resources Board, the Park Service saw the 1936 study act as the opportunity to redeem itself. To cap the individual state efforts that were coming to fruition about this time, the NPS produced a landmark report from the national perspective entitled, "A Study of the Park and Recreation Problem of the United States." The document was published in early 1942, but, again, because of world events it never received the attention and use that it might have under more favorable conditions.

With the nation's total commitment to the war effort, just about every nonessential government program was drastically scaled back or terminated altogether. This was the fate of the Civilian Conservation Corps, which went out of existence in July 1942. And because it depended entirely on CCC funds, the recreation study program simply withered on the vine. In submitting a summary report on the CCC to Secretary Ickes in January 1944, Conrad Wirth lamented the program's passing and offered these parting comments:

For insurance of the success of any future Federal aid program, regardless of what agency administers it or the methods used, the provisions of the Recreation Study Act should continue to be carried out, at least to the extent of assisting the States in keeping the studies and plans alive and abreast with the developments of the time. This would permit rapid resumption of development work on a sound basis, either with or without Federal assistance.[7]

Wirth was among the many who had grown fond of the Civilian Conservation Corps, the Recreational Demonstration Areas, and the recreation study initiatives, and he hated to see them go.

The End of an Exciting Era

By 1937, Roosevelt's New Deal, which had debuted with such excitement and anticipation (and more than a little apprehension) just four years before, was tottering. A convergence of adverse political and economic forces had become too formidable for even the popular president to overcome. From that point on, many of the recovery programs were doomed, and it was only due to their immense popular (translated into political) support that those of direct concern to state parks were able to survive until the bitter end. Inevitably, though, the redirection of the nation's interest, energies, and assets to the single purpose of victory in the World War would bring about swift and certain closure for them all.

Of the three principal New Deal programs that directly benefited state parks, the Civilian Conservation Corps easily stands out as the most significant by far—but the other two are fully deserving of honorable mention. The Recreational Demonstration Areas—an imaginative adaptation of what was conceived as an agricultural resettlement effort—made a tremendous contribution in the form of almost three hundred thousand acres of new state park land, and could have had even greater impact had the axe not fallen so quickly on the parent program. Likewise, in providing the basis for ongoing federal assistance to state recreation planning efforts, the 1936 Park, Parkway, and Recreational Area Study Act gave a degree of legitimacy and continuity to the long-cherished concept of an intergovernmental, nationwide park and recreation program.

But there can be no denying the supreme importance of the CCC program where the state parks are concerned. NPS director Arno Cammerer, even as early as 1935, was crediting the CCC with advancing state parks by fifty years. I would

7. Wirth, "Report to Harold L. Ickes," 44.

not presume to quantify the CCC's impact in quite that way, but without doubt the contributions the program made during that exceptional nine-year period, 1933–1942, constitute the greatest defining influence in the history of state parks to date. It would not be an overstatement to say that the CCC is an essential and inseparable part of the state park heritage. That is so not just because of the more than $300 million spent in building and improving over four hundred parks in forty-two states—nor even because of the hundreds of new park properties the states were able, by hook or by crook, to round up for themselves in order to qualify for CCC camps. The most enduring legacy of the CCC lies in the intrinsic state park culture that germinated, took root, and flourished during that brief period. It is unlikely that such a compressed evolution could have occurred in any other situation, and in that respect the Civilian Conservation Corps did more than anything else to shape the state park movement as we know it today.

And that is quite a legacy indeed.

10

A Major Interruption
Wartime Distraction and Postwar Rebound

It Was Great While It Lasted

The latter years of the 1930s were indeed heady times for state park advocates in America. While wishful thinking and good intentions alone had produced few or no parks in most of the forty-eight states, the sudden availability of direct federal aid in 1933 had worked wonders. Now, less than a decade later, almost every state in the union was firmly committed to a state parks program. The number of individual parks had increased by the hundreds and the total acreage had more than doubled. Probably just as important, state park administrative agencies had been established in every state but one—even in several that still had no parks—and all but three were receiving fairly regular, albeit modest, appropriations of funds.

New Deal largess, ministered principally through the Civilian Conservation Corps, had wrought a truly amazing transformation in America's state parks movement. Where the National Conference on State Parks had merely publicized the state park idea, the CCC had given it real stone-and-timber substance.

But, as some pessimist once concluded, all good things must come to an end. The decline of the CCC program had started with political opposition to the New Deal in the late 1930s, but the reality of war brought it to an abrupt end in 1942. At the program's zenith, in 1935, the National Park Service was operating 475 CCC camps in state parks around the country. By the beginning of what was to be its last budget year, in July 1941, the number of state park camps had already dropped to 113, and at the end of that year there were but nine. Only a small amount of new recreational construction was undertaken during the year,

155

and that was limited to completion of work necessary "to assure maximum operation and protection to facilities already provided."[1] Everything else was redi-
rected to support national defense and the rapid preparation for war. The CCC
program was now history, and state park administrators would both lament its
passing and glory in its accomplishments.

Although the CCC had proved to be something of a one-shot effort (but indeed a potent one), the New Deal era also had laid groundwork for continuing federal aid to state park programs through the 1936 Park, Parkway, and
Recreational Area Study Act. For several years the National Park Service had been
helping the individual states conduct comprehensive analyses of their respective
park and recreation needs, and in 1941 it produced its own nationwide assessment
under the title *A Study of the Park and Recreation Problem of the United States.*

The National Park Service had obviously savored its role in working with the
states in both the CCC program and the park studies, and this fact clearly influenced the tone of its final report. Its principal thrust was toward implementation
of a coordinated federal-state-local program to meet the nation's park and recreation needs. To help bring this about, the report made a strong pitch for a permanent federal aid program for state parks analogous to other programs already in
existence. Said the report: "Every reason, of human need and of equalization of
burden, which can be adduced in support of such aid for highways, education,
forestry, wildlife, etc., applies also to the preservation of our scenic, historic, scientific, and outdoor recreational resources and their development for human use."[2]

The comprehensive approach proposed by the National Park Service seemed sincere, well-intentioned, and even visionary. State park administrators, generally
pleased with the harmonious relationship they had enjoyed with their federal counterpart, might have taken great comfort from the findings of the report except for
one thing: the timing, though entirely accidental, could not possibly have been
worse. America was now at war, and everything else was figuratively out the window.

Is This Park Necessary?

Although it had been barely a short generation since the last great conflict had
ended, the onset of World War II was seen in America as an almost unprece-

1. Federal Security Agency, "Annual Report of the Director of the Civilian Conservation
Corps," 1942, unpublished report in the U.S. Department of the Interior Library (SD143 .A2),
Washington, D.C., 36.
2. U.S. Department of the Interior, National Park Service, *A Study of the Park and Recreation
Problem of the United States,* 132.

dented event (probably due to the nature of the Pearl Harbor attack), accompanied by widespread uncertainty as to its likely effects on the daily lives of the people. Determined as they were to prevail on the battlefield, Americans resigned themselves to make whatever adjustments and sacrifices might be necessary—they just didn't know what that might entail. This was an immediate concern for the park and recreation profession. In the sobering context of global war, could parks be considered anything but frivolous and unimportant—even unpatriotic?

As isolationist as they may have seemed at the time, the American people were nonetheless very much aware of the situation developing in Europe in the 1930s, and most assumed that the country would be drawn into the inevitable conflict sooner or later. A national defense mentality had beset the nation long before actual hostilities erupted. Such an attitude was reflected in a resolution adopted on October 31, 1940, by the board of directors of the National Conference on State Parks, which stated:

> WHEREAS, past and present experience indicates the likelihood that effort will be made at many points to take over for national defense purposes lands and facilities which have been acquired and dedicated to provide healthful outdoor recreation for the people of America, and
>
> WHEREAS, particularly and especially in times of stress, park and other areas developed and dedicated for recreation are vitally needed in maintaining the health and morale of the general population and specifically of those engaged in defense activities, therefore be it
>
> RESOLVED, that the National Conference on State Parks, acting through its Board of Directors, most strongly urges that all agencies charged with administration of areas dedicated to park and recreation purposes maintain a definite stand in opposition to any alienation of these areas for which it cannot be conclusively shown that such alienation is necessary for the national defense, and we further earnestly urge that the defense authorities in determining their land requirements for military purposes give the fullest consideration to the defense values of park and recreation areas.[3]

Because in 1940 America was not yet actually at war, it was possible for the NCSP to get away with protecting its turf without seeming to be unpatriotic. With Pearl Harbor, however, everything changed abruptly. Now, instead of simply paying lip service to national defense considerations, every official action had

3. National Conference on State Parks Board of Directors Resolution, October 31, 1940, in National Conference on State Parks Minutes of Policy Making Bodies, series 1, box 1, NRPA Library.

to be subordinated to the interests of the war effort, in appearance as well as in fact. This was illustrated by the "supplemental foreword" that Secretary of the Interior Harold Ickes prepared for the 1941 National Park Service report referred to above. The report was actually printed before Pearl Harbor and contained a foreword by Ickes that spoke glowingly of the country's park and recreation needs, but not a word of qualification in recognition of the impending world crisis.

By the time this almost three-hundred-page book was ready for distribution in early 1942, however, the only thing on America's mind was the war. Apparently sensing the awkwardness of the situation, Ickes quickly prepared (and had inserted in each book by hand) a new foreword, giving proper deference to the new national priorities but at the same time reasserting the importance of parks and recreation, especially in wartime. It read, in part:

> The accompanying report is presented at a time when our energies and resources are centered in one objective—victory in war. While our present war effort must take precedence over all other activities, planning to meet our park and recreational requirements must continue to receive consideration. The inspiration experienced through visiting the Nation's scenic wonders and historic shrines instills a love of country and maintains morale, and participation in recreational activities is vital to the welfare of the people, both military and civilian.[4]

Secretary Ickes may well have been taking his cue from his boss, President Franklin Roosevelt. Reacting to the same concern about the propriety of something as seemingly frivolous as recreation—particularly spectator sports—with the whole country now absorbed by the subject of war, the Major League Baseball commissioner, Judge Kenesaw Landis, wrote to Roosevelt in early January 1942, seeking the president's opinion about whether the baseball season should proceed. Roosevelt responded immediately, heartily endorsing baseball as usual. "I honestly feel that it would be best for the country to keep baseball going," he said. "There will be fewer people unemployed and everybody will work longer hours and harder than ever before. And that means that they ought to have a chance for recreation and for taking their minds off their work even more than before."[5] Clearly, the same argument could be made for other legitimate forms of recreation as well—and it would be, again and again.

---

4. Harold L. Ickes, supplemental foreword to *Study of the Park and Recreation Problem of the United States*.
5. Franklin D. Roosevelt to Kenesaw M. Landis, January 15, 1942, Franklin D. Roosevelt Library, Hyde Park, N.Y.

Wartime emergencies established new priorities for use of many of America's state parks in the early 1940s, especially for military training purposes. Strategically located in San Francisco Bay, California's Angel Island State Park served as a staging area for troop and equipment movements to the Pacific, as shown here in 1942. © CALIFORNIA STATE PARKS, 2003

However the importance of parks and recreation in a wartime emergency might be defended and justified, it was abundantly clear that the war itself would necessitate many changes, some drastic, in the way such programs were operated. America's state parks girded their loins and prepared to make the best of it.

The State Parks Go to War

For the growing number of state park users, the news on the eve of World War II was both good and bad. On the plus side, there were now—thanks to the Civilian Conservation Corps' efforts of the last decade—hundreds of new and improved parks for them to enjoy. The bad news, though, was that the nation's rapid conversion to a wartime mode would render many of these new recreation areas all but inaccessible. In the face of a critical rubber shortage, tire rationing was instituted almost immediately, with Roosevelt even threatening to have private citizens surrender the tires from their cars for use by the military. Gasoline rationing soon followed for the eastern United States and was extended to the entire country before the end of 1942. Car owners without a justifiable need for more (the "A" windshield stickers) were limited at first to four gallons of gasoline per week, and this was soon reduced to three—hardly enough to meet the barest commuting needs. Continuing use of the nation's parks and playgrounds might well be desirable as a health and morale booster in wartime, but getting to them was going to be a serious problem.

Attendance at state parks did indeed plummet during the early years of the war, but it started to rebound before war's end. All states and all parks did not follow the same pattern, of course, as there were many factors affecting visitation. Parks readily accessible to military bases and big defense plants were generally well-used, and in many cases service personnel were admitted free as a patriotic gesture. Some states—such as Georgia, Tennessee, and Texas—reported that wartime conditions had actually increased attendance at some parks because the local population was tending to visit close-to-home facilities in lieu of taking distant vacation trips. Interestingly, use of overnight facilities—especially lodges and cabins equipped for longer stays—seems to have been affected to a lesser degree than day-use activity, presumably due to the visitors' desire to get maximum recreational benefit for the miles they had to travel.

Personal transportation for any purpose was a sticky subject throughout the war, and especially so at the outset when patriotic fervor, along with apprehension and uncertainty, gripped the country. Gasoline allocations were particularly controversial and suspect. In some eastern states, for a time anyway, fines were actually levied on cars bearing "B" or "C" stickers (those allowed extra gasoline for critical needs) that happened to be found in the parks. The assumption was that these drivers were unfairly taking advantage of their special status purely for personal pleasure, but the practice of fining them for visiting the parks was soon seen as an overreaction and discontinued.

Because of the drastic curtailment of private automobile travel, though, thoughts necessarily turned to other possible forms of transportation. A special panel convened by the National Conference on State Parks to deal with this and other wartime issues recommended that weekday mass transit schedules be extended through the weekends to accommodate day users on Saturdays and Sundays. It also suggested that supplemental bus service be considered for peak-use times, and even that school buses might be pressed into service as park transport without losing their "priority rating on tires."

But getting people to the parks was to become almost a moot issue as the war dragged on. A more fundamental question was whether the state parks would be able to operate at all. Manpower shortages came right on the heels of tire and gasoline rationing and posed just as great a problem, especially in areas where industry and other war-related activity quickly absorbed the available workforce. Numerous state park employees went into military service, voluntarily and otherwise, and many others left to take higher-paying jobs in the factories and shipyards. With no one left to run the shop, many parks were closed outright, and others operated on a reduced schedule. Indiana's Richard Lieber, writing in the NCSP 1943 yearbook, offered this description of the situation: "In every state the authorities are short-handed, due to the War, and the operating staffs are carrying extra loads. In some states, the State Parks are serving directly and indirectly the war effort. In others, the parks are lying fallow, as it were, with little or no patronage, due to gasoline rationing and limited transportation facilities."[6]

And instead of idly sitting on their hands and crying the blues, state park authorities were indeed "serving the war effort." Parks in Connecticut, Kentucky, Louisiana, Oklahoma, South Dakota, and elsewhere were turned over to the military for national defense, training, and recreational purposes. Some were used on an ad hoc basis as training grounds, while still others made their overnight facilities available to relieve temporary housing shortages around newly developed military installations. Almost every state park system welcomed military personnel with free or reduced admission, hosted special programs and activities, and otherwise did all it could to aid the national cause. South Dakota's Custer State Park, however, would surely get the prize for the most unusual contribution. To help relieve the country's "critical meat shortage," it increased the number of animals that could be taken in its annual winter buffalo and elk slaughter (but taking care to point out that it would not unduly reduce the size of the native herds).[7]

With wartime needs taking priority over everything else, and with the desire of state park administrators along with every other patriotic citizen to go all out for the war effort, there naturally were misgivings about what the parks would look like when returned by the military after the war. This concern was expressed early by the NCSP panel in 1942:

> The Conference commends the action of those responsible for the protection of State Parks, who, subject to Park regulations, have agreed to use of parks by

6. Richard Lieber, introduction to *Park and Recreation Progress: 1943 Yearbook.*
7. National Conference on State Parks, "Use of State Parks during War Time," 169.

State parks made a variety of contributions to the home-front war effort during World War II, but increasing the buffalo slaughter at Custer State Park to help ease the nation's meat shortage was probably the most unusual. CUSTER STATE PARK

the Military forces on condition that the areas be returned to the States in the condition in which they were found. We protest, however, against use of State Parks for any purpose which will injure natural scenery which it would be impossible to restore after intensive use, especially in view of the fact that in most or all cases there would be available [other] land whose natural features would not be injured or could easily be restored.[8]

In his comments on the subject the following year, Lieber obviously was feeling better about the situation—or perhaps he was merely indulging in wishful thinking: "In all the States where state parks are being utilized by the Army, provision is being made for post-war restoration of the terrain." He noted further that "The use of state parks for recreation by the Armed Forces and war workers is stimulating the habit of using the parks and will tend to increase state park visitors after the war." Nor was Lieber willing to let state park personnel fall back on wartime conditions as an excuse for not doing their jobs. After first observing that "There is no evidence that custodial care of the physical plant in any state has been

8. National Conference on State Parks, resolutions adopted at the roundtable on "Wartime Uses of State Parks," Chicago, Ill., September 23–24, 1942, in Minutes of Policy Making Bodies, series 1, box 1, NRPA Library.

reduced to the danger point," he continued: "All state park agencies realize that they are trustees for the state parks and, insofar as manpower and appropriations permit, they are preparing for the peace patronage which is bound to be unleashed when the park-hungry public is again free to travel."[9] With the prospect of victory already on the horizon, that time would not be long in coming.

Elsewhere on the State Park Front

Although the frontline operation of state parks clearly was disrupted and curtailed by the events of World War II, the movement in its broader sense continued to develop and mature. It was now being served, and influenced, by the twin engines of the National Conference on State Parks and the National Park Service—sometimes working in concert, sometimes not. As the only national organization devoted specifically to state park matters, the NCSP remained the focal point for most of the professional dialogue; but the NPS, after years of involvement with the CCC program and implementation of the 1936 Park, Parkway, and Recreational Area Study Act, could make a strong claim for being the real motivating force behind the state park movement. Both entities, however, could agree on the number one priority for maintaining momentum in the movement, and that was some kind of continuing federal aid program for state parks across the board.

With the demise of the CCC program, the NCSP board had appointed a special committee under the chairmanship of Robert Kingery of Illinois to consider prospects for getting some other type of assistance bill through Congress. The committee reported its findings at the NCSP board meeting in May 1943. The board concluded that federal aid could be justified by the "inter-state character" of state parks and directed that a draft bill be submitted for review by the state park directors.[10] The proposal was patterned after an existing program that provided federal aid to states for highway constuction, and it called for distribution of funds according to a preset formula, to be matched by the states. The idea was kicked around for several years with no conclusive results. In October 1944, then-NCSP president Harold Lathrop of Minnesota tried to breathe new life into the proposal as a means of revitalizing the state park movement after the war. In urging immediate feedback from the states, he warned: "public statements have been

9. Lieber, introduction to *1943 Yearbook*.

10. Robert Kingery, chairman, report of "Committee on Federal Aid to State Parks" to National Conference on State Parks officers and directors, July 3, 1943, in Board of Directors Papers, series 2, box 1, NRPA Library.

made by members of Congress suggesting several different forms of Federal Aid to State Parks, some of which may not be in accord with the views of state park authorities."[11] Even then, the appeal accomplished little, if anything, because a year later the board was still seeking consensus on how to proceed.

In September 1945, however, the board decided to go ahead and act. In fact, it acted twice. In addition to meeting as the NCSP board, the several members present also were representing the NCSP membership at a joint session with the Association of Southeastern State Park Directors (see next chapter). As it happened, NPS director Newton Drury (who had succeeded Arno Cammerer in 1940) was present for the Southeastern meeting and had commented on the proposed bill and its advantages to the states. In addition to acting on its own, the board also received a resolution of support from the joint group reacting to Drury's favorable comments. Both actions called for steps to be taken immediately to have the bill introduced in Congress and be given the full endorsement and support by the NCSP and all of the states individually.[12]

As a practical matter, the NCSP board decided to ask Conrad Wirth, who handled much of the congressional liaison for the NPS, to find sponsors for the bill. Apparently through Wirth's efforts, the bill was introduced in October 1945 by the chairman of the House Public Lands Committee, J. Hardin Peterson, of Florida, and in the following April by Senator Claude Pepper, also of Florida. Unfortunately, that's about as far as it got. The NPS nominally supported the measure, but the Bureau of the Budget apparently did not. No hearings on the proposal were scheduled, and the 79th Congress adjourned without taking any action. To hear Wirth tell it, the failure was sort of his fault: "I was the principal advocate of the bill in the National Park Service, but twelve days after the bill was introduced I left for Vienna, Austria, on an assignment by Secretary Ickes. Nothing really happened to that piece of legislation after my departure."[13]

Although Peterson reintroduced the bill in the next Congress, efforts to pass the legislation would ultimately fail—just as those to continue the CCC program had done a few years earlier. However, there was still the possibility of reinvigorating

11. Harold W. Lathrop, communication to National Conference on State Parks membership, October 30, 1944, in Minutes of Policy Making Bodies, series 1, box 1, NRPA Library.

12. National Conference on State Parks, minutes of "Meeting of Board of Directors and Joint Session with the Association of Southeastern State Park Directors," Cumberland Mountain State Park, Tenn., September 21, 1945, in Minutes of Policy Making Bodies, series 1, box 1, NRPA Library, 4–5.

13. Wirth, *Parks, Politics, and the People,* 174.

the 1936 act as a means of providing federal assistance to state parks. Immediately after the war, the National Park Service renewed its request for funds to resume recreational planning and coordination under that existing authority, but there was a potential threat brewing in that area as well. The culprit was in the form of legislation pending in both houses of Congress to, in effect, set up a new federal recreation service in the Federal Security Agency. This was the recommendation of a fifteen-agency Federal Inter-Agency Committee on Recreation, which had been set up administratively in the fall of 1946. The NCSP and most of the state park directors disliked the measure and actively opposed it, citing the work already being done by the National Park Service pursuant to the 1936 act. Although the legislation failed to pass, the idea for a separate federal recreation agency would pop up again from time to time, ultimately achieving success in the 1960s (the emergence of outdoor recreation as a separate program will be discussed in the next chapter).

The National Park Service continued to assert its desire to work with and to assist the state park programs in a "two-way relationship," but it was limited in its ability by the failure of Congress to provide funds and personnel. It recognized the need to update the state recreation studies of the late 1930s and encouraged the states to proceed with this task on their own, although few of them were in a position to do so. There were, however, some other developments at the federal level that offered potential for assisting the park programs of those states that happened to be favorably situated. One of these was the Flood Control Act of 1944, which authorized state and local governments to provide public recreation areas on federal water projects, including the numerous freshwater reservoirs. Another boost for state parks came in the form of a 1948 act authorizing the conveyance of surplus federal real property—including many recently abandoned military sites—to state and local governments for park, recreation, and historic preservation purposes. The number of state parks subsequently made possible by these two measures would certainly be counted in the hundreds.

It seemed that the "big war" was barely over before a lesser one broke out in Korea. While this new national emergency had far less of an impact on state parks than had World War II, of course, it still threw a small monkey wrench into the works. Many states were just getting their park development efforts back in gear when, in November 1950, the National Production Authority of the Department of Commerce issued its Order M-4, which threatened to derail much, if not all, of the planned park construction work. The order was intended to prohibit construction that "does not further the defense effort, either directly or indirectly,

Congressional action in the 1940s enabled many new state parks to be established on surplus military properties and on federal reservoir projects. The latter was especially important in view of the rapid postwar increase in boating and other water sports, as reflected
here at Oklahoma's Lake Texhoma State Park. OKLAHOMA DIVISION OF STATE PARKS

and does not increase the nation's productive capacity."[14] By liberal interpretation and application, this prohibition could have been disastrous for new state
projects, especially considering that no one knew how long it might be in force.

Fortunately, the NPA understood the potential magnitude of the problem and
was willing to work with state and national park interests to exempt most construction that could be considered more for "conservation" than for pure "recreation." A case was made that "state parks were essentially conservation projects . . .
acquired and established by the States primarily to preserve outstanding examples of the State's scenic, scientific and cultural features . . . [and] should not be
considered as recreation facilities in the sense of city playgrounds."[15] The accommodation reached must have been sufficient, as there is no evidence that the
order resulted in any significant curtailment of state park construction.

14. U.S. Department of Commerce, National Production Authority, "Order M-4, as amended
Nov. 15, 1950: Title 32A, Chapter 1, 'What This Part Does'" (Washington: Government Printing Office, 1950).
15. National Conference on State Parks, memorandum to "State Park Authorities," November 17, 1950, in Board of Directors Papers, series 3, box 1, NRPA Library.

State Parks Expansion in the Postwar Years

The loss of the Civilian Conservation Corps and the distraction of a world war, coming in quick succession, dealt the state park movement a double blow and left it reeling for several years. By 1945, though, signs of recovery were everywhere apparent. State park attendance was again on the rise (although nowhere near its prewar levels), more park personnel were on the job, and park expenditures were up in almost every category over the previous two years.

One of the most encouraging signs was the renewed emphasis being placed on park land acquisition. Even during the war years, state parks had managed to add ninety-two new areas and some 350,000 acres overall. Relatively little of this had been accomplished through purchase, but in 1945 land acquisition expenditures jumped to $2,645,000 as compared with only $178,000 for the year before. In 1946, according to data collected by the National Park Service, there were about 1,549 areas loosely categorized as state parks, with a total acreage of approximately 2,251,449. By 1950, these figures had increased to 1,723 and 2,407,716, respectively, and by 1960, to 2,587 and 3,153,767.[16] Even allowing for the obvious weaknesses in the NPS survey, it is clear that state park expansion was again on the upswing.

Through the decade of the 1950s, improved economic conditions and renewed interest in state parks led to steadily increasing appropriations to purchase new park properties (rising to a postwar high of almost $15 million in 1959). But now there were other significant factors contributing to overall expansion as well. Most notable among these were two federal initiatives already mentioned: the Flood Control Act of 1944, which in effect opened up federal lands on reservoir projects operated by agencies such as the Corps of Engineers and the Bureau of Reclamation for public recreational use; and the 1948 act (Public Law 616 of the 80th Congress) which helped steer many of the surplus and abandoned military properties into recreational use at the state and local levels. Obviously, not all states were fortunate enough to take advantage of these new programs, but those that were exploited the opportunities to the fullest.

At war's end, there were still five of the forty-eight states without a state park. Delaware was the first of these to join the ranks, in 1951, and the others would follow in less than a decade. Delaware's first acquisition was Trap Pond, a former CCC site in the southern part of the state, followed by the federally surplused

16. U.S. Department of the Interior, National Park Service, "State Parks and Recreational Areas, Acreage and Accommodations as of June 30, 1946," "State Parks Areas, Acreages, and Accommodations, December 31, 1950," "State Park Statistics—1960."

Fort Delaware later that same year. Kansas was next, in 1955, leasing 1,500 acres on a Corps of Engineers reservoir for its Kanopolis State Park. Utah, in 1957, with its Territorial State House, and Arizona, in 1958, with the Tubac Presidio, started their state park programs with historic sites. Colorado, although it had been anticipating a state parks program at least since 1937 and had legislatively provided for establishment of a state parks board in 1957, did not get its first park, Cherry Creek, until 1959 under a lease from the Corps of Engineers.

With those five additions, all of the contiguous forty-eight states were now formally and officially in the state parks business. In 1959, of course, Alaska and Hawaii joined the union. Hawaii brought with it an existing parks legacy, with a number of park areas dating back as early as 1952. Alaska, on the other hand, still very much an undeveloped frontier, had not seen a need for territorial parks, but it would initiate in 1970 what would quickly become the largest state park system of all in terms of included acreage.

While most of the states were busy creating and expanding their park holdings, they were not neglecting park development, either. The momentum started by the CCC program had whetted a desire to improve and open for use other park properties as soon as that could be accomplished. Expenditures for park improvement work increased from $2,304,000 in 1946, the first postwar year, to $19,026,000 in 1960, and actually spiked to over $27 million in 1957. Much of the new construction was devoted to providing more and a wider range of overnight accommodations. Hotels and lodges, for instance, increased from 60 in 1950 to 82 in 1960, and their capacity from 3,556 guests per night to 4,526. Cabins increased at an even greater rate during that decade, from 2,808 to 3,801, while tent and trailer campsites more than doubled, from 24,582 to 56,321.

New park improvements were clearly being aimed at the tourist trade, with facilities designed for longer, more comfortable stays, and they were quickly put to use. With the resumption of normal travel patterns after the war, attendance at state parks skyrocketed, and overnight users steadily increased as a percentage of the total. State park visitations numbered 92,507,000 in 1946, but only 4 percent of those were overnight; by 1960, the total had risen to 259,000,000, and overnight users now accounted for almost 8 percent. An accelerating trend was definitely under way, and America's state parks would hasten to take advantage of it.

11

The Continuing Search for Direction
The Ever-Resilient National Conference on State Parks

Even without a federal financial aid program, the course of America's state park movement during and in the years immediately following the World War II was still influenced to a significant degree by its close involvement with the National Park Service. Near at hand on a parallel track, however, trying to keep up with the times and provide useful service, was the venerable National Conference on State Parks.

In 1941, the NCSP marked its twentieth year of existence, yet the organization now bore scant resemblance to itself during the dynamic Mather years. The fact that it still survived at all as a considerable player in the state parks arena was due almost entirely to the strong, capable leadership it had somehow been fortunate enough to attract. That was indeed the case in the early 1940s, with the redoubtable Richard Lieber at the helm as chairman and the ever-dependable Harlean James still minding the store as executive secretary. Together, they made a formidable team.

The NCSP did not always follow a consistent path, however, and at times it was difficult to know exactly what its agenda was. This confusion prompted Newton Drury, still somewhat new in his position as National Parks director, to submit his resignation from the NCSP board in October 1941. His apparent concern was that certain policy issues at the time might put the NCSP and the NPS on opposite sides and prove "mutually embarrassing." Following Drury's lead, two of his subordinates—Conrad Wirth and Herbert Evison—also offered to resign.[1] This potential abandonment by the NPS brain trust, which had been

1. National Conference on State Parks, minutes of board of directors meeting, October 31, 1941, in Minutes of Policy Making Bodies, series 1, box 1, NRPA Library.

a dominant factor in the success of NCSP since the very beginning, left the board in a temporary state of shock. The matter was amicably resolved, however, by an agreement for Wirth, who was a "life" member of the board, to stay on and represent the NPS. Although this action signaled a definite, though gradual, withdrawal by the NPS from NCSP affairs, Wirth himself would continue his deep personal involvement, eventually serving as chairman of the board from 1964 until the position was abolished in 1971.

Despite an array of problems, the NCSP managed to accomplish many worthwhile projects during the 1940s and 1950s. When wartime budget restrictions forced the NPS to suspend publication of the *Park and Recreation Progress Yearbook,* which it had initiated in 1937, the NCSP picked up the project with the 1942 edition and continued to publish it randomly for a number of years. In a related venture, the NCSP and the NPS cooperated on a technical publication called *Park Practice,* although it was sometimes a strained partnership due to the difficulties in producing such a demanding, labor-intensive document. The idea for the publication reportedly originated at the 1950 NCSP conference, and a committee was subsequently appointed to oversee the project. After several years of struggling largely by itself, however, the NCSP happily accepted a formal offer of assistance from the NPS in 1955 and eventually withdrew almost totally from any practical participation in the collaborative effort.

Since its beginning in 1921, the annual conference had continued to be the highlight of the NCSP program. During World War II, though, the organization decided that transportation problems, if nothing else, would severely limit attendance and called off its 1942 meeting. Instead, it sponsored what it called a "Round Table on Wartime Uses of State Parks" (discussed in the previous chapter) in September of that year. As no one knew how long the hostilities might continue, the decision on subsequent meetings was left on a case-by-case basis. No general meeting was held in 1943 or 1944 either, although the board of directors continued to meet once or twice a year. There was some talk about resuming the annual conferences in 1945, but instead the board elected to sit in with the Association of Southeastern State Park Directors at the latter's regular meeting that year in Tennessee. The theme chosen for the joint session was "Postwar State Park Policies." The annual NCSP meetings were resumed on a regular basis the following year, 1946, with an eleven-day "Pacific Coast Pilgrimage," starting in Los Angeles and proceeding northward into Oregon.

Even before its meeting with the Southeastern group—in fact, going back almost to its inception—the NCSP had variously advocated some kind of regional affiliates as a means of taking its message closer to its constituents. Several regional conferences had indeed been held, but no formal organizations established. The Association of Southeastern State Park Directors, organized in March 1942, was the first regional state park group, but it was in no way directly connected to the NCSP. Rather, it was influenced more by contacts with the National Park Service, as evidenced by Conrad Wirth's attendance and active participation in its organizational meeting.

However, Wirth may well have been acting to some degree in his capacity with the NCSP, as he had been appointed by Chairman Lieber not long before to head up a committee to look into the feasibility of dividing the country into subordinate regional affiliates, possibly to be called "chapters." In October 1943, Wirth submitted for Lieber's consideration a fairly detailed regional proposal, providing for five groupings of states with generally similar geographical characteristics and each containing a combination of "strong states and weak states from the standpoint of park organization."[2] I have seen no record of any action being taken by the NCSP on this specific proposal (possibly because Lieber did not get around to it before his death some months later), but an article eventually included in the NCSP constitution provided that the NCSP "may encourage the formation of regional organizations" with similar objectives. A Midwest State Park Association was organized in late 1947, and there have been others since then—but none formally affiliated with the NCSP.

Without a cohesive national constituency or any kind of regional or local substructure to bolster it, the NCSP continued essentially as an oligarchical organization, its fortunes ebbing and flowing with the interests and energies of its leadership. As already noted, it managed to accomplish some useful work—particularly in the area of publications—but it also at times got so bogged down in tangential, even trifling, matters as to obscure and frustrate its larger agenda. As state park personnel became more and more dominant in the affairs of the Conference, it increasingly took on the character of a fraternal organization—almost like a "benevolent and protective order of state park administrators."

An inordinate amount of attention was devoted to internal matters such as membership classes and qualifications, dues structure, and means of governance. Its constitution provided for eight different categories of membership and six levels of dues. Even an incumbent state park administrator would not automatically

2. Conrad Wirth to Richard Lieber, October 7, 1943, in Board of Directors Papers, series 3, box 1, NRPA Library.

qualify for membership. First, that person would have to be nominated by two members in good standing and then be approved by the "qualifications committee" in accordance with standards and requirements set by the board of directors. One has to wonder what on earth all of this elitist minutiae was designed to accomplish.

At times, the NCSP took a very active interventionist role in matters of concern to individual states. In 1953, for instance, it adopted resolutions and wrote letters of protest deploring or outright opposing state park personnel actions and reorganizations in Florida, Montana, Pennsylvania, and elsewhere. The stated concern was the need for "continuity of responsible park administration," but the regularity with which the NCSP intervened, sometimes almost as a knee-jerk reaction, could easily be seen as a form of self-protectionism among the incumbent state park administrators. But the NCSP's interventionism was not limited to protests. In many instances, it was aimed at applauding or encouraging positive park-related developments, such as efforts to establish state park programs in Arizona, Colorado, and Hawaii.

The program of the National Conference on State Parks may have been uneven, inconsistent, erratic, even mystifying at times, but, as noted earlier, it was still virtually the only game in town. Even so, it could be used or ignored by its constituency as circumstances suggested, and it suffered from this volatile and uncertain base of support. It seemed always to be broke and looking for money just to remain solvent, and it was forced repeatedly to at least consider affiliation or merger with other organizations such as the American Institute of Park Executives and the National Recreation Association.

Adamant that state parks should remain its primary focus and the basis of its identity, however, the NCSP managed somehow not only to survive as an organization but also to retain a measure of respectability. Now being run largely by state park professionals themselves, it would muster all of its remaining prestige and influence to help guide the state programs through the chaotic "free-for-all" that the postwar decades would bring.

Old Issues in a New Context

State parks were again on a roll, experiencing rapid growth and expansion in almost every state. But along with the increase in numbers, the subject of parks itself was becoming more complex and confusing for those who had to make the decisions about such matters as which areas should be acquired, how they should

Shown here at a National Conference on State Parks board of directors meeting at Ohio's Lake Hope State Park in 1951 are many of the individuals who were instrumental in further-ing the state park movement in the postwar decade. Front row, left to right: V. W. Flickinger (Ohio), Charles DeTurk (Washington), Ruth Peeler (Washington), Frank Quinn, NCSP president (Texas), Harlean James (NCSP executive secretary), and Arthur Elmer (Michigan). Middle row: Harold Wagner (Ohio), Russell Tobey (New Hampshire), Robert Kingery (Illinois), Charles "Cap" Sauers (Illinois), and Conrad Wirth (NPS assistant director). Back row: Abner Gwinn (Missouri), William W. Wells (Louisiana), Walter Wirth (Pennsylvania), Thomas W. Morse (North Carolina), Lewis G. Scoggin (Florida), and Kenneth Cougill (Indiana). COURTESY OF CATHERINE SCOGGIN FERRELL

be developed and used, and who should manage them. Because state parks were still a relatively new area of responsibility in most states, the need for profession-alism had often been brushed aside in the rush simply to acquire properties. While, to its credit, the National Conference on State Parks had done its best to provide professional guidance for new state park programs, most states still seemed bent on doing it their own way through a trial-and-error approach. As the mistakes, frustrations, and quandaries piled up, it became painfully obvious that there were many ways to run a state park program, but there was no agreement what-soever as to what constituted the best way.

For some of the more advanced states, of course, this was not a new revelation. Serious thinkers on the subject—Albert Turner, Olmsted the younger, Charles Sauers, Laurie Cox, and others—had for years been sorting though the issues, identifying inherent conflicts and offering learned opinions. Their pioneering work was undoubtedly helpful to many states, but possibly confusing to others in the array of arguments and alternatives they presented. It was no longer simply an academic matter, however. In the postwar era, with all forty-eight states firmly embarked on a state parks program, the confusion seemed greater than ever. If the state park movement was ever to have a unified, central thrust, it was high time to start hammering it out.

Interestingly, the National Park Service, sorting through the returns from the New Deal–sponsored state recreation studies, had recognized the problem of too much trial and error in the state park programs years earlier. As a disinterested observer, the NPS was in a better position than the state park agencies themselves to assess the situation on a national basis and offer suggestions of possible nationwide applicability. This it did in its 1941 *Study of the Park and Recreation Problem,* dealing with a number of issues pertinent to the states specifically, but in the context of the total national park and recreation picture. All of those issues were still relevant during the postwar years and remain so even today.

Among the issues raised, probably the most fundamental was the one of dividing responsibility for meeting public park and recreation needs among the several levels of government. The report acknowledged: "At the two ends of the scale—the Federal Government and the municipality—there appears to be general agreement as to certain responsibilities. . . . It is within the vast field between these two extremes that we enter the realm of dispute and uncertainty." The obvious conclusion, of course, was that this middle ground was the proper domain of the states—where they could provide their equivalents of national parks—but the question of gray areas at each end was fully recognized.

How cleanly the lines of responsibility could be drawn—especially between the states and local governments—would depend to a very great extent on the nature of the state concerned. That factor alone would make a significant difference in how, say, Rhode Island and Alaska (two obvious extremes) might approach their state park responsibilities. There could be universal acceptance of the states' responsibility for filling the void between local parks and national parks, but that divide might be a mere ditch in one case and a gaping chasm in another—and therein lay the problem of trying to define the scope of state park responsibility as the same for every state.

A similar situation existed with state park administrative arrangements. One of the first objectives of the National Conference on State Parks had been to push the idea of an independent commission as the best means of overseeing a state parks program, presumably to insulate it from unwanted political meddling. That effort met with only limited success, however, and by the time the NPS took stock of the situation, there were no fewer than nine different organizational arrangements. The two principal approaches, accounting for thirty-three of the forty-seven programs then existing, were the combined conservation or natural resources agency on the one hand, and the independent park board or commission on the other. There were nineteen states of the first type, primarily in the east, and fourteen of the second, mostly in the west. In the rest, state parks generally remained with some other governmental function where they had been placed originally, including seven with forestry and two with fish and game.

This diversity again illustrates the futility of trying to devise a single pattern to fit all state park programs, and indeed in this particular case such an intent is probably the least justified of all. While there is always the possibility that a state parks program might be improperly influenced by the agendas of other governmental functions with which it is administratively associated, in the final analysis it is not the method of delivery but the product itself that is important.

Still another issue of growing interest, if not concern, was how to fashion an assemblage of state parks into a *system* of state parks. Part of the problem lay in just trying to define the term. For some, it was simply a quantitative concept: A system consisted of enough properties appropriately spaced around the state to provide reasonable access to all the people. For others, though, it went beyond that limited definition to include the idea of a balance of property types to provide different kinds of recreational opportunities or to preserve representative samples of the state's resources.

At this point of state park evolution, few states, if any, could honestly claim to have a complete park system by any definition of the term. The NPS in its report openly declared that "None is as yet fully adequate," and the eminent state parks scholar Laurie Cox (by this time engaged in a second career as president of New England College in Henniker, New Hampshire) added in 1948 that "It is not only a fair statement but an accurate one to say that we have no such thing at present as any state with a state park system."[3] Everyone agreed that there were, by this

3. U.S. Department of the Interior, National Park Service, *Study of the Park and Recreation Problem*, 50; Cox, "Nature of State Parks and Parkways," 53.

time, many truly outstanding individual state parks, but the system concept was still not fully understood and appreciated. This was not just a state phenomenon, however; the same assertion could have been made about the national parks as well.

Closely related to the system concept is the matter of classifying state parks for their most appropriate management and use. Excellent arguments had been put forth on behalf of effective classification by Olmsted, Cox, Harold Wagner, and others, dating back at least to the 1920s; and in its 1934 report, the National Resources Board had gone so far as to propose a specific classification system for state parks. The application of this valuable management device had been largely ignored in the past, however, when the number of properties had been small and the need for distinguishing among them not readily appreciated. But by the 1940s and especially the 1950s, at least three factors had emerged to focus more serious attention on the importance of classification.

The first of these was confusion—especially by the public and sometimes even by the park administrators. The ubiquitous use of the term *state park* left doubts as to exactly what characteristics a property might have and what kinds of recreational activities it might support. A second factor was the increasing diversification of state park programs through the inclusion of new functions and more specialized properties—such as historic sites, trails, waysides, boat access sites, and others that did not fit the traditional state park image. The third factor, most significant from the management standpoint, was the constantly increasing and diversifying recreational demands being made on individual properties. These demands tended not only to generate conflicts between incompatible uses, but also to aggravate wear and tear on especially fragile and sensitive parts of the park terrain.

The growing recognition of these problems led many states to start regrouping their park properties along more functional lines. A National Conference on State Parks committee, reporting on a related matter in 1954, noted some sixty different classification categories then in use by state park agencies.[4] Much of this multiplicity was due simply to different terminology rather than to different meanings, and the committee chose to reduce the number to six general categories: state parks, state monuments, state recreation areas, state beaches, state parkways, and state waysides. These groupings were merely for convenience, of course; there is no indication that they were proposed for general use, and if they

4. Kenneth R. Cougill, chairman, National Conference on State Parks Committee on Suggested Criteria, "Suggested Criteria for Evaluating Areas Proposed for Inclusion in State Park Systems," 3.

had been, they likely would have been ignored in view of the growing independence among state park agencies.

As the number of state parks multiplied, so too did the concern about the quality of some of the properties being acquired. The NPS in its 1941 report lamented the lack of policy development and planning as prerequisites for the expansion of state park inventories: "Comparatively few States, unfortunately, have attempted to formulate in specific terms those principles and policies which are to govern the whole process of planning and development, including the first step, that of selection."[5] Actually, this problem had been recognized long before, and some excellent precedents had been laid for site evaluation and selection. John Nolen was way ahead of his time in outlining park selection principles for Wisconsin in 1907, and Albert Turner had proposed a detailed set of criteria for Connecticut as early as 1914. The younger Olmsted had produced a veritable bible on the subject in developing his recommendations for California's state parks in 1928, and similar efforts were to follow in other states such as Iowa and Indiana.

In a further attempt to provide general guidance for emerging state park programs, the NCSP adopted and promulgated a set of comprehensive site-selection criteria for each of the six categories noted above. But here again, there is no evidence that its recommendations were ever used to any significant degree. Even though the need for systematic site selection was given a thorough airing, many of the state park inventories continued to take on questionable properties at times, seemingly influenced as much by political as by professional considerations—an interesting parallel with the situation that vexed Stephen Mather with the national parks decades earlier.

Growing Concern over Park Development and Use

While all of the above issues were receiving fresh attention and consideration, they had been important points in the ongoing state parks debate almost since the beginning. There were at least two others, however, that, although perhaps not new, were just coming into their own as major professional concerns. Actually, the two may be seen simply as two manifestations of the same issue. Both had to do with threats to park natural values, one from commercialism and

5. U.S. Department of the Interior, National Park Service, *Study of the Park and Recreation Problem*, 65.

overdevelopment, and the other from demands for more active (or physical, as it was often called) use of the parks.

Outdoor recreation, as distinguished from the state park movement, had enjoyed a brief time in the sun in the 1920s as a result of President Coolidge's national conference on that subject. Little of any lasting import had come of that effort, but in the wake of World War II, interest was revived with the creation of the Federal Inter-Agency Committee on Recreation and its proposal to establish a federal recreation agency. That initiative had failed—in part due to opposition from state park interests—but it did succeed in stimulating a more spirited dialogue on the question of active recreational use of America's parks.

Opposing sides of the recreation issue began to form within the state park ranks as early as 1946, when New York's state parks director, James Evans, and the NCSP chairman, Tom Wallace, squared off on the subject at a board meeting.[6] Evans took the position that state park agencies had been too negative and that they should have made greater effort to accommodate the growing public desire for more outdoor recreational opportunities. Wallace countered that the true state park tradition was one of providing more passive uses in an essentially wild and natural setting, and that many of the desired forms of recreation would not be appropriate. It quickly became apparent that neither was going to change the other's mind, and their standoff undoubtedly reflected the conflicting attitudes of the profession as a whole.

The following year, 1947, the NCSP took it upon itself to set up a committee on state park standards, facilities, and services to develop some guidelines in this sticky area. It is significant that this committee was chaired by Charles "Cap" Sauers, who had been a protégé of Indiana's Richard Lieber before moving on to manage the Cook County Forest Preserve in Illinois. As his report would amply indicate, Sauers's views tended to be even more traditional than those of his distinguished mentor.

The report acknowledged the legitimacy of outdoor recreation but held that the more active forms should be provided for in separate types of areas other than the scenic or natural state parks, preferably located closer to centers of population. All areas, regardless of their purpose, should be minimally developed with only the simplest types of facilities. "The expense for flush toilet installations is rarely justified," he proclaimed. Some other excerpts from his report:

6. National Conference on State Parks, minutes of the board of directors meeting, September 26, 1946, in Minutes of Policy Making Bodies, series 1, box 1, NRPA Library, 2.

"Elaborate hotels or inns are generally not justified in a state park . . . [s]leeping rooms should be mere cubicles"; "Special play facilities such as tennis courts, shuffleboard courts, play apparatus, golf courses and amphitheaters in general, are functionally related to hotels or inns and the exclusion of one excludes the other"; "Supervised Recreation has no place in any park category above that of a municipal park."[7] From these few samples, it is fairly easy to catch Sauers's drift.

Sauers's rather extreme views would not go unchallenged, however. While most of his committee at least acquiesced in the substance of the report, one, L. L. Huttleston of New York, felt compelled to take issue with almost its entire contents. Expressing concern that adherence to the report's philosophy would likely cause state parks to "degenerate into a chain of remote field museums," Huttleston counterattacked with equally provocative prose. Again, some examples: "subduing structures and manmade facilities to a trivial or non-existent landscape rapidly reduces itself to an absurdity"; "Nature study is a weak 'may' instead of a strong 'must.' This sort of gratuitous educational or cultural activity has no place in state park work"; "This doctrine [as expressed by the report] is sort of a double cousin to the idea which I have heard propounded in high park circles, that a park would be a wonderful place if you could keep the people out of it"; "It is time we . . . laid to rest the idea that [preservation of landscape] is a sublime Article of Faith—the Apostle's creed for all park planners."[8] No mincing of words there, either.

Sauers's and Huttleston's positions presumably represented the two poles on this particular issue. More pragmatic state park administrators would likely have been satisfied to seek a middle ground by recognizing the need for both natural parks and active recreation areas and let it go at that. Sauers, however, was apparently not at all disposed to compromise. He submitted his report essentially as it was originally drafted, but in fairness appended Huttleston's minority comments, which he allowed were "considered and well sustained." So much for another episode in the continuing saga of "preservation versus use" in America's state parks.

Too much use was one aspect of the perceived threat; too much development was the other. Actually, the issue was even broader than that. The NCSP had gone

7. Charles G. Sauers, chairman, National Conference on State Parks Committee on State Park Standards, Facilities, and Services, committee report submitted March 10, 1948, in James Truncer collection (unprocessed), NRPA Library, 3–5.

8. L. L. Huttleston, comments on Sauers committee report on state park standards, in James Truncer collection (unprocessed), NRPA Library, pages unnumbered.

so far as to set up a "vigilance committee" in the early 1950s to be on the lookout for "encroachments and incongruous developments" in state parks.[9] The main weapon in the defense of state parks, however, came in late 1951 or early 1952 with the formation of a joint committee appointed from four organizations of allied interest: the National Conference on State Parks, the American Institute of Park Executives, the National Recreation Association, and the National Park Service.

This committee was given a broad but somewhat vague and open-ended charge. When it first released its report, in July 1952, its title subject was "State Park Policy on 'Overdevelopment and Commercialization.'" Later, the report was formally published as a "Suggested Policy Statement Relating to Development, Use, and Operation of State Parks." As might be expected, the contents covered a wide range, but its opening paragraph serves as a preamble:

> Many park people are deeply concerned over the possibility that some recent developments and trends may lead to impairment or destruction of state park values for which the parks have been established. Included among these trends are: (1) continuing increase in attendance and use, (2) aggressive advertising of parks as tourist attractions, (3) non-conforming uses, (4) development of overnight accommodations, (5) over-emphasis on development of income producing facilities, (6) attempts at self-support, and (7) inappropriate forms of commercialism.

In suggesting specific policies to deal with the above issues, the statement was careful to make the distinction between state parks and state recreation areas, and to specify that the policies were meant primarily for application to the parks. On the whole, however, the suggestions were relatively innocuous and not likely to generate much controversy. It did come down fairly hard on overdevelopment, admonishing that "state parks are reserves, not resorts," and cautioning against trying to make the parks self-supporting, lest that lead to "installation of catchpenny devices, over-emphasis on the sale of souvenirs, and the development of resort-type facilities primarily to attract tourists and make a profit."[10] This was an almost complete reversal from the parks-for-tourism days of a generation before.

9. National Conference on State Parks, minutes of the board of directors meeting, February 13, 1953, in Minutes of Policy Making Bodies, series 1 and 2, box 1, NRPA Library, 5.

10. Sydney S. Kennedy, chairman, joint committee of the National Conference on State Parks, the American Institute of Park Executives, the National Recreation Association, and the National Park Service, "Suggested Policy Statement Relating to Development, Use, and Operation of State Parks," 57–59.

A Trend toward Commercialization?

As with other instances in which the NCSP sought to develop guidelines for general application, there is no indication that these suggestions were seriously considered, much less followed. Several years later, in addressing the 1955 NCSP meeting in Vermont, Conrad Wirth, now director of the National Park Service, was still raising similar concerns. "Since World War II," he said, "another trend which may bear careful watching and analysis seems to be developing. I refer to the development of the state parks primarily for tourist revenue." He went on: "The use of [large hotels and ultramodern cabins] is tending toward that of the conventional resort hotel and the conventional resort, with considerable emphasis on monetary profit." And finally: "I simply wish to indicate that in a searching analysis of our state park programs, we should look carefully at the extent to which the commercial motive can be useful to our fundamental and long range objectives and the extent to which it can be detrimental. I call this to your attention as a grave warning."[11]

There would be other Cassandras from time to time with essentially the same words of caution, but for the most part their words would fall on deaf or dubious ears. The handwriting was already on the wall, and, in general, there would be no turning back from the trend toward increasing commercialism in America's state parks.

11. Conrad L. Wirth, "National and State Parks," *Planning and Civic Comment*, 6–7.

12

A New Era of Federal-State Cooperation

An astute observer once pointed out that the growth pattern of state parks was not unlike that of children: "Growth does not usually occur at a consistent rate, but in spurts." Both children and parks, he acknowledged, were also susceptible to "growing pains."

It is true that state parks experienced a modest growth spurt in the mid-1920s as a result of the promotional efforts of the newly organized National Conference on State Parks, and a really stupendous one a decade later thanks to the Civilian Conservation Corps. But by the late 1950s, after twenty years of respectable but hardly spectacular progress, America's state parks were clearly in need of another "spurt"—something to reenergize the program, to stimulate interest that would prime the budget pumps in state legislatures.

Growth of any kind presupposes a source of nourishment, of course, and whence would such nourishment for state parks expansion come? A few states were financially able—and sufficiently motivated—to support dynamic state park programs on their own, and these were already outdistancing the pack. For the great majority, though, it was apparent that little would be done without the impetus of some external encouragement and support. The CCC experience certainly had left little room to doubt that fact. If help was to come in the form of another big juicy carrot, though, it would have to originate with the federal government somehow. Fortunately, some creative minds and persuasive voices were already at work on the matter. Separate, largely unrelated, federal initiatives that would benefit state parks were well underway, "racing" along parallel tracks.

Parks for America

Now under the firm leadership of Director Conrad Wirth, the National Park Service still considered itself the nation's principal outdoor recreation agency and, as always, a friend and patron of the state parks movement. Wirth, in fact, remained a "life" member of the NCSP board and actively participated in all of its affairs. As one of the instigators of the 1936 Park, Parkway, and Recreational Area Study Act, he also was constantly mindful of the special responsibility the Park Service had under that law to cooperate with and assist the states in pursuing their own park and recreation goals. It was not uncharacteristic, then, that in putting together his ambitious "Mission 66" program for modernizing the national parks, he would also include something for the state parks as well. That something was to be an initiative launched in 1957 called "Parks for America."

Parks for America, as Wirth envisioned it, would be the third in a series of nationwide assessments of state park and recreation programs and needs conducted by the National Park Service, following generally in the pattern of the 1934 "Recreational Use of Lands in the United States" prepared for the National Resources Board and the 1941 *A Study of the Park and Recreation Problem of the United States.* The primary purpose was to assess the situation in each of the states and lay a factual basis for further acquisition and development efforts, presumably to be assisted with federal technical and financial aid. The prospect of federal assistance ensured the full cooperation and participation by the states, and over the next several years a tremendous volume of information was compiled, including the inventory of some 4,800 existing nonurban park and recreation areas and the identification of almost 2,800 potential new areas.[1] By early 1961, the impressive report was completed and ready for publication—but it was not yet to have its day. The political situation in Washington had changed, and the National Park Service was destined for a rude shock.

Apparently Wirth sensed that the Park Service's report might need an organized show of support in view of other developments taking place in Washington at the time (more about that later). He got Secretary of the Interior Fred Seaton to invite representatives of the National Conference on State Parks and the American Institute of Park Executives to meet with himself and other NPS personnel on October 31, 1960. After Wirth presented his ideas for an action plan to implement the recommendations of the forthcoming report, the group agreed to organize itself as the "Committee of Fifteen," with five members from each of the

1. U.S. Department of the Interior, National Park Service, *Parks for America*, vii.

three organizations.[2] That this was seen as at least a quasi-permanent arrangement is borne out by the fact that the group met again in early December and developed operating procedures, a staff plan, and a budget. Wirth's role as puppet master in all of this was blatantly transparent—not only did he handle all of the logistical arrangements and provide a NPS staffer to serve as secretary for the committee, he also agreed personally to seek out donors of funds to cover the committee's budgetary needs.

Among the first items of business to come before the Committee of Fifteen was a proposed bill (undoubtedly drafted by the NPS) to provide funding for park and recreation programs at all levels of government. In concept, it would allocate 20 percent of the funds for federal programs, administered through the NPS, and the rest to state and local governments on a fifty-fifty matching basis. The proposed distribution of the latter portion was to be 25 percent for state parks and 75 percent for local programs, but this immediately met with opposition from the NCSP delegation.[3] In many of its features, this proposed legislation was similar to that which was recommended a year later (1962) by the Outdoor Recreation Resources Review Commission (see below), but it is not clear as to which version, if either, might have influenced the other.

On January 21, 1961, Stewart Udall succeeded Fred Seaton as Secretary of the Interior. Wirth, who had already briefed Udall personally, arranged a meeting for the Committee of Fifteen on March 15 to discuss its program and get Udall's reaction. In reporting the results to the NCSP Board, V. W. Flickinger of Ohio, NCSP's chief delegate to the Committee of Fifteen, was upbeat: "Secretary Udall indicated his interest in the program, outlined his desires, and advised the committee as follows: 'Get your trumpets ready, get your people ready, in a few weeks we will be ready to go.'"[4] The big unanswered question, though, was, *Who* was going *where?*

Following the meeting with Udall, the Committee of Fifteen did not convene again before the regular NCSP meeting in September 1961. Flickinger took that latter occasion to submit a further progress report. Although he clearly tried to put a positive face on subject, he nevertheless tipped his hand by weaving in several references to precautionary statements attributed to Udall and his Assistant Secretary for Public Land Management, John Carver. Flickinger's own assessment

---

2. V. W. Flickinger, chairman, "Parks for America Committee of Fifteen Report" [undated], in Board of Directors Papers, series 3, box 1, NRPA Library.

3. Ibid.

4. Ibid.

seemed less than hopeful: "The problem of getting the PARKS FOR AMERICA program launched involves timing and agreement of all concerned in government."[5]

Taken literally, the ramifications of that statement would be enough to discourage anybody, but during the course of the meeting, the group received a telegram from Udall that again seemed to provide some cause for optimism. It read in part: "In the next few months we will see the issuance of the final report of the Outdoor Recreation Resources Review Commission; definite progress on the nationwide plan for nonurban recreation resources by the National Park Service; and more specific proposals by the 'Committee of Fifteen.'"[6] It appeared to be anybody's guess as to what really was in the works. Within a matter of months, though, the air would start to clear—and Conrad Wirth, for one, would not be happy.

The Outdoor Recreation Resources Review Commission

While the interest the National Park Service had taken in the broader aspects of America's outdoor recreation needs was indeed laudable, it nevertheless devolved from a rather narrow and now somewhat dated statutory authority, the 1936 study act. By the 1950s there was a growing realization by others that the problem was now far too complex and would have to be addressed on a much more comprehensive basis. Outdoor recreation demand had surged in the postwar era, and scholars such as Marion Clawson of the newly established research group Resources for the Future were already warning of an impending crisis unless timely action was taken to provide more public recreational opportunities. The time was clearly ripe for some kind of bold stroke, and in 1958 Congress responded.

The resulting legislation, Public Law 85-470, signed by President Eisenhower on June 28, 1958, proved to be exactly what was needed. Cited as the "Outdoor Recreation Resources Review Act," it was broader in scope and more generous with its means for implementation than anything that had been enacted previously. Principal credit for its authorship is generally given to Joseph Penfold, the conservation director of the Izaak Walton League, and Edward Crafts, an official with the U.S. Forest Service, both of whom would also play instrumental roles in

5. V. W. Flickinger, chairman, "Parks for America Committee of Fifteen" report to National Conference on State Parks annual meeting, Lake Texoma Lodge, Okla., September 1961, in Board of Directors Papers, series 3, box 1, NRPA Library.
6. Ibid.

subsequent developments. Although neither of them at the time might be considered predominantly an outdoor recreation specialist, the bill they drafted reflected both a perceptive understanding of the problem and a practical knowledge of how to deal with it.

Although the act itself was skillfully crafted, it was the commission it created that really made a difference. The Outdoor Recreation Resources Review Commission, or ORRRC, was a fifteen-member body (eight members of Congress and seven citizens appointed by the president), given a three-year time frame and a $2.5 million authorization, and told to identify the country's outdoor recreation needs and propose recommendations for meeting them. To assist it with this daunting task, the act also provided that the commission could select individuals from certain general-interest categories to serve on an advisory council. One of the categories specified was "State park departments," although only one state park professional—Kenneth Cougill, director of Indiana state parks—was actually appointed.

The ORRRC hired a competent staff and went to work. Three years later, on January 31, 1962, it submitted its report—actually, one basic report with twenty-seven appurtenant study reports that covered in great detail almost every important aspect of the subject. In seeking to assign responsibility for appropriate follow-up action, the report recognized a particularly important role for state governments:

> In a national effort to improve outdoor recreation opportunities, State governments should play the pivotal role. They are more advantageously situated than either local units or the Federal Government to deal with many recreational problems. . . . Moreover, the States occupy a key position—the middle level in our complex system of government.[7]

After discussing the similarities and contrasts, strengths and weaknesses, of state programs, the report concluded:

> But most State park programs are in difficulty. Practically all State park agencies report trouble in securing adequate funds, even for minimum operations. Facilities at some State parks have not been substantially improved since 1940. Personnel is severely limited. Management tools, such as planning and modern

7. Outdoor Recreation Resources Review Commission, *Outdoor Recreation for America,* 137.

accounting systems, are often lacking. Underlying all of these difficulties is the absence, in many States, of well-developed civic and political support.[8]

The Commission made many recommendations, including a number specifically directed to states for strengthening their programs internally. But the most significant recommendation of all, in terms of its likely impact on state parks generally, was one calling for a federal grants-in-aid program to assist with outdoor recreation planning and with the acquisition and development of additional parks and recreation areas. And to administer the grants program, among other duties, the commission also recommended the creation of a new "bureau of outdoor recreation" within the Department of the Interior.

The commission had done its job in admirable fashion, and with the above recommendations it had deftly bounced the ball back to the United States Congress.

The Bureau of Outdoor Recreation

The ink had hardly dried on the ORRRC report before exciting things started to happen. On March 1, 1962, President Kennedy in a special message to Congress strongly endorsed the creation of a new bureau of outdoor recreation. Several weeks later, the issue of a new federal outdoor recreation agency was taken up by the NCSP board. It was pointed out that NCSP had consistently opposed the creation of a federal department of recreation in the past, but the board decided to go ahead and support, in principle, the ORRRC recommendation for a bureau of outdoor recreation anyway. Apparently, Horace Albright's views on the matter had been persuasive. Although he was not present for the meeting, he submitted his comments in writing, and it is obvious that his position placed him in direct opposition to his colleague Conrad Wirth.

Albright had served on the ORRRC advisory council along with Kenneth Cougill and others, and he was strongly supportive of the commission's report and recommendations. This was emphatically so in the matter of creating a new federal agency, as his words clearly attest:

> I realize that the recommendations regarding future relations of the Federal Government to the state parks may have disappointed some people, perhaps

8. Ibid., 138.

many of them, including my good friends in the National Park Service. I am sure that every person concerned with the work of ORRRC fully appreciated the great work accomplished by the National Park Service under the 1936 Act of Congress, and I certainly cannot too highly commend its achievements under that law, but I have never felt that the National Park Service could ever play a guiding role in recreation policy and practice outside of its own areas or in co-operation with state and municipal park authorities. I have never been able to see how it could accomplish anything with or without cooperation of the Forest Service, the Army Engineers and other agencies in the areas under their control. The National Park Service could not, for more than one reason, become *THE RECREATION BUREAU* of the Federal Government. Hence the need for a Bureau of Recreation in the Interior Department.[9]

It is doubtful that either Albright's views or the endorsement of the bureau of outdoor recreation by the NCSP board had any bearing on subsequent developments, but both must have been bitter disappointments for Wirth.

Stewart Udall did not wait for Congress to act on creating a new bureau. On April 2, 1962, just a month after Kennedy had made his appeal to Congress, he signed Secretarial Order No. 497, creating the Bureau of Outdoor Recreation himself. The fact that he used the 1936 study act as the legal basis for this action was a further insult to Wirth, but there was worse to come. That same day, President Kennedy appointed Edward Crafts—a forester, not a park and recreation man—as director of the just-created bureau. Crafts's selection from outside of the Interior Department presumably was intended to facilitate cooperation between the new bureau and non-Interior agencies, but that fact probably offered little comfort to the leadership of the National Park Service, which had been largely ignored throughout the whole process.

Although a Bureau of Outdoor Recreation now officially existed on paper, it had only limited authority and capabilities and could do very little but plan and coordinate while it awaited formal establishment by Congress. A number of positions and some $1.5 million of already-appropriated funds were transferred from the National Park Service so the new BOR could assume the Park Service's former duties dealing directly with the states. By October 1962, Crafts had assembled a small staff in Washington and decided it was time to call in a few of the states for consultation. I was one of about a dozen state representatives attending

9. Horace M. Albright to National Conference on State Parks board of directors, date unknown (incorporated in minutes of March 17, 1962), in Board of Directors Papers, series 3, box 1, NRPA Library.

that first meeting, at which we all got our first real insights into what the BOR was and hoped to accomplish. As there was yet no grants program, and very little else for that matter, the discussions generated interest but hardly any excitement.

In early 1963, Congress took up and quickly passed a bill "to promote the coordination and development of effective programs relating to outdoor recreation, and for other purposes." This became Public Law 88-29, more commonly referred to as the Outdoor Recreation Act, or the Bureau of Outdoor Recreation "organic act." For all practical purposes, this act was a replacement for the 1936 study act. Although it did not mention the BOR by name, as the 1936 act had done with the National Park Service, it legitimized the bureau's existence by specifically authorizing the Secretary of the Interior to undertake all of the various functions he had already assigned to the bureau. Among these were developing a nationwide outdoor recreation plan, providing technical assistance to states and other entities, and promoting interstate regional cooperation for outdoor recreation programs.

The administrative apparatus was now firmly in place to coordinate and oversee a massive program of assistance to the states. All that was still needed was a source of money, and that was already in the works.

Parks for America, Continued

Secretary Udall's feeling about the proposed National Park Service report *Parks for America* had seemed ambivalent at best when he was being sounded out by the Committee of Fifteen in 1961. Thus, it was hardly surprising that nothing more had been heard of it; the whole matter had simply dropped off the radar screen. Now, almost three years later, with the Bureau of Outdoor Recreation well up and running, it seemed like an odd time for the report to be resurrected. But there it was, published in 1964 as a five-hundred-page hardback book, almost exactly in its original 1961 format.

Wirth understood of course that the new leadership at the Interior Department would want to hold up release of such a monumental report until it could look it over and decide for itself the document's merit. The official position was that publication should be withheld pending completion of the ORRRC report, presumably to ensure compatibility. But by 1964 the ORRRC report had been around for two years. If it had been decided that the Park Service report did have sufficient merit to be published in addition to the ORRRC report, why wait so long? If Wirth knew the full story, he did not share it with his readers.

When *Parks for America* was finally published, it proved to be a bittersweet victory for Wirth and the National Park Service. A foreword included by Udall seemed to damn the document with faint praise. Wirth called Udall's comments "anything but favorable," and "a slur on the Park Service and the states that helped . . . put the report together." Udall offered the explanation that the report was published "at the request of many of the States to assist in their park planning and legislative programs," but he included so many reservations about the usefulness of the data that it surely must have impugned its credibility.[10] There is also the possibility that the report was finally published simply as a parting sop to Wirth himself—he had just ended his long and distinguished career with the National Park Service by his retirement on January 7, 1964.

The Land and Water Conservation Fund

For years, state parks advocates had been looking to the federal government for more than just moral support and technical assistance—they wanted money. The flush years of the CCC program had whetted an appetite for financial aid that would not subside. But even with the best efforts of the National Park Service and the National Conference on State Parks, success had eluded them. They came close—a variety of bills had been proposed, and a few even introduced—but Congress had not been convinced of the need for or propriety of channeling federal funds into state park programs, especially when it could not keep up with the budgetary demands of an expanding national park system. If by the early 1960s state park people had been conditioned to expect rejection and failure, their pessimism was certainly understandable.

The breakthrough finally came in 1964. As early as 1961, in fact, Congress had evidenced a more sympathetic attitude toward the mounting problems faced by state and local governments. That was the year it passed the Area Redevelopment Act (Public Law 87-27) and the Housing Act (Public Law 87-70), providing matching funds for land acquisition for public facilities and open space, respectively. Thus, when the ORRRC submitted its recommendations a few months later, including a proposal for matching grants to state and local governments for outdoor recreation projects, it was hoped that Congress would respond quickly and favorably. The scope and complexity of such a precedent-setting new program, however, required a higher degree of scrutiny and deliberation, and it would take two more years for the authorizing legislation to work its way through Congress.

10. Wirth, *Parks, Politics, and the People,* 175; Stewart L. Udall, foreword to *Parks for America.*

The payoff finally came on September 3, 1964, with the passage of Public Law 88-578—the Land and Water Conservation Fund Act.

Although creation of the Land and Water Conservation Fund was clearly a direct response to the work of the ORRRC, the grants-in-aid program it authorized differed materially from the one that had been recommended. Some of the changes were strictly political, as with the formula adopted for allocating funds among the states, but for the most part they actually made the program somewhat simpler and more flexible to implement. Instead of appropriating grant funds directly from the general treasury as recommended, Congress created a special fund supported by several earmarked revenue sources, the chief of which was the royalties received from offshore oil leases. This method of funding was potentially both advantageous (in not having to compete with other programs for a share of the general fund) and disadvantageous (in being subject to the vicissitudes of revenue flow), but it also served to give the program a special aura of importance and implied continuity.

Congress generally followed the ORRRC recommendation in providing for the allocation of available grant funds but gave the smaller and lesser populated states a boost by requiring that the first two-fifths be divided equally among all of the states. The remaining three-fifths was to be allocated according to need, as reflected primarily by population characteristics and the extent of existing federal land and program activity. As recommended by ORRRC, the LWCF Act provided that grant funds could be used by the states for outdoor recreation planning, land acquisition, and development of facilities, but on a fifty-fifty federal-state matching basis rather than the proposed forty-sixty for ordinary projects. Whereas ORRRC had suggested that local governments be allowed to make application directly to the federal administering agency after simply obtaining approval from the state, the LWCF Act gave the states more direct control by making them the only official grant fund recipients, even if some of those funds were then transferred to local governments. Both the ORRRC and the LWCF Act called for federal approval of a state comprehensive outdoor recreation plan as a condition of eligibility for receiving grant funds. A proposal by ORRRC for federal loans to complement the grants-in-aid program was not included in the act.

One extremely consequential difference between the grants program envisioned by ORRRC and the one authorized by Congress was the provision in the latter for certain federal agencies also to receive a major share of the available funds. Hindsight would suggest that federal agency participation should have been provided for as an entirely separate program. Congress, however, chose to allocate up to 40 percent of available LWCF funds for land acquisition by the National Park Service, the Bureau of Sport Fisheries and Wildlife, and the U.S. Forest Service. The states (including the District of Columbia and the several territories) would share not less than 60 percent, but for the first five years of the program the president could vary the forty-sixty split by fifteen percentage points either way. Unfortunately, as it tuned out, this arrangement tended to place the federal agencies in direct competition with the states, and changing congressional priorities over the years clearly gave the federal interests the upper hand. At the time, however, this was not foreseen as a problem, and the new LWCF program was received by state and local interests with great enthusiasm and anticipation.

It would seem that the state parks were now poised to be a major, if not the principal, beneficiary of a long-awaited federal grants program. The LWCF program, however, was designed to serve a wide array of outdoor recreation interests, and the relative priority of state park needs was yet to be determined on a state-by-state basis.

A New Program Gets Under Way

Because the revenue sources for the new Land and Water Conservation Fund program were subject to a number of variables, no one could accurately predict how much money would become available. The states' share of the first revenues to flow into the fund during the latter part of fiscal year 1965 amounted to a meager $130,000, and this was applied primarily to a handful of planning grants. The following year saw a significant increase, with the states' share rising to $16.5 million, but still not enough to make much of a splash. Starting with fiscal year 1967, however, and continuing for the next decade and a half, the level of funding for state grants averaged a respectable $174 million per year. Even though the annual revenue flow was variable and inconsistent, at least the amounts of money becoming available were large enough to make a real difference. State park directors no doubt started to lick their chops.

But this was not, per se, a state parks grant program. Rather, the LWCF was designed to address the broader concept of *outdoor recreation,* and not just at the state level, but across the entire public sector. The LWCF Act provided that the secretary of the interior would work with the governors of the states in implementing the grants-in-aid aspects of the program. As a practical matter, the secretary had already decided to ask the governors to appoint a more accessible contact person to serve as the "state liaison officer." Under this arrangement, the state liaison officer, or SLO, thus occupied the key role—potentially, a veritable czar—in determining policies and procedures for distributing and using the state's apportionment of funds. Consequently, the direction and emphasis of the program in each state would be materially influenced by the selection of the SLO, and the position in government that individual occupied. As might be expected, the placement of the selected SLO varied greatly from state to state.

It would stand to reason, of course, that state park officials, with primary responsibility for outdoor recreation at the state level, would be logical candidates for the SLO position. In fact, state park directors, or higher level administrators overseeing parks as part of their duties, have provided probably the largest number of SLOs since the beginning. But many other governmental interests have been represented as well: fish and wildlife, forestry, state planning, local government, environmental protection, state highways, governor's aides, and even citizen board appointees. Some states have moved the SLO job around from one agency to another as governors change, but many others have, through the years, settled on a specific placement, often created or mandated by legislation. The bottom line, though, is that state park interests have never dominated either the SLO ranks or the claim on LWCF money. Instead, they have had to compete for a share of the funds with other outdoor recreation interests, usually without any particular favor or advantage.

In retrospect, the Land and Water Conservation Fund program, or at least its grants-in-aid component, proved to be a case of boom and bust. From its inception through fiscal year 1981, it generated some $2,625 billion for state and local projects; but for the twenty years since, the total has amounted to less than $700 million. During its heyday, though, the program was a glowing success, frequently compared with the Civilian Conservation Corps in terms of the numerous new and expanded park and recreation projects it made possible. For state-level projects alone, some $551 million has been applied to acquisition of 2.1 million new acres, the vast majority going for state parks. Probably even more of the total has been used for state park development, but the exact figures are difficult to break out. The impact of all of these grants, moreover, has been at least doubled by an equal amount of nonfederal matching funds.

Overall, almost two-thirds of the LWCF grants have been used for development, suggesting something of a paradox in light of the program's name. Many sponsors of the original legislation felt that saving scarce and threatened recreational properties should be the highest priority, hence the name *Land and Water*

Conservation Fund. When it appeared that most of the money was being used to provide new facilities, concern voiced by powerful members of Congress, such as Colorado's Wayne Aspinall, caused the Bureau of Outdoor Recreation to issue a directive calling for two-thirds of all grant funds to be used for land acquisition. That goal was never achieved, however, and the increasing popularity of the program for developing city and county recreational facilities eventually caused the emphasis on acquisition to be relaxed and, later, actually reversed. Where state parks were concerned, this shifting emphasis was seldom a problem; most states had sufficient needs for both new parklands and additional facilities to effectively utilize all of the funds allocated to them.

One of the real beauties of the Land and Water Conservation Fund program is that it does leave to the individual states maximum discretion in deciding when and how to apply its grant funds (presumably, however, in accordance with its approved comprehensive outdoor recreation plan). Initially, a significant amount of most states' apportionments were used for state projects, but over the years, as less money became available, a larger portion—all of it, in some cases—was "passed through" to local governments. Because the records maintained by the BOR (and later, the NPS) do not permit an appropriate analysis, it is difficult to determine just how much state parks have directly benefited from the LWCF program—but it is substantial. By their own count, state park agencies acknowledge LWCF assistance at some 1,400 separate park properties, or about one-fourth of the total. During the period of peak LWCF grant activity, state park inventories expanded significantly, from 3,202 areas and 7,352,322 acres in 1967, to 4,376 areas and 9,259,686 acres in 1981—increases of 37 percent and 26 percent, respectively.

As the record clearly shows, the Land and Water Conservation Fund was never intended to be specifically a state parks assistance program. It was administered during the most productive part of its life by a new "outdoor recreation" agency rather than by the National Park Service, and it involved the states through a special "state liaison officer" rather than the state park director. Still, it channeled a vast amount of welcome financial assistance into state park programs at a time when most of those programs were sorely in need of a helping hand and thereby provided another important impetus for the continued growth of America's state parks movement.

Dramatic Changes on the Organizational Front

By the time the Land and Water Conservation Fund program really hit its stride, though, the state park movement was experiencing something of an adolescent change of personality. It seemed to be asserting itself as a more independent, self-confident enterprise, fully capable of determining its own course. If the movement was now in fact reaching maturity, its timing was indeed fortunate. It no longer, after Wirth's retirement, had a real champion in the National Park Service, and the rising Bureau of Outdoor Recreation clearly had a much broader agenda than promoting state parks. Moreover, the so-called National Conference on State Parks was now anything but that, as it floundered around in search of a relevant purpose and a cohesive constituency. Whether they were weaned, abandoned, or simply flew the coop, the state parks were now essentially on their own for the first time in almost half a century.

It was bound to happen. For some time, a growing number of state park directors had been expressing concerns about the ability, or even the desire, of the National Conference on State Parks to effectively represent their interests. Many felt that the time had come for the state park directors themselves to form their own organization to deal specifically with their issues and needs. Although some of the directors were still active in and supportive of the NCSP, they recognized that the organization was changing under the influence of recreation interests other than state parks. One source of concern, for instance, was an alleged "de facto domination . . . by the Washington representatives of some federal agencies," meaning, of course, the National Park Service.[11] As a case in point, the NCSP board had recently obliged NPS director Wirth by passing a motion to "condemn" three articles in the February 1961 issue of the *Atlantic Monthly* simply because they were critical of the Park Service's management.[12]

Things finally came to a head at the NCSP annual meeting in October 1962, held at Illinois Beach State Park, near Zion, Illinois. Interestingly, it was at that meeting that the NCSP amended its constitution to broaden the scope of outdoor recreation in its mission statement by deleting the limiting modifier *non-urban*. Whether that apparent change of emphasis in the organization's mission was contributory or purely coincidental, it was also at the 1962 conference that the state park directors present decided to "defect." An impromptu meeting was called (in a furnace room for lack of a better place) to consider setting up a separate organization, but support for the idea proved initially to be less than unanimous. Concerns were raised that such a move could prove disastrous for the NCSP, which was struggling just to survive. The discussions reportedly became

11. William A. Parr, "A Brief Organizational History."
12. National Conference on State Parks, minutes of the board of directors meeting, March 18, 1961, in Board of Directors Papers, series 3, box 1, NRPA Library.

"heated" at times, but in the end a majority voted to form a new, completely in-dependent organization to be called the "Association of State Park Directors."[13]

The following year, at its first official meeting, the name was changed by adding the word *National,* and under that banner the new organization quickly began to supplant the NCSP as the principal support group for America's state parks. It was hard to break old ties completely, however, and the park directors agreed to continue to meet annually in conjunction with NCSP, both for conve-nience of their mutual members and also to maintain an effective working rela-tionship. In fact, there may actually have been some second thinking on the matter of separation. Two years later, at the 1964 NCSP meeting, the president of NASPD announced that his organization "has determined to become a strong professional section of NCSP and hopes to be able to integrate its program more completely with that of the Conference."[14]

With the creation of NASPD as a separate entity, though, the identity of NCSP as a state parks organization became even more tenuous. There followed an ef-fort to find another, more appropriate name, and several possibilities were con-sidered, including "National Conference on Parks for America." None managed to gain enough support, however, and in 1963 the NCSP board accepted the rec-ommendation of its ad hoc committee to stick with the original. But while the name remained the same, almost everything else affecting NCSP was in a state of flux. In early 1965, the American Planning and Civic Association—NCSP's part-ner for almost thirty years, with which it had shared offices, staff, and publica-tions—metamorphosed into something called "Urban America" and parted ways with its longtime soul mate. NCSP thus found itself virtually without a home and with no place to go.

As one door closed, though, another one opened for NCSP. A movement had been in the making for several years to bring together the various recreation and park groups under a single umbrella organization for increased efficiency and ef-fectiveness. Allied interest groups such as the American Institute of Park Execu-tives and the American Recreation Society were closely involved in the merger effort and actively supported creation of the resulting conglomerate, the National Recreation and Park Association. NCSP was not so sure about joining, however, concerned that as a relatively small and narrowly focused organization it would get swallowed up or ignored by its larger and more powerful counterparts. But an

13. Parr, "Brief Organizational History."
14. Ben Bolen, Remarks at the National Conference on State Parks 1964 annual meeting, in Board of Directors Papers, series 3, box 1, NRPA Library.

ad hoc committee appointed to study the matter concluded that affiliation with the new NRPA was NCSP's best option, and recommended accordingly.

At its 1965 annual meeting, NCSP voted unanimously to join the new NRPA as a branch of its "lay division," but the following year it decided to switch to the NRPA's "professional division" instead—possibly an acknowledgment that its constituency and its operational emphasis were continuing to change. Interestingly, the minutes of the 1965 NCSP meeting also noted that NASPD had applied for membership in NRPA as a branch of the professional division but would continue also to function as a professional section of NCSP. Both NCSP and NASPD, however, were insistent on retaining their separate names and identities. It is not clear, though, that NASPD ever followed through with formal membership in NRPA; if so, it was only temporary.

After a decade of turmoil, change, and redirection among the country's leading recreation and park interest groups, the two major new organizations—the National Association of State Park Directors and the National Recreation and Park Association—both continued to thrive and to strengthen their identities. The venerable veteran—the National Conference on State Parks—however, never recovered from its long period of decline caused by confusion of purpose, inconsistent leadership, and an erratic constituency. Even the redoubtable Conrad Wirth, who assumed the role of chairman in 1964, shortly after his retirement from the National Park Service, could not breathe needed life into the sadly deflated organization. In 1974, after much anguish, resignation, and probably a few tears, it was reconstituted as a purely professional body called the National Society for Park Resources and ceased to be a major player in the further development of the nation's state park movement.

A New Task Ahead

For state parks generally, the decade of the 1960s was most notable for the creation of the Land and Water Conservation Fund and for the major realignment of professional support organizations. But behind the scenes, state park administrators were awakening to an awesome realization that the whole role of state parks was changing, or about to change, in a very fundamental way. For most of the twentieth century, as the state park movement gained momentum and spread across the country, the primary goal had been to acquire scenic areas and historically interesting sites for casual public enjoyment. The concern had been one more of quality—and, probably in too many instances, simply of availability—

A pioneer in outdoor recreation research and policy development, Marion Clawson was among the first to voice concern over the burgeoning postwar demand for public outdoor recreation opportunities, and to recognize the important role for state parks in meeting that need. PHOTOGRAPH BY FABIAN BACHRACH, COURTESY OF RESOURCES FOR THE FUTURE

than of quantity and distribution. While there is no questioning the validity of that approach to state park selection—to find the very best park properties wherever they lay—it was, by pure necessity, about to change.

The postwar spike in outdoor recreation demand had not been unexpected. After all, the American people had been largely distracted and preoccupied by more pressing concerns for ten years of economic depression and four years of war, and they were eager to return to a more leisurely and carefree lifestyle. But few prognosticators could foresee that an enormous, sustained outdoor recreation boom lay in the offing, the dimensions of which were totally without precedent. Fair warning was quick to come, however, first in the pioneering work of Marion Clawson, Burnell Held, Jack Knetsch, and others with Resources for the Future, and, right on their heels, in the monumental report of the Outdoor Recreation Resources Review Commission. Even the popular press pitched in. *Time* magazine devoted its cover and a major article to the subject in its July 14, 1961, issue: "Across the whole expanse of the U.S., the wildernesses where once only the hardiest of outdoorsmen trod now shuddered under the invasion of hundreds of thousands of families hungering for a summertime skirmish with nature."

Clawson referred to the expected deficiency in outdoor recreation supply as a "crisis." In 1959, he noted that recreational use of the public lands had already trebled since the end of the war, and he called the task of meeting future demand a "national problem of the first rank." "The greatest need of all," he said, "is for a more co-ordinated attack on the whole problem of outdoor recreation." The ORRRC likewise called for a comprehensive "national outdoor recreation policy" to assure recreational opportunities for all the people, the implementation of which would "require the cooperative participation of all levels of government and private enterprise."[15] Never before had the problem been so well identified and documented, nor the strategy for confronting it so clearly enunciated. An all-out, coordinated campaign would be required to meet the country's burgeoning outdoor recreation demand, and no one doubted that America's state parks would have to be a major part of that effort.

Unfortunately, in the 1960s most of the state park systems were ill-prepared to assume their appropriate share of responsibility. True, they had accumulated many desirable properties, but few states had given much thought to distribution and accessibility—or, just as important, whether those properties were capable of providing the specific types of legitimate outdoor recreational opportunities that the people wanted. Individual park master plans were not uncommon at the time, but comprehensive statewide park system plans were almost unknown. Little effort had been made to assess specific outdoor recreation needs within the states, or to ensure balance and adequacy among park property types. In other words, there were at the time very few, if any, state park "systems" truly deserving of that title.

Still, the state parks were widely recognized as potentially the most important component of a balanced nationwide outdoor recreation supply system, as envisioned by Clawson, the ORRRC, and others. Clawson, in fact, commented in 1963 that the state parks had the greatest flexibility of all, capable of being developed at numerous locations from land and water resources rather easily available. He added, not too flatteringly, that their "convenient location goes a long way to offset any resource mediocrity." Clawson concluded that state parks "can be expanded almost without limit and can provide an increasingly larger part of

15. Clawson, "Crisis in Outdoor Recreation"; Outdoor Recreation Resources Review Commission, *Outdoor Recreation for America*, 6.

the total recreation supply in the future," but he admonished that "To achieve their potential, however, state park agencies must be much better organized, staffed, and financed than they have been in the past."[16]

What Clawson was advocating, in effect, was that, in order to make their greatest overall contribution, traditional state "park" programs would also have to become state "outdoor recreation" programs. To do that, state parks would now have to determine and address outdoor recreation needs in a "quantitative" as well as a "qualitative" sense. This evolving concept would create a whole new dimension for America's state parks and would greatly influence the direction of the movement in years to come.

16. Marion Clawson, *Land and Water for Recreation: Opportunities, Problems, and Policies,* 21–25, 91–94.

13

Signs of Maturity

A Point of Convergence

An evolutionary process, by definition, does not ordinarily culminate with a neat and precise final product, but goes on indefinitely with never-ending change and refinement. Such undoubtedly will be the continuing course of America's state parks. But sometime during the 1970s, a series of factors converged to suggest that the state park movement was at last coming of age. After a century or so of trial and error, of innovation and emulation, the pieces seemed to be falling comfortably into place. State parks, as a national phenomenon, apparently had found their niche.

For one thing, the fold was now complete. With the addition of Alaska in 1970, all fifty states had established state park programs, and all seemed to be sufficiently motivated and self-reliant to ensure their likely permanence. Most, if not all, enjoyed the benefit of capable professionals within their ranks to provide sound advice and guidance—not only for day-to-day operations, but for political decision making as well. Moreover, the National Association of State Park Directors itself was maturing into an effective and much-needed support organization for a diverse and often beleaguered group of state park leaders. The perennial funding problem also was less of a concern. The new Land and Water Conservation Fund, now hitting its full stride, was providing almost unprecedented amounts of money as matching grants for capital expansion of reenergized state park systems across the country. It was truly an exciting time for state parks everywhere.

But of all the positive signs that the state park movement had indeed achieved its majority, probably the most compelling were also the most subtle. There was now a definite aura of self-confidence and a spirit of equality and independence permeating the movement. State parks clearly were here to stay. In the eyes of many, they were as essential as any other public service, and they must be pursued just as aggressively and vigorously as the rest, with an equal claim to legitimacy. At this pivotal point in its history, the state park movement had truly solidified—bolstered by a time-tested tradition, a clearly defined mission, a dedicated corps of professionals, and a collective determination to succeed.

Evolving Roles and Changing Relationships

A degree of maturity does not necessarily predicate a comparable degree of perfection, of course, and this obviously was the case where state parks were concerned. For all that had been accomplished as a national movement, there still were vast differences in the rate of progress and the level of quality among the fifty state park systems. Even more fundamental, there still was no consensus on major aspects of state park policy and philosophy, or on the place of state parks in the hierarchy of outdoor recreation providers. These and other elusive issues seemed to defy definitive resolution, and even in the 1970s, as the state park movement was settling into a comfortable groove, they were still being debated as if for the first time.

One of the players in this debate was the seemingly moribund, but still persistent, National Conference on State Parks. Under its new president, Lemuel "Lon" Garrison (another legendary figure from the ranks of the National Park Service), the NCSP was still groping for some purposeful agenda; and in the early 1970s it started negotiating with Marion Clawson of Resources for the Future for a "re-examination of the function and role of state parks." Clawson, who was in fact acting on behalf of NCSP's Finance and Budget Committee rather than RFF, expressed the hope that the proposed study would result in "a new orientation, a new course of action, a new purposefulness for state parks as a whole."[1]

When the idea for such a basic rehashing of state park issues was circulated, however, it met with formidable opposition from some of the more practical state park leaders. One of these was the sometimes irascible William Penn Mott—then director of California state parks (and later NPS director)—who questioned

---

1. Marion Clawson to Lemuel A. Garrison, April 24, 1973, in Board of Directors Papers, series 3, box 1, NRPA Library.

the usefulness of the proposed study and offered a number of more pressing topics in its place. Of particular concern to Mott was "not *our* role but the *political* role which the National Park Service seems to be playing at the present time in trying to relate the National Park Service to the urban centers of population."[2] This was a direct reference to the recent creation of the Golden Gate National Recreation Area in California and the Gateway National Recreation Area in New York, urban-oriented projects that signaled a marked departure from the traditional national park role and further clouded the distinctions among federal, state, and local park responsibilities (which had never been adequately clarified in the first place).

As president of the NCSP, though, Garrison was determined to find something useful for the organization to do. At its board meeting in March 1973, Garrison appointed a committee to consider the possibilities and make recommendations. Appropriately, five of the eight appointees were state park directors, and the NASPD—which was steadily eclipsing the NCSP as the primary forum for state park issues—actually put up the money to enable the committee to meet in Denver two months later. Recognizing the inevitable, the committee recommended that the NCSP abandon its confusing state parks identity and broaden its scope to embrace the interests of the entire outdoor recreation profession—and to change its name accordingly. The name first proposed was "National Society for Parks and Outdoor Recreation Resources," but when ultimately adopted it was shortened to "National Society for Park Resources," which it remains today.

The following year, in April 1974, Garrison—possibly sensing that a major change in state parks–national parks relations was about to result from the loss of the traditional NCSP forum—was instrumental in convening a special conference for invited representatives of the two groups. Nine state park directors were present, including Charles "Chuck" Odegaard of the state of Washington, who had just been elected president of NASPD and was also scheduled to succeed Garrison as president of the newly reconstituted NSPR later that year. The NPS was represented by its regional directors and several of its Washington, D.C., staff. Interestingly, the venerable Horace Albright also was included.

Billed as "Common Ground for Common Goals," the conference dealt primarily with the need to clarify respective roles and improve communications between the two levels of government. In the course of the discussions, though, National

---

2. William Penn Mott to Lemuel A. Garrison, May 24, 1973, in Board of Directors Papers, series 3, box 1, NRPA Library.

Park Service director Ron Walker brought up the matter of NPS's venture into urban recreation projects. Since 1972 when the first two such projects were authorized, he advised, "the Service has had requests from some 10–15 cities wanting us to do the same thing for them." If that announcement had Steve Mather shuddering in his grave, he would have been quickly relieved by Walker's next remark. He and Secretary of the Interior Rogers Morton, Walker stated, "do not think this should be the responsibility of NPS and have recommended that states handle these projects themselves."[3]

As might be expected from such a diverse group, the reaction of the state park directors to Walker's assertion was somewhat mixed. Some welcomed the withdrawal of NPS from the provision of essentially local recreation; a few expressed concern that they would now have to assume a role for which they were unprepared; and still others seemed to readily acknowledge a responsibility for helping to meet local recreation needs.

At any rate, the dialogue really didn't settle anything. The NASPD, at its annual meeting the following year, passed a motion urging "a moratorium on federal activity in urban parks," but neither Walker nor Morton stuck around long enough thereafter to make any difference. The political climate during the subsequent Carter administration was more conducive to nontraditional measures, and the roles distinction was muddled even more with the creation of other questionable national park projects of a local or even an urban character.

Although the newness of national park involvement in the local recreation arena made it a high-profile issue at the time, it was merely indicative of the fundamental need to determine more precisely how the lines of responsibility among the levels of government—especially between the federal and the state—should be drawn. This proved to be the central theme of Garrison's 1974 conference, and significant progress was made at least in recognizing the problem and agreeing on a wide range of needed actions. The pity is that there was very little follow-up, and the same frustrating exercise would be repeated time and again over the years with similar results—a lot of good intentions and mutual agreement, but no constructive action.

There is a larger point to be made here, though. The relationship that prevailed between the National Park Service and the state park directors over most of the previous half-century was now distinctly different. No longer was the NPS the "big

3. "Common Ground for Common Goals," Minutes of the National Park Service/State Park Directors Meeting, Washington, D.C., April 24–25, 1974, in Board of Directors Papers, series 3, box 1, NRPA Library.

brother," the mentor, the dispenser of largesse to the struggling state park programs. Having now come of age, the state parks could command their own seat at the table and be treated as equals. The body of knowledge and experience accumulated by the numerous state park systems was now comparable to that of the national parks, and in many cases their achievements were even superior. There is little evidence of any national park properties being conveyed to the states for management, but many examples of the reverse. The ready acceptance of various state parks into the national park system may be seen as a clear acknowledgment of the growing parity between the quality standards of the two programs.

There was, however, one interesting twist to the apparent trend in park "take-overs." In the face of growing publicity about funding problems and possible national park closures in the mid-1990s, South Dakota made a formal, well-considered proposal to the Interior Department to take over the operation and maintenance of the four national parks in that state as a means of forestalling "draconian" consequences. Soon afterwards, Arizona made similar overtures concerning its possibly taking over Grand Canyon National Park. Both South Dakota and Arizona had excellent state park programs, headed by competent, experienced directors, but neither of the proposals was received as seriously as it was offered (although legislation was actually introduced in the U.S. Senate on behalf of the South Dakota bid).

There were some, though, who did take the matter seriously. The National Parks and Conservation Association, the national parks' venerable watchdog organization, called on its membership to help "stop state takeovers," warning that such moves would set a "frightening precedent" for the whole national park system. "Many state parks are simply not managed with as much attention to preservation of critical resources as are national parks," the NPCA asserted, and "state [park] employees are not trained to operate a complex park" such as the Grand Canyon.[4] From a logistical standpoint, it would indeed have been difficult for the states concerned to assume such a greatly expanded workload (as the NPCA pointed out, the staff of Grand Canyon National Park was larger than that of the entire Arizona state parks department); but in expertise and dedication, the majority of state park personnel need yield to no one.

This changed relationship is not solely attributable to the rise in stature of the state parks, as impressive as that may have been. In fact, the role and the attitude

4. National Parks and Conservation Association, "Arizona Governor Aims for the Grand Canyon."

of the NPS vis-à-vis the state parks were also being affected by other factors. One of the most obvious, of course, was the Bureau of Outdoor Recreation's replacement of the NPS as the administering agency of federal grants to the states for park and recreation projects. This created a new bond between the states and the BOR at the expense of the NPS, and it greatly reduced the need and the opportunity for frequent dealings with the latter. The situation would change again in a few years, however. In the early 1980s, the BOR—or, rather, its successor, the Heritage Conservation and Recreation Service—was abolished and its functions transferred to the NPS. By that time, though, there was so little federal money to dispense that it barely made any difference.

Of a more subtle nature was the gradual decline in the sustained, paternalistic interest the NPS had taken in the state parks almost from the beginning. This change in institutional attitude no doubt reflected the absence of strong individual state park supporters in the NPS, such as Mather, Albright, and Wirth. Although several of the subsequent national park directors would come to that office with extensive, firsthand state park experience, none would ever rise to the level of those early pioneers as true champions of the state park movement.

Over many decades of growth and development, the state park movement had interacted with and been supported by a number of allied interest groups and organizations. Clearly, the two most prominent of these had been the National Conference on State Parks, through its several incarnations, and the National Park Service. Now the NCSP was no more, having metamorphosed again into a National Society for Park Resources, no longer with any special ties to state parks. The NPS, too, had changed. With no further need to nurture and guide its fledgling counterparts, it had largely withdrawn to deal with its own internal priorities. The postadolescent, if not quite yet adult, state park movement was thus left alone on wobbly legs to seek its further fortune. For fifty widely disparate state park systems to succeed as a unified national movement, it obviously would need a coordinating vehicle and support group of its own. All eyes would now turn to the largely untested National Association of State Park Directors.

The Rise of NASPD

The National Association of State Park Directors had been born in 1962 as an almost spontaneous spin-off from the National Conference on State Parks. The NCSP was obviously losing its focus and effectiveness, and the state park directors among its membership sensed a need for having an organization to represent their own specific interests. For most of its early years, though, the NASPD existed more in name than as a potent player on the park and recreation scene. But by the early 1970s, it clearly was time for NASPD also to change.

I had been the state parks director in Florida for several years before I knew anything about NASPD other than that it existed. In 1974, I was asked to attend the annual meeting in Missouri that year and give a report on the status of state parks in the Southeast (such regional reports, I learned, were a standard part of the annual meeting program). As a veteran attender of meetings, I thought I was prepared for anything, but I confess to being underwhelmed by my first experience with NASPD. There were twenty-three directors present—about average for those years—but the meeting was held in conjunction with the NSPR (its first conference under its new name) and was largely dominated by that connection. Part of this perception, however, may have been due to the fact that Chuck Odegaard was the presiding officer of both meetings, and some of the events tended to fuse together in my mind. But even after twelve years, it seemed, NASPD was still behaving like an appendage of the older group. The business agenda was short and informal, but professionally conducted, and several worthwhile actions were taken. In the end, I concluded that the organization might have enough potential to give it a second try, and I never missed another meeting during the balance of my career.

The way I saw it, in 1974 the NASPD had nowhere to go but up. Fortunately, most of the other directors seemed to feel that way as well, and efforts to mold the group into a more systematic, effective, and *independent* organization were undertaken in earnest. Already, in 1972, Odegaard had seen the need to allot more time expressly for NASPD business—separate from NCSP/NSPR—and two days had been set aside subsequently for that purpose. When the subject of meeting locations came up at the 1974 conference, a motion was passed for NASPD to "have its own conference, not necessarily tied to the NSPR meeting." Accordingly, while NSPR met in Dallas the following year, NASPD opted for a separate location at Lake Texoma State Park, some distance away in Oklahoma.

Although Odegaard and others were still encouraging NASPD to affiliate with the National Recreation and Park Association, of which NSPR was already a branch, the die was now cast for full independence. Traditionally, the NASPD "executive committee" (now "board of directors") meetings also were held each year in conjunction with the NRPA/NSPR midyear meetings. When I assumed the presidency of the NASPD in 1977, I decided it was time for a change. The practice was discontinued starting in 1978; and at the annual conference the next year, a motion was passed formally divorcing NASPD from NRPA and NSPR scheduling altogether. The NASPD was now, finally and completely, its "own" organization.

Another important organizational step was taken in 1978, when the association's constitution was amended to provide for dividing the country into six multistate "political" regions. Prior to that time there had been a tendency—inadvertent, to be sure—to concentrate leadership responsibilities in a relatively few areas of the country. The new arrangement required that the officers be elected from different regions, and that each of the six regions have its own member on the executive committee.

Other reform measures were undertaken over time as circumstances warranted and permitted. It was not until 1988, however—over a quarter-century after the organization was founded—that NASPD abandoned its nomadic ways and put down some semipermanent roots. Up until that time, the association had no place to call home except the office of the president, limited to a two-year term. Many of the files were lost in the biennial transfer from one president to the next, and it was almost impossible for outsiders to know how or where to contact the organization.

In 1988, the association decided to create a position of "executive director" to help remedy these problems and provide a variety of services for its membership. As I had announced my plans to retire as director of Florida's state parks in early 1989, I was "recruited" to fill the new NASPD position (as a volunteer initially, as the minimal budget did not allow for a stipend). By 1997, the association had advanced sufficiently to afford a regular half-time staff position, and Glen Alexander, recently retired as chief of Ohio's state parks, assumed the executive director's duties from me at that time. Upgrading of the position proved to be an important step in enhancing the professionalism of NASPD's expanding operations.

While getting its house in order was top priority, the NASPD also turned its attention to ways in which it could better serve the profession. One glaring need was for more accurate, complete, and up-to-date statistical information on all of the nation's state park programs, which could be used in a wide variety of applications. For years, sporadic efforts had been made by others to compile such data, and in fact the National Conference on State Parks and the National Park Service had collaborated on such an exercise from 1939 through 1961 (followed by the Bureau of Outdoor Recreation for the single year 1962). But these and the few later attempts, for all their usefulness, still had severe limitations caused by a lack of standard definitions, inconsistent reporting and processing, and various other problems. The data these surveys produced may have been better than nothing, but they simply could not be used without strict qualification.

Interest by the NASPD in taking on this project itself surfaced at its annual meeting in 1974. As part of my report on park activities in the Southeast, I described the statistical exercise that Florida had been conducting for several years on behalf of the Association of Southeastern State Park Directors. The membership was intrigued by the idea and voted to adopt it as a trial project. The state of Missouri volunteered to conduct the national survey for the year 1975, and the NSPR agreed to publish the data, which it did in 1977. Although not easy, the task went smoothly enough to encourage the NASPD to initiate it as a regular project, starting with the year 1978, and it has been continued without interruption ever since. The state of Indiana handled the exercise for the association through the year 1986, and then Texas through the year 1991. As executive director, I took over the task until 1996, when it was contracted out, first to the Eppley Institute for Parks and Public Lands at Indiana University, and later to Indiana State University.

Referred to simply as the "Annual Information Exchange," the compendium of state park statistical data compiled by the NASPD is still far from perfect, but it has been improved to the point that the information may be used for most purposes with a high degree of reliability. Because the included data present a more comprehensive picture of America's fifty state park systems than any other source document, producing and continuing to refine the Annual Information Exchange undoubtedly will remain a high priority for the association.

The NASPD took another important step in 1979, when it began a regular interchange with its counterpart representing the provincial parks of Canada. Actually, the Canadians took the initiative. I was in my second year as NASPD president when I received an invitation to participate in the annual meeting of the Federal Provincial Parks Council, in Winnipeg, Manitoba. I had never heard of the FPPC and knew next to nothing about Canada's parks, national or provincial, so I gladly accepted the opportunity to see what they were doing. Thoroughly impressed by what I had learned, and recognizing the potential for a mutually beneficial relationship, I extended a reciprocal invitation for members of the FPPC to attend the annual NASPD meeting in Louisiana later that year. We were delighted that a three-member party did attend and participate actively in our sessions, and the precedent was established for a regular exchange of delegations that continues to this day.

The relationship with the Canadian park professionals has been a valuable one. We found that our approaches to park management are similar in many ways and strikingly different in others, and we learned from both. That same characterization applied to our organizations as well. The FPPC, we quickly observed, seemed much more formal and structured than the NASPD. It conducted its meetings in a more orderly and businesslike fashion, delved into subjects much more technical and academic than we were used to, and published its proceedings and reports in much greater volume and detail.

Some of these differences were simply a reflection of cultural influences, but others had a more practical basis. Because the FPPC included Parks Canada (their national parks agency) along with the twelve (now thirteen) provinces and territories, the organization enjoyed the prestige and the financial support of the federal government. They were thus able to support a full-time coordinator, or manager, and carry out a broader and more systematic program. The relationship between the federal and provincial levels also was different. Although Canada is a vast and diverse country geographically, its relatively small population and number of political subdivisions seems to create a more intimate atmosphere for intergovernmental

A smaller but somewhat more formal group than its American counterpart, the Canadian Federal Provincial Parks Council is shown here in session at its 1994 annual meeting at Whitehorse, in the Yukon Territory. NASPD president Ed Koenemann of Vermont (left) and the author (right) sit attentively at the far end of the table. AUTHOR'S PERSONAL COLLECTION

activities. The resulting impression is that Parks Canada is just another "one of the group" in FPPC, along with the provincial representatives.

With similar commitments to the preservation and protection of their superb park resources, the state parks of the United States and the provincial parks of Canada have much to gain by working together and sharing information and experiences. The cordial and productive relationship that has been established between the NASPD and the FPPC has contributed much toward that end. Already, there have been two joint plenary meetings of the two organizations—in 1985 at Banff, and in 1993 on the two sides of the international border at Niagara Falls— and the spirit of cooperation and mutual support first kindled in 1979 will surely grow stronger as the years go by.

There can be no question that the NASPD has served a valuable purpose for the state parks profession since it became a fully independent, sharply focused organization in the late 1970s. With very limited budget and staff capabilities, it has in fact achieved far beyond any reasonable expectations. From its early days, however, when it served only as a vehicle for bringing some of the state park directors together once a year, it has become more complex and multifaceted, raising questions as to exactly what its purpose and program ought to be. The mission statement and objectives articulated in its constitution are clear and logical enough, and they seem to focus specifically, and even exclusively, on the direct interests of state park programs. But there appears to be an increasing desire on the part of some of the newer state park directors, especially, to broaden the organization's scope, outreach, and even its composition.

The issue of what the NASPD should be boils down essentially to a question of internal versus external orientation. Good arguments can be made for each position, and possibly even for a combination of the two. But the evolving "outside the box" philosophy seems to advocate a more active, all-encompassing role for the association, even to the extent of changing its name and membership to support a redefined mission. On the other side of the issue is the conservative, introspective case for keeping the association narrowly focused as a service and support organization for state park directors themselves. To reinforce this latter position, the association amended its constitution in 1991 to add the following objective: "To enhance the ability of the individual state park directors to perform their responsibilities for administering state park programs of the highest quality for the benefit of both the state park resources and the public."[5] With fifty individual

5. National Association of State Parks Directors, "Minutes for the 1991 Annual Meeting," 7.

state park directors involved, each with a somewhat different view of the world, it is unlikely that total consensus on this issue will ever be achieved. It is safe to say, though, that with such a dynamic field of endeavor as the state park movement the NASPD will have to remain flexible and resilient to adjust to the needs of an ever-changing constituency.

State Parks Expansion—A Continuing Success Story

Much can be said or written about the state park movement in general, but for the recreation-seeking American public the real action is on the ground—or in the water—of the thousands of diverse park areas around the country. This is, to use the modern vernacular, "where the rubber meets the road." Probably the best measure of how successful the state parks have been in satisfying the public's outdoor recreation appetite is the number of people using them year after year. Similarly, the potential for meeting an even greater demand can be estimated on the basis of the number, size, and degree of development of the parks available for use. To be able to make such assessments as these is one of the reasons why it is important to compile accurate statistical data on the complete inventory of state park areas and facilities.

The first full survey of *all fifty* state park systems was conducted by the National Conference on State Parks for the year 1970 and thus represents a baseline for what might loosely be called the "modern" state park era. Comparing data from that survey with those compiled subsequently provides a general idea of the state parks' rate and direction of growth during the latter part of the twentieth century, as reflected in the table below:

	Number of Parks	Acreage	Operating Expenditures	Visitors	Capital Expenditures
1970	3,371	5,901,824	478,263,000	176,387,000	195,255,000
1975	3,727	7,107,574	507,057,000	313,321,000	317,586,000
1980	4,178	9,468,284	548,912,000	495,360,000	525,305,000
1985	4,778	10,122,740	639,115,000	740,637,000	275,788,000
1990	4,599	10,346,113	725,307,000	1,060,401,000	435,051,000
1995	5,541	11,807,076	745,602,000	1,244,903,000	275,771,000
2000	5,382	12,807,195	786,610,000	1,627,941,000	525,477,000

Source: NCSP/NSPR and NASPD statistical surveys.

The trend line for the first four categories is steadily upward over the thirty-year period, reflecting increases of 60 percent in number of parks, 117 percent in acreage, 82 percent in visitation, and 823 percent in operating expenditures. In the last category, capital expenditures, the trend is a series of peaks and valleys due to the widely fluctuating pattern of land acquisition and new construction funding. Even so, the increase between the two outside years, 1970 and 2000, is an impressive 169 percent. It should be noted, of course, that in the last two categories the figures are inflated by the declining value of the dollar.

Park visitation figures of any kind must always be taken with a grain of salt. Most state park directors are candid enough to acknowledge the problems, and their effect on the results, of collecting such data without adequate controls. Many state park systems charge no entrance fees at all, and most have at least some areas that are wide open, or on the honor system, with no reliable means of counting the "gate." These problems have existed since year one, however, and there is no reason to believe that they have gotten worse over time. It can be reasonably asserted, then, that the overall trend in state park attendance is generally reliable, with the degree of confidence in the count remaining approximately the same from year to year.

The most significant statistical indicators of state park expansion, of course, are those dealing with tangible assets: lands and facilities. In spite of the compilation difficulties previously noted, the data produced by the NASPD's surveys over the past twenty years or so have gotten progressively more comparable, especially for areas and acres. For this reason, it is possible to look at the huge increases reported since 1970 and know that, by and large, they represent actual on-the-ground accomplishments: There really is a park out there somewhere for each one of those numbers! In a quantitative sense anyway, this is a measure of real progress.

Even with a lackluster economy for extended periods since the 1970s, and the consequent impact on state park capital budgets, the aggregate size of the fifty state park systems more than doubled over that time, adding almost seven million acres. Before that statistic generates too much excitement, though, it calls for some further analysis. First, 2,344,000 acres of that total increase, or 34 percent, was in Alaska alone—due primarily to the transfer of lands from the federal public domain. Another 2,182,000 acres, or 32 percent of the total increase, is accounted for by just seven other rapidly expanding systems (California, Colorado, Florida, Michigan, New Jersey, North Carolina, and Texas). Those two sums make up two-thirds of the increase, and at least half of the remaining third is accounted for by inclusion of other public lands (such as state forests and wildlife preserves) in the state parks total for the first time. This leaves just over a million acres of new additions distributed among the other forty-two states. Several states actually reported slight decreases in acreage between 1970 and 2000 (New Hampshire, Oklahoma, Rhode Island, Vermont, and Wyoming), but all of the others registered modest to highly significant gains.

Part of the difficulty in trying to get an accurate handle on state park statistics was, and is, attributable to imprecise or changing definitions. This problem has existed from the very first inventory efforts in the early 1920s and has been commented on already. But one particularly puzzling aspect involves those "state parks" that are *not* state parks. A number of states have created parks that, for various reasons, they have not placed under the same administrative jurisdiction as their regular state parks program. Some notable examples are Custer State Park in South Dakota, Baxter State Park in Maine, Jekyll Island State Park in Georgia, and Mackinac Island State Park in Michigan, but there are other, lesser-known ones as well. Using the same or similar terminology in such cases tends to create even more confusion for inventory purposes than, say, distinguishing state parks from state forests or state wildlife areas (the Adirondack and Catskill Forest Preserves in New York also are often included but are not formally designated as "parks"). And because many of these areas are extremely large compared to most state parks, deciding whether to include or exclude them in the inventory process can make a significant difference in the results. While this is clearly a matter for the individual states to work out for themselves, following a consistent practice would go a long way toward averting unnecessary confusion.

However the numbers are crunched, though, the bottom line is that America's state parks, as a whole, experienced tremendous growth and expansion in the final decades of the twentieth century. True, that growth was not evenly distributed among the states—far from it. As might be expected, the needs, means, opportunities, and motivations for park land acquisition vary widely from state to state, especially when acquisition involves a significant cash outlay. Real estate markets boomed in most parts of the United States during this time, particularly in areas of rapid growth. The resulting competition not only drove up land prices, but in many areas of critical recreation need it severely diminished the availability of suitable park properties. That so much land was acquired and preserved under these circumstances—for what many might even regard as a nonessential purpose—is a true testament to the foresight, initiative, and perseverance of state park advocates everywhere.

One important reason for this success was that the state governments had a lot of help from a variety of sources. Many states forged ahead on their own, of course, floating bond issues, appropriating general funds, soliciting donations of cash and properties—all in recognition of the critical importance of preserving park-lands while it was still possible to do so. Others, however, required a little more in-centive—and in most cases this came in the form of money. Federal financial support through the Land and Water Conservation Fund was certainly a major fac-tor. During its heyday in the 1970s and early 1980s, this program helped the states acquire some two million acres of recreation land—much of it for state parks—at a total cost (half federal, half state and local) of well over a billion dollars.

Comparable assistance materialized from another important source as well: the nonprofit land preservation organizations. The Nature Conservancy, for in-stance, beginning as early as 1959, helped fund land acquisition projects in every state—some 3.6 million acres in all, valued at almost two billion dollars. Starting somewhat later, the Trust for Public Land actively assisted in saving over 340,000 acres in thirty-two states, with a total value of three-fourths of a billion dollars. The Conservation Fund followed, aiding in the protection of over three million acres valued at $1.8 billion. The state parks were the beneficiaries in many of these projects as well.

Lands, with all of their included resources, are the very essence of the state parks. To a large degree, the ability of the state parks to meet their obligation to provide appropriate public outdoor recreation opportunities is directly propor-tional to the amount (and types) of land available. This is why so much emphasis is placed on continued expansion through acquisition of additional properties. The success in this regard over the past three decades has certainly made Amer-ica's state park systems bigger—but are they getting better? Trying to evaluate and compare the quality of state parks, or especially of state park systems, is a tricky business—as we shall see.

The Rating Game: Looking for the "Best" State Parks

With so many state parks to choose from, it was inevitable that someone would eventually decide they should be competitively ranked to determine which were the "best." Their sheer numbers made it impractical to treat them all equally for any kind of descriptive coverage, so some means had to be found to narrow the field to a manageable few. How on earth do you go about conducting a con-test for objects as diverse as the state parks? Wise men probably wouldn't even try, but the tendency to compare, judge, and declare the "winners" apparently is a cherished American tradition that will not be denied. And nowhere has this been more evident than in the so-called popular literature.

As the state park systems have grown and matured, they naturally have generated more interest from the publishing world—much of it initiated or encouraged by increasingly effective park publicity efforts. During my time as executive director of NASPD, I had the opportunity to work with several national publications pursuing stories on the state parks, each looking for its own special slant on the subject. When faced with the magnitude of the task and the need to pare it down to size, they invariably started asking about the "best," or the "most important," or the "most spectacular." Always facing deadlines, they could never afford the time to delve into the inherent differences of state parks, so I simply told them there was no such thing as the "best" state parks and to find another "hook" for their articles. To their credit, they all complied.

In 1994, *National Geographic Traveler* magazine decided to do an article on the "best" state parks in the country. After further thought, they neatly finessed the issue of ranking by focusing on "10 *of* America's Best State Parks."[6] Even then, though, they were careful to select only one park from any one state; and, not to offend anyone, they also listed a park for each of the other forty states as "outstanding pieces of America."

A similar approach was taken in 1994 by *Family Fun* magazine, in an article called "America's Great State Parks." Avoiding the use of superlatives in favor of all-inclusive adjectives like "great" and "grand," this article also selected one park from each state for brief description, but it singled out seven on some unknown basis for special attention. The following year, *Frommer's America's 100 Best-Loved State Parks* was published. This well-organized guidebook also originally intended to focus on the "best" state parks, but at my suggestion backed off a little bit with the "best-loved" approach. The hundred selections covered all fifty states, ranging from only one each for fifteen states to five for New York. "Best-loved" presumably equates to "most popular," but as Jones Beach State Park was not included among those for New York, it is highly doubtful that popularity was indeed the main criterion for selection.[7]

Without doubt, the most important popular work on state parks to come out in recent years (possibly ever to be published) was the 1997 *National Geographic's*

6. K. M. Kostyal, "America's State Parks: Ten of the Best."
7. Barbara Rowley, "America's Great State Parks"; Robert Rafferty, *Frommer's America's 100 Best-Loved State Parks.*

Guide to the State Parks of the United States. This 249-page, copiously illustrated volume describes over two hundred parks, representative of all fifty states. Other than the typically high quality of the finished product, what makes this project distinctive is that it was a cooperative effort with NASPD and the individual state park directors themselves. The directors had a major hand in selecting the parks for their respective states, using their own judgment to recommend those sites they deemed most representative of their state park systems.

In these various attempts to feature state parks for commercial publication purposes, the publishers obviously are trying to grab readers' attention, and certainly not to pass considered judgment on the qualitative merits of the parks they select. On the basis of reader appeal, these lists invariably contain mostly the "high-profile" parks: the biggest, the most unusual, the most spectacular, and so forth. Although these superlatives are still somewhat subjective, they are easier to reach consensus on; and for this reason many of the same parks keep popping up in every publication: Custer in South Dakota, Baxter in Maine, Franconia Notch in New Hampshire, John Pennekamp Coral Reef in Florida, Fall Creek Falls in Tennessee, Itasca in Minnesota, Chugach in Alaska, Anza-Borrego in California— to mention only a few of the most prominent. While they may occasionally confuse their readers as to the basis for selecting the parks they feature, these publications more than offset that small transgression with the excellent publicity they provide for state parks generally.

But it is one thing for travel writers to take a few liberties in telling us which state parks are better than others, and quite another for state park professionals to try to do it themselves. Wine tasters and diving judges may get away with such arbitrary exercises, but state parks are far too diverse and complex for such folly. No one has yet come up with a satisfactory means for rating state parks on qualitative grounds, and the idea should simply be abandoned. Still, the delusion persists, and the obvious case that proves the point is the Gold Medal Awards program conducted by the National Sporting Goods Association's Sports Foundation.

The idea for a competitive award exclusively for state parks was first raised at the NASPD annual meeting in 1987. At that time, state park systems were eligible to compete with other public recreation agencies for more general awards, but very few of them did. The thought behind creating an exclusive award was that more states would participate if the program were geared specifically to their interests. The matter was deferred for further study and did not come up for action until 1994, when NASPD unanimously rejected the Gold Medal program as not being suited to the state parks situation.

Two years later, however, at its 1996 annual meeting, the association received a report that a Gold Medal Awards program for state parks had been established anyway. The competition was initiated the following year, on an alternate-year basis. Ohio was proclaimed the first winner, in 1997, followed by Florida in 1999 and Virginia in 2001.

While the Sports Foundation's awards program obviously has a certain popular appeal, representing itself as the arbiter of the nation's "most outstanding state park system" is a gross and unsupportable presumption. The awards program is not truly representative, as only a few states have so far opted to participate. And because the winner is then ineligible to enter the competition for another five years, it cannot be the "most outstanding" for more than two years at a time.

Although fraught with questionable procedures that challenge its authority, the Gold Medal program does serve to publicize state parks; and receiving the award can be parlayed into a veritable public relations bonanza for the recipient. For the sake of honesty and fairness, though, the sponsor of this awards program

Although trying to rank state park systems is a questionable exercise at best, winners of such voluntary competitions as the Gold Medal Awards may at least claim temporary bragging rights. PHOTOGRAPH BY THE AUTHOR

should seriously rethink its overstated claim of "honoring the most outstanding state park system in our fifty states."

Whatever the reason or the method used, trying to evaluate the quality of any aspect of state parks, and especially that of entire state park programs, is inherently risky. There are too many diverse factors at play to allow for easy analysis and comparison. For a truly adequate understanding of what makes the state park programs tick, it would be necessary to examine all of those determinative factors in some detail. Such an exhaustive study is beyond the scope of this work, but in the following chapter we will at least take a quick look at some of the most basic issues that bear on the quality and substance of a typical state parks program.

14

A Look behind the Scenes
Issues and Influences that Shape the State Park System

There is long-held truth among state park administrators that courteous personnel and clean restrooms make for happy visitors. Although admittedly simplistic, this maxim reflects a general assumption that most park users do not really see beneath the surface aspects of a park operation—that as long as conditions *appear* to be satisfactory, then they *are* satisfactory. Such a perception may be all right for visitors, but it could lead to all kinds of grief if park managers themselves succumbed to such a notion.

For many purposes, though, appearances are the paramount concern. This is why so much emphasis is placed on designing attractive structures, maintaining clean and serviceable facilities, and training personnel to keep a smiling face in spite of frequent aggravation. Above all, the parks must look good and meet at least the minimum requirements of a demanding clientele. Success in these endeavors will go a long way toward reducing visitor complaints and keeping the parks director happy as well.

Unfortunately, planning and operating a modern state park program in a thoroughly professional manner is not nearly as simple as that. While the visitors see only the superficial side of the parks, the administrators must deal with far more complex issues that materially affect the quality and efficiency of a whole system of parks. Such issues and how to cope with them are the grist for an increasingly sophisticated state parks profession and, for the most part, are beyond the scope of our concern here. But there are a few factors that bear so directly on the course a state park system takes that they deserve at least some cursory consideration.

The Politics Factor

State parks are the creatures of government, and government is the matrix of politics. It follows, then, that state parks have been, are, and always will be directly affected by politics in all of its myriad manifestations. In a practical sense, this can be good or bad—and for state parks it has been both. Because of its impact, it is important to consider the role of politics in shaping the status of America's state park programs, and to make a clear distinction between that political role and the different one occupied by the state parks professional.

The fundamental purpose of a state park system—and often its specific policies and procedures—is determined in the political arena, usually by the state legislature. In making this determination, the general tone is normally set by where the state parks function is placed within the organizational structure of state government. That organizational placement was discussed earlier, in the context of the maturing state park movement, and it was noted that it generally reflected the state park "tradition" adopted by a particular state. By the latter years of the twentieth century, however, the pattern had pretty much solidified, with a preponderance of the states (twenty-eight) placing state parks within a department charged almost exclusively with natural resources or environmental management.

Emphasis on tourism and economic development had declined by this time, as only five state park systems were placed in agencies with major responsibility for those functions. In two states, parks were lodged in departments responsible for other combinations of programs: "resources and economic development" in one case, and "conservation and recreation" in the other. Parks in six states remained allied with fish and wildlife departments; but, although parks and forestry shared equal status within the same department in twenty-three states, in only one of these was forestry the principal departmental thrust. In what may prove to be a slight reversal of the trend, eight states now had their parks programs in functionally independent agencies—usually under a board or commission.

All across the country, it seemed, state parks were finding their organizational groove. Even the Oregon program, the last major anomaly, was removed from its traditional home in the state transportation department (where it had been made a separate division in 1980) and placed under an independent department in 1989.

As controlling as it would seem to be, however, the organizational placement of the state park function does not necessarily dictate the direction the program takes. All states enjoy a great deal of latitude within the scope of their legislative mandates, especially since new projects and programs are often specifically provided for by special or supplemental legislation. More significant in the short run is the appointment of the key personnel who will direct the inner workings of the program. In most states, such appointments are politically determined, usually by the governor directly or with the governor's advice and consent.

There was a time, not too long ago, when state park staff in many states, right down to the individual rangers, were subject to replacement with each change of administration. Fortunately, civil service protections and just plain common sense have largely curbed such irresponsible mass turnovers, but most state park directors and some of their higher level aides are still vulnerable to the vagaries of political whim.

Over three-fourths of directors today serve at the pleasure of their appointing authorities (usually the governor or one of his department heads). The rest claim to enjoy some degree of career protection, but experience has shown that even they can be removed if higher level desire is strong enough. This would seem to be borne out by the turnover frequency of state park directors: The average length of service of current directors is just over six years (less than the typical two-term gubernatorial administration), ranging from a minimum of a few months to a maximum of seventeen years. Only ten directors presently have served as long as ten years in that capacity.

Some directors are more competent than others, of course, but the good are often terminated along with the not-so-good. The value of longevity is that it not only gives the incumbent an opportunity to grow (and presumably improve) in the job, but also provides adequate time for the appointing authority to fairly assess that individual's competence and worthiness for retention. But longevity can cut both ways; keeping an ineffective director too long is likely to be more counterproductive than the premature ousting of an outstanding director for purely political reasons.

In a sampling of opinion in 1998, the state park directors themselves concluded that they, more than any other entity—including the legislatures and the governors—influenced the policy direction taken by their programs.[1] I hold to the same belief, and the high probability that it is accurate highlights the importance of finding the best person for the job. But even if it were not the case, the wisdom of placing and keeping an able administrator at the state parks' helm should be self-evident. Fortunately, the trend in hiring proven professionals in

1. Survey of all state park directors, conducted by the author in the summer of 1998.

recent decades suggests that this obvious truism is now more widely recognized by political decision makers.

From a purely practical standpoint, probably the most critical area of political influence exerted on state parks is in the budget-allocation process: parks can be built and operated only in proportion to the amount of money they receive. For many years, most states sustained their programs with appropriations from the general fund, augmented by park-generated revenues and sporadic grants and donations. This pattern would start to change with the economic downturn of the 1970s and the frantic search for new revenue sources (discussed in the following chapter); but even then the legislatures in most cases would still retain control over the allocation of funds, regardless of the source. This control allowed legislators to decide not only how much money the parks would get, but also how it would be used—and it is difficult to say which has had the greater impact on the direction state park programs have taken.

Clearly, the amount of money appropriated for parks is important—and the usual attitude of the state parks director is "the more, the better." There are always critical needs to be met, especially with a constantly growing backlog of deferred maintenance projects. In recent decades, though, there seem to have been more lean than fat budget years, and never enough funds to take care of all the items on the "wish list." Where capital appropriations (for acquiring and developing new parks) are concerned, though, this is not necessarily a bad thing. Too much available money can lead a state parks agency to make questionable judgments in the mad scramble to spend every last dollar—and in many instances those judgments are influenced, or even dictated, by overly helpful legislators.

Parks are undeniably among the most popular of state government programs. The people might oppose the location of a new road, office building, or prison, but they will almost always welcome a new park. And if the people like parks, the politicians will love them! This fact of life—combined in most cases with genuine personal interest and a sense of civic responsibility—has led many a governor and legislator to become a state parks champion.

Without such champions, of course, state park programs would never have attained their present status—but often they become overly zealous and forceful in pursuit of their pet projects. Almost every state park system today contains a few dubious monuments to those well-meant but patently inappropriate endeavors. Most of these gratuitous projects are harmless except for the waste of funds that could have been better used elsewhere; but some are so clearly inappropriate and unneeded that they constitute lasting embarrassments for park staff that have to live with them long after the ribbon-cutting ceremonies are over.

Politics has also been responsible for numerous other projects that, regardless of their quality, are not well suited for state park management because of their type, size, or location. Most of these probably should be county or even city parks, but were foisted off on the state for greater prestige or, more likely, financial support. State park directors are aware of these various misfits, although not all are willing to admit it. When asked not long ago if their park system contained any "nonrepresentative" areas (a euphemism intended to cover any park they considered undesirable), two-thirds responded affirmatively (although some, understandably, were reluctant to identify any such areas).[2]

As with every government program, direct political involvement in state park matters is clearly a mixed bag. Because of the parks' great popularity, though, such involvement in this case is usually well-intentioned and benign. Occasionally, responding to constituent concerns or some special-interest goal, legislators will push policy changes that the professional staff considers unwise or inappropriate. But, overall, interest in state parks by the governor and the legislature has been regarded as an asset and is cultivated in such a way as to facilitate the program's goals. Whatever its form, wanted or not, politics is a permanent part of the state parks picture. Learning to accept this and deal with it effectively has been a key to the state park director's survival and the success of the state parks program.

The State Parks Mission: A Confusion of Purposes

Probably the most basic requirement for prosecuting a successful state parks program is the clear delineation of the purpose it is to serve. Theoretically, at least, the mandate for such a program and the general guidance for its implementation come from an enabling statute or a mission statement derived from some legislative authority. From a practical standpoint, though, most state park statutes seem broad enough or ambiguous enough so that they neither specifically dictate nor materially inhibit the direction the program actually takes.

Mission statements, however derived, also appear far less controlling in actual practice than the term might imply. The overall result is that many of the state park programs lay out and follow a course that serves short-range rather than long-range interests, dictated by fluctuating political and practical considerations

2. Survey of all state park directors, conducted by the author in the spring of 1999.

rather than strict adherence to a time-tested statement of purpose. This lack of consistency makes it all but impossible to predict which way state parks might turn in the future. To further complicate matters, many of the mission statements themselves tend to be too general and vague to be very helpful. And, as might be expected, they vary considerably from one to another.

State park mission statements range from the very detailed and specific to the very brief and general. Take Iowa's, for instance:

> To provide a diversity of natural communities that provide multiple benefits for society; provide permanent protection with sound conservation of histori-cal, biological, scenic and geological qualities; contribute to the quality of life of Iowa's citizens by providing areas for healthful outdoor recreation and nature appreciation; acquiring, protecting, developing and managing Iowa's best nat-ural areas for the benefit of Iowa's citizens and other visitors; and providing leadership in outdoor recreation through good management, planning services, grant programs and other services.

Or Pennsylvania's:

> To provide opportunities for enjoying healthful outdoor recreation and to serve as outdoor classrooms for environmental education. In meeting these purposes, the conservation of the natural, scenic, aesthetic, and historical values of the parks should be given first consideration. Stewardship responsibilities should be carried out in a way that protects the natural outdoor experience for the enjoyment of current and future generations.

On the other hand, consider New Hampshire's:

> To protect, maintain and expand a comprehensive system of state parks.

Or Utah's:

> To enhance the quality of life in Utah through parks, people and programs.

A mission statement is typically condensed from some more comprehensive planning document, so it does not need to be overly long or detailed; as a matter of fact, too much verbiage can defeat its purpose of helping to maintain program focus. The statement should include only the essential points, preferably in a crisply worded single-sentence format. There are quite a few good ones, including California's:

> To provide for the health, inspiration and education of the people of California by helping to preserve the state's extraordinary biological diversity, protecting its most valued natural and cultural resources, and creating opportunities for high-quality outdoor recreation.

And Tennessee's:

> To preserve and protect, in perpetuity, unique examples of natural, cultural, and scenic areas and provide a variety of safe, quality outdoor experiences through a well-planned and professionally managed system of state parks.

While the state park programs in all of the above cases might actually be quite similar in many respects and very different in others, it would be difficult to find the basis for either similarities or differences in the specific language of their mission statements. And that is generally true for the rest of the states as well. Looking for useful correlations among the fifty state park mission statements may be a fruitless exercise, but there are a number of key terms or concepts that commonly appear. Some of these are listed below in descending order of frequency, expressed as a percentage of the statements in which they appear:

Recreation	90%
Conservation/preservation	80
Natural	76
Cultural	56
Interpretation/education	54
Historic	42
Management	42
Outdoor	38
Health/quality of life	30
Scenery/scenic	24
Environment/science	20
The economy/economic	14
Experiences	12

Tourism	10
Resource-based	8

The list is instructive not only for the range of different concepts it reveals, but also for the relative popularity indicated by their frequency of occurrence. For instance, *providing recreation* (90 percent) and *preserving nature* (80 percent) appear to be the most favored concepts, while *stimulating the economy* (14 percent) and *promoting tourism* (10 percent) are among the least emphasized. On its face, this would seem to comport with conventional wisdom on the purpose of state parks. But, unfortunately, what a state says its parks are supposed to do and what they are actually made to do may not always be the same.

Most state park directors today seem generally satisfied with the direction their programs are taking. All but a few are pleased with their current mission statements, whether they helped develop them or not, and feel that their programs are adhering closely to their stated missions.[3] But the real problem with mission statements is that in many cases they are not articulated in a way to provide explicit and adequate guidance or they simply are not followed religiously enough to effect their stipulated purpose.

Pragmatism and flexibility certainly have their place in the government arena, and they may even be prerequisites for the state park director's political survival. Still, experience has shown that the best way to ensure the success and long-range stability of a state parks program is to clearly identify a sound and defensible goal and pursue it as consistently and conscientiously as the scope of the director's authority will allow. In testimony of which, I point to such classic cases as Albert Turner's experience in Connecticut and Richard Lieber's in Indiana;[4] but I could also cite a number of more recent success stories as well.

Questions of Policy

State park policy, especially development policy, is another important factor that should influence program quality but which, unfortunately, often lacks clarity and consistency. The NCSP recognized this early on and made repeated attempts through the years to promote the adoption of a set of recommended policies for consideration

---

3. Survey of all state park directors, conducted by the author in the summer of 2000.

4. Turner and Lieber were arguably the most influential of the actual state park *practitioners* of the early twentieth century. (This would exclude such luminaries as the two Olmsteds, Laurie Cox, and others who did not directly administer state park programs. Major W. A.

by the states. Even so, many states still do not have nor consistently apply formal
state park policies on such matters as site selection, site planning, unit classification, and so forth. Because state park policy is an often misunderstood and controversial matter, almost nothing has been done in recent years to assess the
situation on a state-by-state basis (although individual state positions on certain
policy issues are solicited voluntarily for the NASPD's Annual Information Exchange).

In 1966, a team from Southern Illinois University, led by Dwight McCurdy,
took a hard look at the state park programs with an eye to producing a set of
standard policy statements on many issues of general concern. In their report, released in 1967, the authors concluded that:

> Today, development and management policies governing state park systems
> not only vary among states, but change according to public demand, political
> pressures, and economic and social imperatives. . . . The result is a diversity of
> development and management practices, some duplication and gaps, and in
> many cases, less than optimum resource utilization. This situation constitutes a
> major obstacle to a balance of local, state, and national programs.[5]

To help alleviate this perceived problem, the authors offered a set of twenty-
four recommended policies that they felt, if universally applied, would result in
greatly improved operating procedures for all state park programs. McCurdy and
company, however, were not so brash as to think superior state park policy could

---

Welch probably should be included except for the fact that he administered only a single project, the Palisades Park, rather than an entire state park system.)

Albert Turner, who started the Connecticut state parks program in 1914 and directed it until
1942, was especially notable for the pioneering work he did in all phases of state park administration, particularly in the fundamentals of state park philosophy and planning. Richard
Lieber made a similar contribution to state park development in Indiana. He served as the first
chairman of the State Park Commission from 1915 until 1919, when he was appointed the first
director of the Indiana Conservation Department, where he continued to oversee the state
park program until his retirement in 1933. Lieber is better known than Turner today because
of his active participation in the National Conference on State Parks, serving in almost every
capacity over an eighteen-year period. But both men established exemplary park systems in
their respective states and left enduring legacies that are probably unequalled in the annals of
the state parks profession.

I am reluctant to name any of the outstanding state park directors of the past several
decades for fear of either making the list too long or omitting the names of some who are fully
deserving of the recognition.

5. Dwight R. McCurdy and Larry K. Johnson, *Recommended Policies for the Development and
Management of State Park Systems*, 2.

be developed in an isolated academic milieu. What they proposed was really a synthesis of policies already in use by the various states—although not all of them yet embodied in officially adopted form.

There is no evidence that the SIU recommended policies were ever considered, much less adopted, by any state park agency; and, not surprisingly, there have been no similar exercises undertaken since that time. However, as a way of testing current thinking on the same issues, incumbent state park directors were recently asked how they felt about SIU's specific policy recommendations.[6]

None of the proposed policy statements received unanimous agreement, although all of them were supported to a degree. Widest approval (92 percent on a weighted basis)[7] went to the proposed policy on *maintenance and operation:* "All state parks should be maintained in a clean, neat, sanitary and orderly manner, and operated in such a way as to protect public health, safety and welfare and provide for and enhance the use and enjoyment by visitors." It's hard to see how such an innocuous statement as that could elicit anything short of total agreement, but it did.

At the other extreme, there was less than a 75 percent concurrence with the statement on *planning:* "The state park system should have a comprehensive statewide plan, a master plan for every major park, a site plan for all developments, and an interpretive master plan for every major park—all periodically reviewed for needed changes." Taken literally, that policy could lead to a tremendous amount of work and expense, which might easily make it off-putting for many directors strapped for staff and cash—even though they might otherwise agree with the intent.

Much of the disagreement by today's directors with the recommended policy statements could be due to the wording rather than the substance, of course. But, if nothing else, the exercise serves to further illustrate that views on such important matters not only vary from state to state, but are constantly changing over time as well. So much depends on the background and perspective of the individuals who happen to be serving as state park directors at any given time.

Although not restricted to matters of policy, as in the above case, a study conducted by the Conservation Foundation in 1985 did seek to test state park directors' opinion on a wide range of "diverse issues confronting state park

6. Spring 1999 survey.

7. State park directors were asked to rank the extent of their agreement with each policy statement on a five-level scale, ranging from a low of "not at all" (a weight of 0) to a high of "completely" (a weight of 4). These weight factors were then applied to the fifty state responses to determine a weighted average percentage of agreement for all fifty directors.

systems."[8] Coming as it did during a period when almost every state park system was challenged by severe budget cuts, it is not surprising that most of the issues discussed were more practical and transitory than they might have been during more ordinary times.

The shortage of funds and the immediate consequences thereof, particularly in the area of repair and maintenance, dominated the list. Even so, it is interesting that a number of issues—some ranked fairly high by the park directors—spoke directly to fundamental policy matters. For instance:

- "need to identify and protect distinctive ecological areas" (80 percent support, on a weighted basis)[9]
- "some units very crowded, some very underused" (79 percent)
- "concentrated visitor use in some parks is causing resource degradation" (74 percent)
- "need to develop better standards to guide decisions about what lands to buy" (61 percent)
- "some state parklands becoming too developed" (52 percent)

Recognition of such problems is the first step toward solution, and it cries out for the development of practical policy guidance to help the states deal effectively with these and similar issues. Some states, of course, are way ahead of others in such policy development, and it is essential that those that may be lagging in this regard take full advantage of the wealth of information and expertise available to them—even if a little pride has to be swallowed in the process.

A Case for State Park Self-Evaluation

America's state parks are undeniably popular, but are they being effectively managed? Unfortunately, in a categorical sense no one can truly say. In spite of the interest noted in the previous chapter, no means has yet been devised for assessing and evaluating state parks quality across the board—and certainly not for any attempt at competitive ranking. For such an exercise to claim any real legitimacy, it would have to be developed and conducted by the state parks profession itself,

8. Phyllis Myers and Ann Christine Reid, *State Parks in a New Era: A Survey of Issues and Innovations,* 14–16, table II–2.

9. See note 7; the same procedure was used in this case, except that there were six levels involved in the ranking, ranging from a low of "unimportant" (a weight of 1) to a high of "extremely important" (a weight of 6).

and, so far, there has been no apparent interest expressed in the idea. The impracticality and the questionable usefulness of a process to rank the fifty state park programs are reasons enough to reject it. On the other hand, there is potentially a real benefit to be derived from having the individual state park agencies assess and evaluate the quality of their own programs, and in 1993 the NASPD took tentative steps to do just that.

The idea for a self-evaluation exercise originated with Wilbur LaPage, in 1993 the director of New Hampshire state parks. One of the more erudite of the state park directors, with a distinguished prior career in federal outdoor recreation work, LaPage was concerned about the lack of a means for monitoring the overall quality of state park management. As a starting point, he came up with a procedure for what he called a "stewardship survey," and tested it in a number of the northeastern states. Finding the results sufficiently satisfactory, he then took the idea before the NASPD at its 1993 annual meeting for consideration as a nationwide project.

Some of the directors did not share LaPage's enthusiasm for grading their own management success, however, and expressed various misgivings about the purpose and methodology of the survey and how the results were to be used. A major concern was the possibility that negative findings might be leaked to the press and create public relations problems for the directors involved. In the end, though, the membership adopted a "state of the parks" assessment as an association project, at least for a one-time trial.

The inaugural "stewardship survey" of the nation's state parks was undertaken in the fall of 1993 under LaPage's personal direction. It was designed to measure, in a general and largely subjective way, three principal areas of state park management: resource stewardship, park maintenance, and public service. In reporting his findings to NASPD the next year, LaPage noted that, compared with the results of a similar exercise recently conducted for the national parks by Colorado State University, the state parks on the whole had fared much better. Sufficiently impressed, the state park directors voted to continue conducting the survey every other year. But, still skittish about how the results might be used, they agreed that the findings would be released only as national averages, and that all directors would be asked not to divulge their own state's data, even on a voluntary basis, until after the survey had been tested over several years.

Although nobly conceived, the NASPD's "stewardship survey" never really got off the ground. Never suitably refined, not well-understood, and only reluctantly supported by the state park directors, it was simply ignored and eventually forgotten, without ever going through a second trial. One reason for its quick demise was LaPage's departure from state parks in 1994 to pursue an academic career at Colorado State University. To his credit, he did attempt to resuscitate the survey project the following year under the aegis of the National Recreation and Park Association's Environmental Task Force, but by that time interest at the state parks level had largely dissipated.

Thus ended the one substantial effort ever made to institute a systematic process for evaluating qualitative aspects of state park programs. But it is still an object well worth pursuing. State park administrators need some means of critically examining their own management methods and results in as honest and objective a way as possible. This, too, is an area in which the more progressive states can offer a helping hand to the others if a suitable medium for such an advisory service can be provided. One can only hope that another Wilbur LaPage will come along soon to revive this important endeavor.

Looking Back and Looking Forward

In spite of the many challenges along the way—dealing with internal policy and procedure as well as with external perceptions and pressures—the American state park movement had proved itself a phenomenal success. And while it may not have yet peaked in the waning years of the twentieth century, it certainly had reached a lofty plateau on which it could pause, take stock of its accomplishments, and look to its future with confidence and optimism.

Much progress had been made—possibly as much by chance as by design—over the previous hundred or more years. The movement had indeed solidified and oriented itself; now, with viable park programs in all fifty states, it was for the first time truly national in scope. The numbers of parks and the total acreage they embraced were steadily increasing, as were the crowds of enthusiastic and appreciative visitors. Surely this must be the realization of the vision that had motivated and inspired the state park pioneers so many years before. If the movement had not fully matured, it was certainly on the verge of doing so.

This might well be the point at which to end the story of America's state parks. But, in truth, even as it celebrated its long and successful history with quiet satisfaction, it was about to enter into one of the most volatile and challenging periods of its existence. The state parks had indeed become increasingly more self-reliant and self-sufficient through the years, and it was that fact that shaped their destiny in the final decades of the twentieth century. And it also provides the subject for the chapter that follows.

15

Anything Goes
An Age of Expansion, Experimentation, and Expediency

A Point of Divergence

For five decades or so following the first unifying influence of the National Conference on State Parks, America's state park programs forged steadily ahead, generally pursuing a common goal: to get bigger and more popular. The multi-fold increases in acreage and visitors during that time would suggest that they had succeeded admirably on both counts. The NCSP's once ambitious slogan of "a park every hundred miles" had long since become obsolete. It was now virtually impossible to venture even half that distance without encountering one or more state park properties of some sort—and the people were flocking to them in droves.

Although more difficult to measure, the state parks had probably gotten better as well—but how much, and in what ways? Lacking any reliable means for evaluating park quality, the determination of what is good (or better, or best) must, for now anyway, be left to the subjective judgment of the park users. But if specific evidence of quality improvement was elusive, other signs on the horizon were crystal clear: Many of the state park programs were indeed changing, whether for better or worse.

Having achieved a degree of maturity, most of the state park programs were now ready to spread their wings and test their newfound independence and self-confidence. There were a number of factors at play here. Gone from the scene were the NCSP and—for all practical purposes—the National Park Service, which for so long had effectively held sway over the dimensions and the direction of the state park movement. In their place was a new organization, the National Association

233

of State Park Directors, created by quiet rebellion of the directors to be their servant and not their master. The directors themselves were more likely to be trained park professionals than political patronage appointees, and many of them were drawn from park and recreation programs of local governments and universities to replace old-school, up-through-the-ranks state park veterans.

New concepts, practices, and even whole philosophies were introduced and quickly diffused through the movement. Public interest in state parks, too, was intensifying, with new advocate groups forming to promote environmental goals, support specific recreation activities or hobbies, and carry the banner for a variety of other purposes. Interest and oversight by legislative bodies soon followed. Clearly, in this mix of interacting circumstances, the situation was ripe for change.

Blending the Old and the New

To suggest that rampant change in state parks occurred abruptly in an overnight groundswell would be inaccurate, of course. Park concepts and programs had been evolving in spurts for a long time. But in the second half of the twentieth century, a particularly significant transformation took place as the state park movement shook off its long-standing image (if not a reality) as a protégé of the National Park Service. State parks, to be sure, owed much to the NPS and the various programs it had administered. The Civilian Conservation Corps alone was responsible for the start of many state park programs, and much of the planning, design, construction, and personnel training in state parks was assisted by the NPS. Even to this day, most of the states are still proud of their CCC parks and other tangible reminders of that long and productive association with their federal counterpart agency.

But all that was now history, and the states were ready to break out of the mold and express themselves in ways of their own. It is significant—although perhaps not surprising—that in their continuing search for their appropriate place in the linkage between the local, user-oriented parks and the more remote, resource-based national parks, many of the states would now turn more toward the former.

In aiming their programs more toward the broader, more sophisticated clientele they hoped to attract, many states now saw the traditional state parks as being too limited and one-dimensional. It was no longer enough just to acquire a scenic tract of land and open it to the public with an access road, some restrooms, and a few picnic tables and campsites. To broaden its appeal, that tract

Equipment innovations such as the snowmobile create new and greater demand for the activities they make possible, and many state parks have responded with appropriate programs and facilities. MICHIGAN DEPARTMENT OF NATURAL RESOURCES

must be made multidimensional with additional amenities and a variety of user programs. Experience quickly demonstrated that the public would indeed respond to such innovations in greater numbers, and much of the parks' planning effort and budget was accordingly directed toward that end.

State park planners turned to this new challenge with vigor, and their imagination and creativity were boldly reflected in the variety of both traditional and nontraditional activities introduced or expanded in the nation's parks. The more innovative projects and programs provided bragging rights for the states concerned and gave rise to the "show-and-tell" sessions that were a standard feature of the NASPD meetings during the 1970s and early 1980s. The race was now on, it seemed, to see which of the states could be the most creative.

Upgraded campsites were added in vast numbers to accommodate the booming camping demand, made ever more sophisticated by the variety of new recreational vehicles and other apparently indispensable amenities the industry turned out. In some cases, camping clearly came to dominate rather than complement the parks. In Michigan, for instance, one of the nation's leaders in state park camping, the forty-five-acre Traverse City State Park alone supports a total of 342 campsites. Linear activities such as hiking, horseback riding, mountain biking, and even rollerblading prompted a great expansion of trails of every kind in response. Similarly, aquatic facilities from simple boat ramps to full-service marinas were constructed in growing numbers to cater to the increasing popularity and diversity of water sports. Ohio moved way out front in this category, with forty-two marinas in its seventy-three state parks.

Except in degree of magnitude, the above developments did not represent a departure from the standard state park fare of the time. But they were just the beginning. With equal momentum, along came a proliferation of user-oriented facilities such as playing fields of every sort, golf courses (regulation and miniature), petting zoos, skeet ranges, swimming pools, and even water slides, wave-generators, and snow-making machines. Not all states followed the same pattern, of course, and the degree of emphasis on certain activities varied greatly. Golf courses, for instance, are not a major feature of state parks generally, but New York stands out as a principal advocate of that particular activity, operating twenty-eight courses at nineteen of its parks.

No one has ever counted, but probably at least half of the state parks today

An absence of surf or snow is no impediment where wave generators or snow-making machines can be installed. Such artificially provided recreational opportunities open the door to new possibilities for state park use. MISSISSIPPI DEPARTMENT OF WILDLIFE, FISHERIES AND PARKS

have incorporated some type of artificial, user-oriented facilities to diversify their recreational offerings and enhance their visitor appeal. Some parks, such as Nebraska's Eugene T. Mahoney State Park, have been developed almost entirely around such man-made recreational facilities. This may be a deliberate alternative in some cases (as with Mahoney Park), necessitated by having a site with few undisturbed natural assets to work with; but in other instances gratuitous placement of user-oriented facilities (even such seemingly innocuous ones as swimming pools and ball fields) can seriously detract from the natural qualities of the area they occupy.

New York, ever the innovator, took the user-oriented approach to the ultimate by creating an almost totally artificial environment for its Riverbank State Park in Manhattan. That unique park occupies the twenty-eight-acre rooftop of a sewage treatment plant on the Hudson River, complete with athletic building, cultural center, skating rinks, swimming pools, a carousel, and a riverfront restaurant. And in a minor concession to "Mother Nature," a few real trees and lawns also were included. As a novel adaptation of an unorthodox recreational setting, Riverbank State Park is a tribute to human imagination and ingenuity; as a *state park,* however, its only distinguishing characteristic may be the signs identifying it as such.

Overnighting in Comfort

Of all the trends involving the physical development of state park properties over the past quarter-century or so, probably the most noteworthy are those having to do with overnight accommodations—especially the upscale variety so common in state parks today. No one doubts the importance of an overnight stay as an integral part of the park experience. This has been recognized at least since Olmsted, Muir, and Mather camped out under the big trees of California generations ago. Campsites, modest cabins, and rustic lodges have been a feature of some state parks dating back to the days of Lieber, Welch, and Sauers. Ample precedents already existed by the time the CCC perfected the art of designing and constructing such park-enhancing facilities during the 1930s. Many of those handsome structures, in fact, survive today to remind us of the great contribution they make to the enjoyment of a park visit.

But if it's possible to have too much of a good thing, some of the state park systems today may be pushing the limit where overnight accommodations are concerned. The CCC may be fairly cited for whetting the appetite, but, for the most part, the cabins and lodges the CCC constructed in state parks were carefully designed and sited to blend with their natural settings. Similarly, their numbers and sizes were scaled appropriately for the specific parks in which they were located. In these important aspects, the CCC facilities were true to the theory of public parks—that their primary purpose is to respond to the legitimate recreation needs of the citizenry they serve. A better example than that could not have been hoped for, but, regrettably, it would not prevail in the years to come. Rather than serving legitimate recreation need, stoking the area economy or increasing park revenues would become the driving force behind ever more elaborate state park developments.

Stephen Mather himself had advanced the idea years before in promoting the lodges at such parks as Yosemite and Yellowstone: If you build them fancy enough, the well-heeled visitors will come. He was proved right, of course, even before the automobile age had hit full stride—and the concept would be enthusiastically resurrected by some of the states several decades later.

Kentucky led the way. It started building resort-type facilities as early as 1942 with the reconstruction of a fire-destroyed CCC lodge at Cumberland Falls, and by the mid-1940s, by its own acknowledgment, "the state park system's focus had swung to overnight accommodations."[1] Kentucky went on to construct seventeen "state resort parks" of varying sizes and degrees of elaborateness, making it clearly the leading exponent of this particular state park genre.

Other states pursued a similar course, although not nearly to the same extent. The concept has been particularly popular in the South, where Alabama, Arkansas, Georgia, Oklahoma, Tennessee, and West Virginia have developed several resort parks each; but the Midwest states of Illinois, Indiana, and Ohio also have made it an important aspect of their park systems. California and New York, too, operate several lodges apiece, but they are relatively minor in terms of their overall programs.

A lodge by itself does not a "resort park" make, of course, but it is usually considered the central component of such a facility. The idea is to create a major, self-contained vacation destination capable of drawing visitors from great distances and for extended stays. In addition to the lodge (also variously called inns or hotels), the typical resort park will also have such amenities as a golf course, tennis courts, swimming pools, restaurants, a marina, and occasionally even its own landing strip for private aircraft.

1. Ney C. Landrum, ed., *Histories of the Southeastern State Park Systems,* 61.

Because the resort business is a highly competitive one, the parks have to be aggressive in attracting and holding an adequate share of the market. Conventions and other group functions have become an almost indispensable part of the clientele mix, and elaborate meeting facilities have been added in some cases to support such functions—not always in harmony with the rest of the park. In all of the numerous resort parks that I have seen, though, commendable efforts have been made to maintain a parklike ambience through careful landscaping and the retention of adequate natural buffer areas.

Although lodges and the resort parks they support are more attention-getting because of their scale and visual impact, the addition of cabin or cottage accommodations in state parks has increased at an even greater rate in recent decades. Cabins cost less, are more adaptable to the landscape, and offer a wider range of configurations than a multiple-unit lodge. They may also be easier to rent. With so many practical advantages and a long association with primitive or "backwoods" living, it stands to reason that they would be a popular option for state

Resort parks that cater to a comfort-seeking tourist clientele are a major aspect of state park development in some states. With such facilities as this one at Dale Hollow Lake State Resort Park, Kentucky has pursued this approach to the fullest. KENTUCKY DEPARTMENT OF PARKS

park accommodations. Today, only five states have no cabins at all in their park systems. Most modern cabins, however, are a far cry from the rustic structures of the CCC era, and their architecture does not blend nearly so well with their park environments.

Taken together, the construction of new lodges, cabins, and improved camp-sites has been probably the most striking aspect of state park physical develop-ment in recent decades—this during a time when the commercial hospitality industry, particularly the private campgrounds, was also expanding with equal vigor. Between 1980 and 2000, America's state parks added 2,328 lodge rooms (up 59 percent), 2,615 cabins (up 65 percent) and 40,501 improved campsites (up 33 percent). Except on a case-by-case basis, it might be inappropriate to question the need for or the compatibility of these new facilities. But during the same twenty-year period, overnight visitation of the state parks remained almost flat, rising less than 4 percent, from 62,284,000 to 64,547,000. The reader may draw his own conclusion as to whether all of these additional accommodations were constructed in response to *legitimate recreation need.*

Visitor Programs—Enhancing the Park Experience

For sure, many changes were taking place on the state parks landscape during these years—some of them in the "more of the same" category, as with the nu-merous overnight facilities, and others more innovative, like a "rooftop" park in New York. But along with these physical improvements, possibly of even greater importance was the revolution taking place in the provision of visitor programs. In their infinite variety and appeal, visitor programs truly provide the extra di-mension that gives depth and substance to an otherwise static park experience.

Visitor programs in state parks were not exclusively the product of the late twentieth century, but it was during this period that they flourished in a variety of new and exciting forms. Previously, such programs had been limited largely to the straight interpretation of natural and historical sites and phenomena, which was considered important to the understanding, and therefore the enjoyment, of those special park values. In time, though, a twofold realization would broaden the thinking on such matters and open up a world of new opportunities for the use of state parks.

First, there was a practical consideration: with a fixed park landbase filling up with people looking for something to do, it seemed reasonable that a broader range of programs to engage the visitors might help ease the problem. At the same time, it became apparent that many of the people coming into the parks really did not have the knowledge or experience necessary to take full advantage of the recreational opportunities available. By providing a little basic instruction on how to participate in park activities, that problem could be alleviated as well.

Visitor programming is essentially a cross between education and entertainment, often more one than the other. The more the parks got into it, the more they liked it—and the variations on the theme multiplied. "Show-and-tell" sessions at the NASPD meetings in time contained as many presentations on new programs as on new facilities. Effective visitor programs, everyone agreed, could truly bring a park to life.

Depending on the park and the season of the year, a park visitor might learn about camp cooking, fishing or castnetting, snorkeling, skiing, orienteering, or various other participatory recreation skills—or, alternatively, simply enjoy a campfire talk or a knapping (arrowhead-making) demonstration. Interpretation—the original park program—was not ignored but took on new forms. One of the most common, and most popular, was "living history" presentations. Dressed in period costume and using appropriate methods and equipment, park staff and volunteers literally replayed the history of the significant events associated with their parks.

As they entered the final quarter of the twentieth century, America's state parks were indeed changing—simply reinforcing proven practices on the one hand and testing a variety of new ones on the other. But even as they were confidently looking ahead to a promising future, unforeseeable trouble was looming on the horizon. A temporary national economic crisis with lingering repercussions would soon alter, perhaps permanently, the ability of state parks to compete successfully with other public services for an appropriate share of their state's financial resources. Relatively speaking, America's state parks were about to go from riches to rags.

A Whole New Ball Game

The year 1973 began optimistically enough. "Peace with honor" had been negotiated in Vietnam, and the American people looked forward hopefully to the return of better times. But in October the Organization of Petroleum Exporting Countries muddied the water again by abruptly cutting off oil shipments to the United States. The embargo, which lasted until the following April, threw the whole country into a major tizzy and seriously disrupted its

Visitor programs of wide variety are a common feature in today's state parks. Those that involve military exercises and reenactments, such as this one at Maryland's Fort Frederick State Park, are among the most popular. MARYLAND DEPARTMENT OF NATURAL RESOURCES

economy for more than a decade. Runaway inflation during most of that time played havoc with everybody's finances, and state governments suffered along with the rest. Tightened purse strings inevitably would put an especially hard squeeze on state park programs.

The most immediate impact was felt in the dire shortage of gasoline, and the state parks responded by implementing strict conservation measures, such as a drastic reduction in the use of mowers and heavy equipment. But that would prove to be just a petty annoyance compared with the hard times to come. Although appropriations for state parks on the whole continued to rise in total dollars, the declining purchasing power of available funds made it difficult to keep up with inflated costs. Some states suffered more than others, of course, but all increasingly felt the pinch as the economic malaise continued.

Because of their day-to-day operational requirements, parks were among the first to feel the effects of tightened budgets. Unlike some government programs, they could not shelve or even defer their responsibilities without immediate consequences. If the parks were to remain open for public use, some serious adjustments would have to be made. The easiest means of relief was to put construction projects on hold; even if those funds could not readily be transferred to the operating budget, at least there would be that much less physical plant to maintain. Beyond that, however, the problem got really sticky and sent park directors scrambling, first, for quick solutions, then, for *any* solution. What ensued over the next dozen or so years speaks volumes about the resiliency, adaptability, and resourcefulness of state park directors with their backs to the wall.

Very few, if any, of the nation's state park systems were accustomed to being funded at what they would consider adequate levels. Most had long ago learned how to make do with lean budgets by dint of hard work and good economy. But while that conditioning surely helped, it could not fully prepare them for the austerity mode necessitated by the faltering national economy in the mid-1970s. After the initial shock waves subsided, though, the parks did what they had to do: find ways to keep operating with less money, even in the face of growing doubt and uncertainty about prospects for quick recovery.

In many states, budgets were cut or partly frozen almost immediately. This left little time to consider the options and make retrenchment plans in an orderly, systematic way. The result in some cases bordered on temporary chaos, but in time things began to settle down to a familiar, if still unwelcome, routine. The less critical maintenance projects and equipment purchases were put on hold. Dozens of entire parks were closed; hundreds were shut down in part or for certain periods of time. Shorter operating hours were instituted to economize on staff and operating funds. Many programs and services, such as interpretation and lifeguards, were scaled back or eliminated altogether. The number of park employees laid off, full-time as well as seasonal, ran into the thousands. To make matters worse, the supply of temporary workers from various federal employment programs, such as the Young Adult Conservation Corps and the Comprehensive Employment and Training Act, also was sharply curtailed. No matter where you looked, it was not a pretty sight.

Such painful adjustments would continue, to a lessening degree, even into the 1990s and beyond, necessitated from time to time by the erratic effects of a volatile and unpredictable economy. But it did not take park administrators long—especially with vigorous prodding from their legislatures and budget offices—to realize that some permanent retooling would be necessary as well to offset the impact of lost program funding. With the instability brought on by recent economic events, it was clear that the good old days of relying largely on regular general appropriations for support of the state parks were not likely to return. From that point on, the financial fate of America's state parks would lie, to a very great extent, in their own hands.

Whatever It Takes

All of the states were not affected equally, of course. Some suffered immediately with the first oil shortages and skyrocketing prices; in other cases, it took several years for the brunt of the recession to hit. And, depending on their economic base, some recovered fairly quickly while others must have thought that happy days would never return. Where state parks were concerned, however, the relative severity of the recession made little difference in the strategies adopted for stabilizing their funding base. In almost every instance, those strategies ultimately were founded on the assumption that the parks themselves could pick up a large part of their own tab. This was not entirely a new idea, of course; most state park systems had been helping to pay their own way for years. But the scope and extent of the revenue-generating measures now envisioned would far exceed anything that had ever been tried before.

"A period of sharp discontinuity with established policies places a special premium on the capacity of park systems to respond creatively to change," concluded the Conservation Foundation in its 1986 report on how the state parks were dealing with a "new era" of less money and increased demands.[2] Translated, I think that means that as the situation gets worse, the incentive to do something about it increases. It was a valid premise: The situation did get worse, and the responses to it came quickly and in a variety of forms, some more helpful than others.

Faced with the prospect of static or even declining general revenue support for parks, many states turned their attention to possible new funding sources earmarked specifically for their park programs. The concept was not exactly new; such dedicated sources had already been tried in some states years before. Florida, for instance, had enacted a sporting goods tax in 1963 that was earmarked for parks and related purposes and had replaced that with a more lucrative real estate transfer tax in 1967. Maryland followed with a similar approach a year or so later. Other precedents were available in the earmarking of nonpark revenues (such as cigarette and fuel taxes) for retirement of bonds. But as the debilitating effects of continuing retrenchment took their toll, interest in exploring alternative funding sources for state parks intensified accordingly.

2. Myers and Reid, *State Parks in a New Era*, ix.

Many approaches were tried. Arkansas, North Carolina, and several other states adopted their own versions of a real estate transfer tax; Colorado, Arizona, and a few others earmarked some portion of their state lotteries; Alabama, California, Nebraska, and Texas tapped state tobacco taxes; Missouri pulled off something of a coup in 1984 with passage of a public referendum authorizing a small increase in its sales tax for park and related purposes.[3] Most of these measures proved successful, and over time the resulting revenues steadily increased both in total and as a percentage of the state park budgets. Early figures are incomplete and unreliable, but by the year 2000 dedicated funding sources were producing some $330 million, representing 16 percent of total state park expenditures.

Despite the welcome relief in the form of new dedicated funds, the financial situation of the state parks was still dire. Park agencies were being told, in effect, that they themselves would have to take up much of the slack and help see to their own salvation. It was a challenge that they would ably meet, but in doing so it would change the focus, and ultimately the character, of the state park movement itself.

The choice between scaling back their programs or raising more money was an easy one for most state park administrators. Having labored diligently to build a first-class park system, they were not about to let it go down the drain if they could help it—so they turned their attention to the second alternative: generating revenue. Among the various money-making options available to them, the quickest and easiest obviously was to raise their fees.

Most states levied a small charge for entering their parks, and all of them charged for certain services and activities, such as camping and other types of overnight use. In most cases, park administrators were in a position to initiate, if not actually institute, changes to their fee schedules, and they yielded readily to pressure to do so. Some of the states where there was still political resistance to charging entrance fees reluctantly reconsidered, and a few simply dodged the issue by imposing a vehicle parking fee instead.

In the end, a handful of states stuck with their free-entry policies, but almost all of the others began hiking their prices, mostly in modest increments. Between 1980 and 2000, entrance fees jumped from an average of $0.55 to $2.00 for individuals and from $2.00 to $3.67 for passenger vehicles. Other fees were raised proportionately; the average cost of a two-hookup (water and electric) campsite,

---

3. For a more detailed look at state park funding practices and innovations, see the Conservation Foundation's three-volume report, *State Parks in a New Era*, by principal author Phyllis Myers.

for instance, went from $7.40 to $15.77, and that of a typical state park cabin from $44.00 to $81.00.

In spite of complaints about not being able "to see the forest for the *fees*," neither the initial fees nor the increases over the twenty-year period could fairly be characterized as price gouging. Entrance fees and parking fees in every case were kept modest enough to avoid discouraging anyone, regardless of economic status, from using the parks. The cost of renting a campsite, cabin, or other park lodging, although necessarily much higher, also was kept at a reasonable level for the quality of accommodations provided. A few states, though, must have felt they were competing with Hiltons rather than Holiday Inns, the way they kept scaling up their facilities and elevating prices commensurately (at the high end, almost four hundred dollars per night for a cabin, three hundred for a lodge room!).[4]

But while most of the price adjustments seemed relatively mild individually, their combined contribution to total park revenues was substantial. Revenue from entrance fees alone jumped from about $20 million in 1975 to almost $60 million in 1985 and to $150 million by 2000. For all park-regulated fee activity (including use of swimming pools, golf courses, and so on, in addition to general admission and rental of overnight accommodations), the revenue totals increased from about $95 million in 1975 to $195 million in 1985, and to right at $500 million in 2000. Much of this increase was due to concurrent increases in visitation, of course. Even so, considering that total attendance went up by just 39 percent over that twenty-five-year span while revenues increased by 426 percent, it is obvious that fee adjustments did indeed have a substantial impact on revenues.

But upscaling facilities and raising fees was just part of the revenue-enhancement game. Practically every state park system and even many of the individual parks were tasked to find ways to generate more income, even as they were also diligently seeking to institute new cost-cutting measures. In at least one state the situation got so dire that neighboring parks found themselves competing with each other for the same potential visitors in order to jack up their revenue totals. In some cases, unneeded, often out-of-place facilities such as redundant gift shops and vending machines were hastily installed in state parks for the purpose of providing additional income.

Numerous states turned to the private sector as a possible solution. New con-

4. All data on state park fees are from National Association of State Park Directors, *Annual Information Exchange*.

cession operations of a more commercial nature were launched in many parks, not always with satisfactory results. "Outsourcing" of certain activities and services (such as grounds maintenance, garbage collection, and lifeguarding) became almost a universal practice on the assumption that private contractors could do the job more cheaply than the parks themselves. A few states even turned over the operation of major facilities or entire parks to private enterprise. In time, private capital would be courted for increasingly larger park development projects as a means of offsetting the decline in construction budgets, and some states would actively seek "corporate partners," or sponsors, to fund a variety of projects and programs, usually with some form of corporate recognition as the quid pro quo.

Companies that pitch their products to park users, along with others that simply wanted to enhance their civic image, were prime targets for such partnerships. Michigan apparently was the first to test the concept in a major way, cutting a deal with Pepsi to make it "the official state park soft drink." New York was quick to follow, negotiating a similar arrangement with Pepsi rival Coca-Cola. Maryland, New Jersey, and other states tried such approaches on a more limited scale and with varying degrees of success.

By the 1990s, it seemed that practically every state park system was caught up in the near frenzy to turn a few more dollars through various forms of park-related commercial enterprises. Almost all had retail shops in their parks, and some had branched out with their own line of products, mail-order catalogs, Internet sales, and even remote outlets in such places as shopping malls. Many had hired full-time marketing directors and staffs to plan and coordinate a range of entrepreneurial activities. In the urgent push to keep the state parks open to the public, come what may, it seemed that no reasonable prospect for generating needed revenue was beyond consideration.

Turning in a different direction, states began looking for more help from non-commercial sources as well. Some entered into cooperative arrangements with local governments or nonprofit organizations to share the burden of operating certain parks. Hard times also gave rise to new volunteer programs and citizen support groups that aided the parks in a variety of ways. Volunteers working directly in the parks took up much of the slack left by staff layoffs, and when organized and focused they could be especially useful in raising funds and lobbying on behalf of the state parks. California's pioneering state parks foundation, launched in 1968, was particularly successful in such efforts and served as a model that other states copied, but none, unfortunately, with comparable results.

Gift shops and other commercial facilities have become increasingly elaborate in many state parks in efforts to generate more revenue to offset worsening budget shortfalls. PHOTOGRAPH BY THE AUTHOR

Unusual circumstances had demanded unusual responses, and the state parks administrators came through with flying colors. Faced with the need—and the mandate—to raise more money to alleviate their worsening budget woes, they had tried just about everything that was legally and politically permissible. The proof of their effectiveness is in the numbers. Between 1975 and 1980, the state parks increased their operating revenues by 219 percent, from $56,596,000 to $180,574,000, and their cost-recovery rate (ratio of revenues to operating expenditures) from 18 percent to 36.5 percent. By 2000, these figures would climb to $677,911,000 and 41.6 percent, respectively. The state parks had succeeded as entrepreneurs probably beyond anyone's expectations.

Facing a New Reality

The economic chaos triggered by the OPEC oil embargo in 1973 seriously disrupted the orderly progress of America's state parks and turned them on their ears. But the whole nation was similarly affected, and the parks would have to weather the storm along with everyone else. Surely, in a few years things would return to normal and the parks would resume business as usual. But it was not to be. The parks had proved themselves remarkably efficient in responding to the exigencies of the time, and it was that very efficiency that, for all practical purposes, changed the way state parks would operate thereafter. They had, in a very real sense, become victims of their own success.

It took a while, but the economy did recover. In fact, it did surprisingly well, with two prolonged "boom" periods in the 1980s and 1990s, broken only by a relatively short stock market slump in 1987. With the worst now over, it might ordinarily be expected that the nation's state park programs would revert to their prerecession status. In the state budget offices and legislative halls, though, the number crunchers had other ideas: If the state parks could raise so much revenue so readily under emergency conditions, they no doubt could do even better in normal times. Instead of relief, state park agencies were met with expectations that they would continue to generate an ever-increasing share of their operating budgets.

In time, more than a third of the states would adopt policies formally requiring their state parks to raise a stipulated amount of revenue or percentage of their budgets. Others would operate under a tacit understanding that they were expected to do likewise. New Hampshire is one of the more extreme examples. After operating at or near self-sufficiency for years—and even turning over surpluses to the general fund on occasion—New Hampshire state parks were mandated by legislative act in 1991 to go it alone financially, but with the proviso that surpluses might now be retained in a nonlapsing fund for park use only. Vermont's experience was similar. It was cut loose by legislative act in 1992 but was allowed to continue receiving additional revenues from private ski areas operated on state-owned lands.

Neither New Hampshire's nor Vermont's situation is really typical, however. Both are relatively specialized vacation destinations where much of their park revenue is derived from the more affluent visitors who can afford to pay well for value received. Other states, especially those with larger programs and more diverse populations, may find the going a lot tougher, though, and usually set their revenue targets somewhat lower. Even so, South Carolina shoots for 65 percent, Kansas for 70 percent, Oregon for 75 percent, and Michigan for 80 percent of their respective operating budgets. Texas has been cut off entirely from general revenue support and is seeking to become "a financially self-supporting organization," albeit with the help of some nonoperating revenue sources. The important point to be made here is that, even under much improved economic conditions, practically every state park system in the country is still expected to carry a substantial part of its own financial weight—almost without regard to the means employed.

Not everybody, in fact, was unhappy about this turn of events. The arguments for park fees and revenue generation have been going on since California let the first private concessionaires into Yosemite Valley. Indiana's Richard Lieber spoke frequently on behalf of financial self-sufficiency for state parks—even as he was cautioning against the "destructive hand of commercialism."[5] Everyone, it seems, concedes the necessity for park-generated income, but the questions of how much and at what sacrifice of park quality will never be resolved to everyone's satisfaction. What is now clear, though, is that the recession-altered fiscal climate of the past quarter-century has made it eminently easier to justify purely commercial ventures in the state parks. In explaining how various revenue-producing facilities were selected for his state parks, the director of one large system told the *Wall Street Journal:* "We make decisions based strictly on the numbers."[6]

Aggravating the situation are misguided arguments such as those put forth by the Montana-based Political Economy Research Center. PERC advocates a free-market approach not only for the state parks, but for the national parks as well, requiring them to set their fees at the level necessary to make the parks financially self-supporting. To accomplish this, individual park managers would be allowed to adjust their own fees as necessary and to retain and use the proceeds as they see fit. In other words, each park would become an essentially independent business venture in itself, with few checks or controls to inhibit it.[7] Such specious ideas miss the point of having a *public* park system in the first place, and, if actually implemented, could do great violence to the concept of maintaining a balanced park system (including areas with no revenue-producing potential) readily accessible to all people (the deprived as well as the affluent).

But just as there are those who applaud the efforts to make the state parks more self-supporting, there are others who view the trend with great apprehension. Typical of the latter is author William Lowry, a longtime observer of both national and state parks, who makes no bones about his concern: "Parks in many

5. Richard Lieber, "Major Problems of Park Management," address delivered to the National Conference on State Parks annual meeting, Clifty Falls State Park, Ind., May 7–9, 1929, in Board of Directors Papers, series 3, box 1, NRPA Library.

6. Terzam Ewing, "Meet the New Entrepreneurs: State Parks."

7. Donald R. Leal and Holly Lippke Fretwell, "Back to the Future to Save Our Parks."

states have become more expensive to visit and less natural as park managers increasingly focus on generating enough revenue to stay in business."[8] Much of the popular press has noted the increasing entrepreneurialism in state parks as well, but no one has yet come forth with a convincing case for the only reasonable alternative: restoring general government funding support.

State parks today desperately need some eloquent champions to help reestablish some fundamental truths. State parks are not a business; they do not exist to make money. State parks are priceless areas of selected real estate set aside in perpetual trust to provide an essential public service: to satisfy the human need for connection with the natural world and with events of the past that have shaped today's cultural environment. In this regard, they are just as important as schools, highways, and other public services that rightly draw on the state treasury for their financial support. But in the case of state parks, there is one very important difference: as schools and highways wear out, they can simply be replaced in kind; but the state parks of today are likely to be the state parks for all time, and they must be protected and managed with a careful eye to the obligations they hold for future generations as well. The primary object of good state park management must always be the well-being of the parks' resources—both natural and cultural—and not to make the parks economically competitive and financially self-supporting.

A Somber Assessment

From the look of things, the situation in which America's state parks now find themselves may likely get worse before it gets better. If any of the state park directors are disturbed by the obvious trend toward increasing commercialization of the state parks, they seem to have been reluctant (no doubt for valid political reasons) to speak out. More likely, they have simply become inured to a situation they feel cannot be helped; or, because the directorships in every state have turned over one or more times since the mid-1970s, the current directors may just assume that the course they inherited is the preferred way to go. Then, there are undoubtedly some who really feel parks should be run as a business (even a profit-making business) and are motivated by maintaining a healthy bottom line on the financial statement (which, after all, is a lot easier to demonstrate than the intrinsic health of such a complex organism as a state park).

8. William R. Lowry, "Nature under Siege," 9.

Whatever the reasons, whether defensible or not, there clearly is too much emphasis still being placed on the development and management of state park systems for the purpose of generating revenue. As this is being written, my own state of Florida is making plans to add 140 cabins to the 117 it presently has in its state parks. Fifty of the new cabins will be placed in one, little-used park of only modest recreational potential. Surely it is more than coincidence that this park happens to lie almost at the doorstep of Walt Disney World!

Responsibility for this situation must be shared up and down the line—from the legislatures to the governors to the directors, and sometimes even to the individual park managers themselves. But even if some, perhaps many, should admit to a growing concern in this area, it still would be difficult in today's circumstances to buck the trend toward increasing artificiality and commercialism in America's state parks. The evolving culture that tolerates, even encourages, this new approach to resource-based park utilization will first have to change.

Some years ago, the U.S. National Park Service was asked to prepare a special symposium for the International Union for Conservation of Nature and Natural Resources, at its Fourth World Congress on Parks and Protected Areas held in Caracas, Venezuela, in 1992. The subject of the symposium was "Revenue Enhancement and Cost Recovery for Protected Areas." Considering that it was recovering only about 7 percent of its operating costs at the time, the NPS must have wondered about its qualifications for the assignment. So, what did it do? It turned to the acknowledged experts on the subject—America's state parks. Accommodatingly, the NASPD assembled a four-person team to put on a program for that distinguished international audience. The symposium was deemed a complete success, but the point of the story is this: Of all the areas of park expertise for which America's state parks might rightly be acknowledged, it is sad to think that they may now be known to much of the world only for their ability to make money.

16

Looking to the Future
The View from One Observer's Soapbox

Getting Back to Basics

America's state park movement was essentially a product of the twentieth century. Although the seeds had been sown long before, the idea really took root
with the scattered initiatives of the early 1900s. Brought together and given direction by the National Conference on State Parks in the 1920s, the emerging state
park programs were then energized and molded by the federal aid programs of
the 1930s. By midcentury the movement was well-established, and after a few
decades it had achieved a degree of independence and stability that hinted of maturity. Much had been accomplished during that time, and the country was truly
the better for it.

But the state parks today face another identity crisis. For all the good that they
do, as a whole they seem to lack a clear sense of purpose and direction. The
nationwide movement that sustained and guided them for so long has largely
dissipated, no longer serving as a central, unifying force. In its stead are the fifty
individual state park programs it helped beget, each with its own unique traditions and its own agenda for the future.

It would be inaccurate, of course, to imply that all of the state park programs
had come from a common mold and were only now beginning to express their individuality. Clearly, that was not the case. In fact, some evolved so differently from
the rest that they likely were never part of a national movement in the first place.

But the situation that now exists—with each state seeing state parks through
its own specially colored lenses—makes it increasingly difficult to judge their
overall effectiveness and to anticipate the course they might take in the years
ahead. If state parks are to serve some consistent function in each state, and work

in concert with other public park programs to ensure that the people's legitimate needs for outdoor recreation are met, then where are the initiative and the guidance to come from that will orchestrate this overall effort?

No single state can claim leadership authority, and no one school of thought is likely to prevail. The states are simply too different, and the policies and procedures they have adopted for their parks have become entrenched from many years of doing things a certain way. Experience has shown, for instance, that new state park directors—especially those promoted from within the agency—are generally inclined to accept and continue the policies of their immediate predecessors rather than to question the status quo and explore other options. Although there is still much contact and communication among state park administrators—possibly more than ever—the prevailing attitude today is one of "doing it my way," which, in turn, conduces to even greater isolation and divergence among the state park programs.

Given the circumstances, not everyone is likely to agree that the fifty state park programs should be defined by certain common criteria and orchestrated in a way to promote a common purpose. But if that is not done, at least to an appropriate degree, those fifty programs will continue to ply their individual courses with no substantive basis for measuring their progress against any established norms. There will be no accepted model for what an effective park program should look like, and no way of determining success except internally through whatever means a particular state might decide best serves its purposes. Unfortunately, that is likely to be based only on some statistical measure, such as the numbers of parks operated or of visitors accommodated—and that would be about as useful as determining the success of the state's education program by how many school buildings it has, or how many students there are in the classrooms.

As they reassess their relevance and their ability to meet the recreational needs of their future citizens, state park agencies need to go back to the basics—at least long enough for an honest self-evaluation. And that evaluation should begin with a hard look at the purpose their state parks are intended to serve, and a critical check of their own policies and procedures to see if they truly support the state park goals they have set for themselves.

Reaffirming the Fundamental State Park Mission

If there is any one factor that should unite the fifty state park programs, it would be in the legitimate public purpose they are all trying to serve. But, given the diversity of opinion reflected in their mission statements, what *is* the most fundamental purpose of a state park system?

In the beginning, individual state parks were established purely and simply to preserve specific pieces of real estate that contained some special value, either natural or cultural. That limited purpose was expanded significantly through the promotional efforts of the NCSP, which envisioned systems of state parks located at suitable distance intervals to provide relatively easy access for the masses of people who were not able to visit the larger and more grandiose national parks, found mostly in the West.

The national parks, still relatively new and few in number, offered a type of recreational experience vastly different from that of the more numerous and familiar city parks. By providing similar types of recreational opportunities, then, the state parks could serve as close-to-home substitutes for the national parks and provide a complementary alternative to the city parks. Filling that void between the outdoor recreational offerings of the national parks and those of the city parks thus became a major goal, and it is still a valid—probably the *most* valid—purpose that state parks can serve today.

Needed: A National System of Parks

But if there is a clear-cut role for state parks, there must also be a corresponding assumption of responsibility by the federal and local governments for other important forms of public outdoor recreation. For years, the need to coordinate local, state, and federal park programs to effect a balanced "national system of parks" has been recognized as a top governmental priority. The nationwide outdoor recreation plan called for by the 1963 Outdoor Recreation Act was intended to provide a blueprint for such a system, but regrettably it never came to fruition. Much lip service—and even some sincere support—has been given to the continuing need for coordination ever since, but still no one has found a means to make it really work. At this writing, apparently serious discourse on the subject has been resumed at the federal level; it remains to be seen, however, if the idea will be more widely embraced and if the collective desire is strong enough to produce an effective plan of action.

Until a workable plan is actually adopted, though, each level of government must continue to do its own thing as best it can, with little or no coordination or comprehensive guidance. The federal government, being the monolithic behemoth that it is, will no doubt bull ahead with its plans and projects without regard to what anyone else might be doing. Meanwhile, the cities and other local governments—which have an almost exclusive responsibility for providing user-oriented recreation—will be less affected by the absence of coordination and therefore better able to proceed unilaterally.

That leaves the states squarely in the middle. If they wish to pursue the concept of a balanced, coordinated, intergovernmental park and open space program, it will have to be accomplished less by direct action than by *reaction*—informed, judicious reaction to the programs being independently implemented at the other levels of government. While this places a special onus on the states, it also gives them a unique opportunity: to create the vital central link that will make the "national system of parks" a working reality.

Absent any overall coordinating mechanism, the states can have very little direct influence on what happens on the national park and local park scenes. Therefore, the initiative they must exercise lies in planning their state park projects to supplement and complement—rather than duplicate or compete with—the projects at the other two levels. This is the only realistic way to ensure that the optimum range of outdoor recreation opportunities is made available to the American people, wherever they may live. All states should recognize this as a major, if not the primary, responsibility of their state park programs.

Bridging the Gap

The void, or "gap," that exists between the outdoor recreational offerings of the federal and local governments differs greatly from state to state, of course, depending on the degree of activity at the two abutting ends. Many of the more urban states in the East will have numerous well-developed, efficiently run local park programs, but little or no national park presence. Because the local parks will in most cases do a superb job of addressing the user-oriented recreation needs, state parks should direct their efforts toward providing alternative recreation opportunities of the resource-based type. The result will be less duplication and greater variety and balance in the public recreation programs of the states concerned—even without any national park contribution.

In the more rural states, especially in the West, just the opposite situation is likely to occur. Fewer population centers will mean fewer local park programs, but at the other extreme the people will be better served by the greater availability of national parks. In such cases, state parks might be fully justified in seeking to supplement local programs by providing more recreation areas close to the people.

The questions most likely to be raised here, of course, will have to do not so much with means or desire as with opportunity. Some of the smaller, densely populated states might argue that they simply do not have suitable natural areas available to support a predominantly resource-based park system. Conversely, sparsely populated states that already have large national parks might still prefer to create their own natural area state parks, even if duplicative, just because they have abundant scenic resources available to them.

Obviously, each state must sort out these issues for itself, but the important point is to seek a complementary balance among all public park efforts. However, because the distribution of the national parks is far more lopsided (93 percent of the acreage is in states west of the Mississippi River, with 65 percent in Alaska alone) than the spread of thriving local communities, it stands to reason that the preponderant effort of the state parks must be to augment the resource-based recreational offerings of the national park system.

The Task at Hand

America's state park movement today—if indeed it still exists as such—seems to have lost its sense of purpose, bereft of any cohesive identity and without a clear idea of where it should go. The fifty individual state park programs may each have their acts together internally, but collectively they are still something of a hodgepodge. No other function of state government is so amorphous and so malleable as state parks. Education, transportation, social services, and all the other programs may be pursued through different means, but they all have a definite, recognizable goal that all states seek to achieve. This is not necessarily the case with state parks—and it is unfortunate, because a strong nationwide consensus on purpose and direction would in turn lend strength and support to each of the state park programs individually.

This essential fact was fully recognized by Stephen Mather, Richard Lieber, Conrad Wirth, and the other stalwarts who guided the state park movement through its formative years in the 1920s and 1930s. Although many of their efforts to standardize and coordinate state park programs were not universally accepted, they nevertheless succeeded in providing a central purpose, structure, and momentum that materially advanced the state park cause throughout the country. The pity is that with the loss of its champions and its national leadership the whole movement has now lost much of its effectiveness. It is high time for that trend to be reversed.

Much has been made of the fact that the fifty states are all different, and that diversity itself may well be a source of strength overall. But where state parks are concerned, there are—or should be—definite similarities as well. The essential characteristics that define a "state park"—such as quality resources, competent stewardship, proportional and harmonious development, and appropriate user programs—should be guided by the same basic principles in every state. These core values are so important for keeping a state park program on track that they should be recognized as universal and timeless, and steadfastly defended as such.

This is not to say that every state park program has to follow an identical path—far from it. There are countless ways that states might continue to express their individuality. But for those essential aspects of state parks that all can agree upon (be they few or many), there is a critical need for general recognition, adoption, and adherence. Only through broad, unwavering acceptance and support can these "mainstream" principles be molded into a true state park tradition that will stand the test of time. Once firmly established, though, this tradition will prove of immeasurable value to future state park directors in helping them hold the line against unwise and unwarranted interference with sound park management.

What America's state parks need, in fact, is a sort of "academy" to define purposes and set standards for general consideration and guidance—through a collegial rather than an autocratic process. This exercise should be an essential responsibility of the state parks profession itself. Let's face it: Most politicians are not overly concerned with the future beyond their own tenures, and their actions are not always likely to be in the best long-range interest of the state parks program. Only by having some universally acknowledged, fundamental principles to back them up can a continuing succession of professional state park managers hope to keep their programs on a steady course to provide sustained, unimpaired, resource-based outdoor recreation potential for coming generations.

An Essential Role for NASPD

But how will anything so far-reaching be achieved without coordinated nationwide leadership? For lack of any other suitable entity, the National Association of State Park Directors must fill the breach, assuming the role long ago relinquished by the National Conference on State Parks. Heretofore, the NASPD has been reluctant even to consider getting involved in any undertaking that might smack of setting standards or promoting uniformity. Even the development of categories for reporting inventory data for the Annual Information Exchange was challenged by some directors on the grounds that it was an attempt to force all states to use a common classification system. Earlier efforts to revive the work of the NCSP committee on state park policies, and to commend for state park use the guidelines proposed by the Conservation Foundation for national parks, were ignored and forgotten. The NASPD obviously had little inclination to take on anything potentially controversial.

But the NASPD is stronger now than it ever has been. It has effective leadership, permanent staff support, and active participation by all fifty states. What is doesn't have, unfortunately, is a strong sense of mandate, or even of responsibility, for reviving and reinvigorating a dynamic, nationwide state park movement. Somewhere out there among the state parks fraternity there must be potential champions with a crusader's zeal and a reformer's impatience for action. Until they step forward, though, there is little hope that America's state park movement will ever be restored to its former position of influence and effectiveness.

A Final Word

No one can doubt the importance of the state parks as a major, even an indispensable, provider of outdoor recreation for the American people today. Their very popularity is evidence enough. Every one of the more than five thousand state park units serves a valid and worthwhile purpose in satisfying someone's desire for a new recreational experience. And who could argue with that? That is, after all, the ultimate purpose of all parks.

But over time the people's recreational interests change, and inevitably the state parks will change as well to cater to new activities and new patterns of use. In due course, parks that started out as relatively simple, minimally developed natural areas may undergo a complete transmogrification through the constant addition of new facilities and the introduction of new forms of play. Eventually, these parks may be recognizable less as true *recreation* areas, in the original sense of the term, than as mere places of idle *entertainment*. The extraordinary natural and cultural resources that justified creation of the state parks may be all but superseded by an artificially constructed environment like that of a recreational theme park such as Disneyland or Six Flags.

By preserving outstanding examples of an area's natural and cultural treasures, state parks will always remain the best hope for providing close-to-home, resource-based outdoor recreational opportunities for the American people. MISSOURI DEPARTMENT OF NATURAL RESOURCES

So, what is wrong with giving the people what they want? After all, as the expression goes, "parks are for people." The easy, if overly simplistic, answer is that nothing is wrong with allowing any park to provide the types of recreational opportunities *for which it was intended.*

State parks, though, are not "all-purpose" parks, and they were never intended to be adaptable to the whims of ephemeral or constantly changing recreational interests. They have their own special legacy and their own distinct purpose. They are founded on the essential principle of resource preservation and management to support certain forms of compatible outdoor recreation. As priceless specimens of an ever-diminishing resource base, they must not be appropriated and manipulated for the exclusive use of the people of today or of any particular time; they must instead be kept aesthetically and functionally intact for equivalent use and enjoyment by all generations yet to come.

It is in this context that the state parks of every state should be expected to acknowledge and adhere to certain absolute and inviolable principles common to them all. And it is for this reason that the nation's state park programs must con-

tinue to work together as a cohesive and coordinated body to preserve and per-
petuate the legacy, the traditions, and the spirit of the unique state park movement that made it all happen.

The park-loving people of America—both now and for generations to come—
surely deserve no less.

Appendix

Selected Data on America's State Parks

	First State Park	Established	Number of Parks*	Acreage*
Alabama	Cheaha	1933	24	49,710
Alaska	Nancy Lake	1966	140	3,325,939
Arizona	Tubac Presidio	1957	31	58,512
Arkansas	Petit Jean	1923	50	51,293
California	Big Basin Redwoods	1902	273	1,456,732
Colorado	Cherry Creek	1959	113	365,142
Connecticut	Sherwood Island	1914	132	200,458
Delaware	Trap Pond	1951	29	22,039
Florida	Olustee Battlefield	1909	151	591,525
Georgia	Indian Springs, Vogel	1925	70	81,218
Hawaii	Akaka Falls (and 5 others)	1952	67	28,002
Idaho	Heyburn	1908	32	44,643
Illinois	Fort Massac	1903	307	306,066
Indiana	McCormick's Creek	1916	33	178,937
Iowa	Backbone	1920	174	63,200
Kansas	Kanapolis	1955	24	32,300
Kentucky	Pine Mountain (and 3 others)	1926	49	44,290
Louisiana	Longfellow-Evangeline	1934	56	38,267
Maine	Aroostook	1938	127	96,686
Maryland	Patapsco	1922	51	266,136
Massachusetts	Mount Greylock	1898	238	293,821
Michigan	Mackinac Island	1895	102	284,977
Minnesota	Itasca	1891	133	267,209
Mississippi	LeRoy Percy	1934	28	24,287
Missouri	Bennett Spring, Mark Twain	1924	83	138,522
Montana	Lewis and Clark Caverns	1937	374	65,839

Total Attendance*	Operating Expenditures*	Cost Recovery* †	Type of Parent Agency*
5,163,113	$30,691,515	78.5%	envir/res mgt
4,282,770	5,612,862	34.7	envir/res mgt
2,410,383	17,039,500	17.7	parks/recreation
8,217,845	30,448,784	42.2	parks/tourism
85,664,789	333,541,000	21.4	parks/recreation
11,098,367	26,909,824	64.6	envir/res mgt
9,000,955	9,706,392	n/a	envir/res mgt
3,207,162	18,546,847	46.2	envir/res mgt
17,734,774	70,251,254	45.4	envir/res mgt
14,622,544	59,064,876	46.4	envir/res mgt
6,340,254	6,974,306	23.5	envir/res mgt
2,497,165	20,527,600	16.7	parks/recreation
43,623,029	55,466,200	12.6	envir/res mgt
16,878,651	42,591,798	78.7	envir/res mgt
15,439,316	10,130,987	33.4	envir/res mgt
7,990,560	7,210,985	69.3	wildlife/parks
7,872,625	83,318,707	66.6	parks/recreation
2,007,564	17,465,483	1.4	parks/tourism
2,554,006	7,227,666	n/a	envir/res mgt
10,339,575	45,580,644	31.4	envir/res mgt
11,883,637	31,829,335	9.1	envir/res mgt
25,296,650	53,836,422	51.4	envir/res mgt
8,075,641	30,297,000	24.9	envir/res mgt
4,224,669	15,289,067	43.5	wildlife/parks
17,760,077	30,204,161	15.1	envir/res mgt
1,219,191	6,039,946	20.8	wildlife/parks

Appendix

Continued

	First State Park	Established	Number of Parks*	Acreage*
Nebraska	Chadron	1921	85	134,200
Nevada	Cathedral Gorge, Valley of Fire	1925	24	132,524
New Hampshire	Miller	1891	89	84,547
New Jersey	Bass River	1905	116	376,532
New Mexico	Bottomless Lakes	1933	31	90,693
New York	Niagara Falls	1885	830	1,158,960
North Carolina	Mount Mitchell	1916	59	168,241
North Dakota	Fort Abraham Lincoln	1907	30	17,276
Ohio	Buckeye Lake (Licking Reservoir)	1894	74	204,557
Oklahoma	Lake Murray	1933	50	71,667
Oregon	Sarah Helmick	1922	231	95,463
Pennsylvania	Valley Forge	1893	119	289,362
Rhode Island	Lincoln Woods	1907	74	8,748
South Carolina	Cheraw	1934	55	80,459
South Dakota	Custer	1919	129	105,386
Tennessee	Harrison Bay	1938	53	144,013
Texas	San Jacinto Battleground	1883	124	668,269
Utah	Territorial State House	1957	46	114,532
Vermont	Mount Philo	1924	98	68,859
Virginia	George Washington's Grist Mill	1936	37	62,236
Washington	Larrabee	1915	259	262,134
West Virginia	Droom Mountain Battlefield	1929	47	195,831
Wisconsin	Interstate	1900	68	132,725
Wyoming	Hot Springs	1897	36	119,266
			5,655	13,162,230

*All statistical data are from NASPD Annual Information Exchange for the year 2002.
†Operating revenues as a percentage of operating expenditures

Total Attendance*	Operating Expenditures*	Cost Recovery* †	Type of Parent Agency‡
9,802,430	$19,731,584	56.1%	wildlife/parks
3,285,847	8,528,763	25.5	envir/res mgt
6,779,207	7,595,496	100.0	res mgt/econ
15,039,719	36,825,156	8.5	envir/res mgt
3,922,888	16,880,400	25.6	envir/res mgt
56,863,921	162,907,900	29.2	parks/recreation
12,758,396	31,176,142	11.9	envir/res mgt
1,096,666	2,644,221	41.7	parks/recreation
57,246,373	65,361,580	44.4	envir/res mgt
14,057,136	44,985,574	53.4	recreation/tourism
39,438,936	36,543,061	42.2	parks/recreation
36,627,267	79,808,000	21.2	envir/res mgt
7,269,823	5,719,235	n/a	envir/res mgt
8,150,521	23,969,797	69.0	parks/tourism
8,821,691	11,983,559	63.6	wildlife/parks
26,274,529	64,208,100	49.6	envir/res mgt
17,089,692	57,943,313	25.6	wildlife/parks
5,940,741	22,484,200	36.5	envir/res mgt
994,011	6,259,543	93.1	forests/parks
6,856,305	18,049,695	28.8	cons/recreation
48,864,376	43,316,651	23.6	parks/recreation
7,317,734	30,353,992	63.3	envir/res mgt
15,528,496	19,633,370	43.3	envir/res mgt
2,783,965	5,491,871	n/a	commerce
758,215,982	$1,888,204,364	35.9 avg.	

‡Major functions as reflected by agency title (cons=conservation; econ=economic development; envir=environmental protection; res mgt=resource management).

Selected Bibliography

Manuscript Collections

National Conference on State Parks Board of Directors Papers. Series 3, box 1, National Recreation and Park Association Library, Ashburn, Va.

National Conference on State Parks Minutes of Policy Making Bodies. Series 1 and 2, box 1, National Recreation and Park Association Library, Ashburn, Va.

Truncer, James. Collection (unprocessed). National Recreation and Park Association Library, Ashburn, Va.

U.S. Department of the Interior Library, Washington, D.C.

References

Albright, Horace M. "Stephen Tyng Mather." In *Park and Recreation Progress: 25th Anniversary Yearbook*. Washington: National Conference on State Parks, 1946.

Borke, Judith Joy. "Wisconsin's State Park System, 1878–1994: An Oral History." Master's thesis, University of Wisconsin–Madison, 1995.

Clawson, Marion. "The Crisis in Outdoor Recreation." Parts 1 and 2. *American Forests* 65, no. 3 (March 1959): 22–31, 40–42; no. 4 (April 1959): 28–35, 61–62.

———. *Land and Water for Recreation: Opportunities, Problems, and Policies*. Chicago: Rand McNally, 1963.

———. *New Deal Planning: The National Resources Planning Board*. Baltimore: Johns Hopkins University Press, 1981.

Conard, Rebecca. "The National Conference on State Parks: The Early Years." Paper presented at the annual meeting of the National Association of State Park Directors, Asheville, N.C., December 6, 1996. Reproduced.

———. "The National Conference on State Parks: Reflections on Organizational Genealogy." *George Wright FORUM* 14, no. 4 (1997): 28–41.

———. *Places of Quiet Beauty*. Iowa City: University of Iowa Press, 1997.

Cordell, H. Ken, principal investigator. *Outdoor Recreation in American Life: A National Assessment of Demand and Supply Trends*. Champaign, Ill.: Sagamore Publishing, 1999.

Cougill, Kenneth, chairman. National Conference on State Parks Committee on Suggested Criteria. "Suggested Criteria for Evaluating Areas Proposed for Inclusion in State Park Systems." *Planning and Civic Comment* 20, no. 4 (December 1954): 3–9.

Cox, Laurie D. "The Nature of State Parks and Parkways." In *American Planning and Civic Annual,* ed. Harlean James, 50–60. Washington: American Planning and Civic Association, 1948.

Cox, Thomas R. *The Park Builders.* Seattle: University of Washington Press, 1988.

Emergency Conservation, Director of. "Report[s] of the Director of Emergency Conservation Work." Washington: Government Printing Office, 1933–1941.

Engbeck, Joseph H., Jr. *State Parks of California from 1864 to the Present.* Portland, Oreg.: C. H. Belding, 1980.

Evison, Herbert S. "The Birth of State Parks." *Planning and Civic Comment* (December 1963): 5–12.

———. "National and State Parks in the Conservation Field." Address given at the Rhode Island Agricultural Conference, Providence, February 27, 1936. U.S. Department of the Interior Library (S 936, U5), Washington, D.C.

Evison, Herbert S., ed. *A State Park Anthology.* Washington, D.C.: National Conference on State Parks, 1930.

Ewing, Terzam. "Meet the New Entrepreneurs: State Parks." *Wall Street Journal,* February 11, 1997.

Fechner, Robert. "State Park Development under the Civilian Conservation Corps Program." In *American Planning and Civic Annual,* ed. Harlean James, 204–7. Washington: American Planning and Civic Association, 1937.

Federal Security Agency. *Conservation and Recreation.* Washington, D.C.: Government Printing Office, 1941.

Fifty Years: New York State Parks. Albany: National Heritage Trust, 1975.

Fitch, Edwin M., and John F. Shanklin. *The Bureau of Outdoor Recreation.* New York: Praeger Publishers, 1970.

Forrey, William C. *History of Pennsylvania State Parks.* Harrisburg: Pennsylvania Department of Natural Resources, 1984.

Foss, Phillip O. "Recreation." In *Conservation in the United States: A Documentary History,* ed. Frank E. Smith. New York: Chelsea House, 1971.

Harbaugh, William Henry. *Power and Responsibility: The Life and Times of Theodore Roosevelt.* New York: Farrar, Straus and Cudahy, 1961.

Harbaugh, William H., ed., *The Writings of Theodore Roosevelt.* Indianapolis: Bobbs-Merrill, 1967.

Ise, John. *Our National Park Policy: A Critical History.* Baltimore: Johns Hopkins University Press, 1961.

Kennedy, Sydney S., chairman, joint committee of the National Conference on State Parks, the American Institute of Park Executives, the National Recreation Association, and the National Park Service. "Suggested Policy Statement Relating to Development, Use, and Operation of State Parks." *Planning and Civic Comment* 21, no. 3 (September 1955): 57–60.

Kostyal, K. M. "America's State Parks: Ten of the Best." *National Geographic Traveler,* March/April 1994, 54–76.

Landrum, Ney C., ed., *Histories of the Southeastern State Park Systems.* Tallahassee, Fla.: Association of Southeastern State Park Directors, 1992.

———. "State Parks and Outdoor Recreation." In *The Book of the States,* vol. 22 (1978–1979): 501–4; vol. 23 (1980–1981): 518–22; vol. 24 (1982–1983): 615–19. Lexington, Ky.: Council of State Governments, 1978–1982.

Leal, Donald R., and Holly Lippke Fretwell. "Back to the Future to Save Our Parks." In *The Politics and Economics of Park Management,* ed. Terry L. Anderson and Alexander James, 43–67. Lanham, Md.: Rowman and Littlefield Publishers, 2001.

Lieber, Richard. Introduction to *Park and Recreation Progress: 1943 Yearbook.* Washington, D.C.: National Conference on State Parks, 1943.

Lowry, William R. "Nature Under Siege." *State Government News* (January 1995): 8–11.

Mackintosh, Barry. "The National Park Service." Unpublished research paper. Washington, D.C.: National Park Service, 1996.

Maryland State Board of Forestry. *Report for 1910 and 1911.* Annapolis: State of Maryland, 1911.

Mather, Stephen T. "The United States of America and Its Parks." Address presented at the National Conference on Parks, Des Moines, Iowa, January 10, 1921. Reprinted in *Iowa Conservation* 5, no. 1 (January–March 1921): 10–14.

McCurdy, Dwight R., and Larry K. Johnson. *Recommended Policies for the Development and Management of State Park Systems.* School of Agriculture Publication no. 26. Carbondale: Southern Illinois University, 1967.

Merriam, Lawrence C., Jr. *Oregon's Highway Park System, 1921–1989: An Administrative History.* Salem: Oregon Parks and Recreation Department, 1992.

Merrill, Perry H. *Roosevelt's Forest Army.* Montpelier, Vt.: n.p., 1981.

Meyer, Roy W. *Everyone's Country Estate.* St. Paul: Minnesota Historical Society Press, 1991.

Myers, Phyllis. *State Parks in a New Era.* Vol. 2, *Future Directions in Funding.* Washington: Conservation Foundation, 1989.

————. *State Parks in a New Era.* Vol. 3, *Strategies for Tourism and Economic Development.* Washington: Conservation Foundation, 1989.

Myers, Phyllis, and Sharon N. Green. *State Parks in a New Era.* Vol. 1, *A Look at the Legacy.* Washington, D.C.: Conservation Foundation, 1989.

Myers, Phyllis, and Ann Christine Reid. *State Parks in a New Era: A Survey of Issues and Innovations.* Washington, D.C.: Conservation Foundation, 1986.

Nadel, Michael. "Scenic, Historic, and Natural Sites." In *Origins of American Conservation,* ed. Henry Clepper, 160–67. New York: Ronald Press, 1966.

Nash, Roderick. *Wilderness and the American Mind.* New Haven: Yale University Press, 1967.

National Association of State Park Directors. *Annual Information Exchange.* Tucson, Ariz.: National Association of State Park Directors, 1978–2003.

National Conference on Outdoor Recreation. *Proceedings of the National Conference on Outdoor Recreation.* 68th Cong., 1st sess., 1924. S. Doc. 151.

National Conference on Parks. "Organization and Proceedings of the First National Conference on Parks, Des Moines, Iowa, January 10–12, 1921." *Iowa Conservation* 5, no. 1 (January–March 1921): 9–25.

National Conference on State Parks. *Proceedings of the Second National Conference on State Parks.* Washington, D.C.: National Conference on State Parks, 1923.

————. "Use of State Parks during War Time." *Parks and Recreation* 24, no. 3 (May–June 1946): 165–69.

National Geographic Society. *National Geographic's Guide to the State Parks of the United States.* Washington, D.C.: National Geographic Society, 1997.

National Parks and Conservation Association. "Arizona Governor Aims for the Grand Canyon." *Park Watcher,* February 1996.

Nelson, Beatrice Ward. *State Recreation: Parks, Forests, and Game Preserves.* Washington, D.C.: National Conference on State Parks, 1928.

Outdoor Recreation Resources Review Commission. *Outdoor Recreation for America.* Washington, D.C.: Government Printing Office, 1962.

Parr, William A. "A Brief Organizational History." Typescript. Tucson, Ariz.: National Association of State Park Directors, [1979].

Rafferty, Robert. *Frommer's America's 100 Best-Loved State Parks.* New York: Macmillan, 1995.

Rogers, George. "The Might-Have-Been State Park." *Wisconsin Natural Resources* (December 1995): 24–27.

Rowley, Barbara. "America's Great State Parks." *Family Fun,* June/July 1994, 60–73.

Sauers, Charles G. "Some Principles of State Park Management." In *A State Park Anthology,* ed. Herbert Evison, 130–33. Washington: National Conference on State Parks, 1930.

Shankland, Robert. *Steve Mather of the National Parks.* New York: Alfred A. Knopf, 1970.

"State Parks and Forestry." In *Forestry Almanac, Semicentennial Edition,* 193–96. Washington, D.C.: American Tree Association, 1926.

Talbot, David G. "Personal Views on the Development of the State Parks and Recreation Program." In *Oregon's Highway Park System, 1921–1989: An Administrative History,* by Lawrence C. Merriam Jr., 69–146. Salem: Oregon Parks and Recreation Department, 1992.

Thompson, Ben H. "The Park, Parkway, and Recreational Area Study." In *American Planning and Civic Annual,* ed. Harlean James, 210–13. Washington, D.C.: American Planning and Civic Association, 1937.

Tilden, Freeman. *The State Parks: Their Meaning in American Life.* New York: Alfred A. Knopf, 1962.

Tindall, Barry S. "An Interview with Horace Marden Albright." *Parks and Recreation* 5, no. 12 (December 1970): 22–23, 46–47.

Torrey, Raymond H. *State Parks and Recreational Uses of State Forests in the United States.* Washington, D.C.: National Conference on State Parks, 1926.

U.S. Department of the Interior, National Park Service. *The CCC and Its Contribution to a Nation-Wide State Park Recreational Program.* Washington, D.C.: Government Printing Office, 1937.

———. *Parks for America.* Washington, D.C.: Government Printing Office, 1964.

———. *A Study of the Park and Recreation Problem of the United States.* Washington, D.C.: Government Printing Office, 1941.

Wagner, Harold S. "Proper Classification of State Parks." In *American Planning and Civic Annual,* ed. Harlean James, 179–81. Washington, D.C.: American Planning and Civic Association, 1939.

Washington State Parks and Recreation Commission. *A History of Washington State Parks, 1913–1988.* Olympia: Washington State Parks and Recreation Commission, 1988.

Weir, L. H. "Historical Background of Recreation Movement in America." *Parks and Recreation* 24, no. 4 (1946): 238–43.

West Virginia State Parks History Committee, Kermit McKeever, chairman. *Where*

People and Nature Meet: A History of the West Virginia State Parks. Charleston, W.V.: Pictorial Histories Publishing, 1988.

Wirth, Conrad L. "National and State Parks." *Planning and Civic Comment* 21, no. 4 (December 1955): 1–8.

———. *Parks, Politics, and the People.* Norman: University of Oklahoma Press, 1980.

———. "Parks and Wilderness." In *Origins of American Conservation,* ed. Henry Clepper, 146–59. New York: Ronald Press, 1966.

Index

Page numbers in italics refer to illustrations.

Acreage: of national parks, 4, 147, 257; of state parks, 4, 137, 147, 167, 193, 194, 212–15, 262, 264

Adirondack Forest Preserve, 214

Adirondack Mountains, 10, 38*n*10, 53

Agriculture Department, U.S., 127, 129, 146, 148

Alabama: Cheaha State Park, 137; Civilian Conservation Corps (CCC), 137; lodging at state parks, 238; Oak Mountain State Park, 147; statistics on state parks in, 262–63; taxation, 245

Alaska: Chugach State Park, 217; national parks in, 257; state parks in, 168, 201; statistics on state parks in, 262–63

Albright, Horace: and Bureau of Outdoor Recreation, 187–88; and "Common Ground for Common Goals" conference, 203; as director of National Park Service, 115, 119, 129, 135, 206; on Mather's interest in state parks, 76, 79; and National Conference on State Parks (NCSP), 82; and Outdoor Recreation Resources Review Commission (ORRRC), 187; and state parks, 115, 206

Alexander, Glen, 208

American Association of Park Superintendents, 8

American Civic Association, 76, 80, 98, 118, 119

American Institute of Park Executives, 98, 172, 180, 183, 196

American Nature Association, 96

American Park Society, 98

American Physical Education Association, 8

American Planning and Civic Association (APCA), 119–20, 196

American Recreation Association, 196

American Scenic and Historic Preservation Society, 53, 98

American Tree Association, 109

Ancient civilizations, 15

Angel Island State Park, *159*

Antiquities Act (1906), 75

Anza–Borrego State Park, 217

APCA. *See* American Planning and Civic Association (APCA)

Arapaho Tribe, 45

Area Redevelopment Act, 190

Arizona: Grand Canyon in, 9, 75, 80, 205; intervention by National Conference on State Parks (NCSP), 172; lottery, 245; proposal by, for takeover of national parks in, 205; statistics on state parks in, 262–63; Tubac Presidio, 168

Arkansas: lodging at state parks, 238; and Mena National Park, 117; mineral springs and hot springs, 10, 28–29, 101; Ouachita Mountains, 101, 117; Petit Jean State Park, 101, 117; statistics on state parks in, 262–63; taxation, 245

Armed Forces. *See* Military; World War II

Aroostook State Park, 137

Arrow Rock Tavern, 103

Aspinall, Wayne, 194

Association of Southeastern State Park Directors, 164, 170, 171, 209

Athletics, 7–8, 236–37

Atlantic Monthly, 195

Attendance statistics for state parks, 160, 167, 168, 212–13, 240, 246, 263, 265

Automobiles, xii, 160

Babylon, 15, 17

Backbone State Park, 71

Badlands, 117–18

Baseball, 158
Bass River State Forest, 60
Baxter State Park, 214, 217
Berkshires, 45
Bible, 15
Bierstadt, Albert, 10
Big Basin Redwoods State Park, 57–59, 69
Big Horn Hot Springs Reserve, 45
Big Spring, Mo., 102
Black Hills, 63–64
BOR. *See* Bureau of Outdoor Recreation
   (BOR)
Bottomless Lakes State Park, 137
Brice, James Lord, 4
Bridger, Jim, 9
Brower, Jacob V., 41–42
Buckeye Lake, 59
Bureau of Outdoor Recreation (BOR),
   187–89, 194, 195, 206, 208
Bureau of Reclamation, 167
Bureau of Roads, U.S., 150
Bureau of Sports Fisheries and Wildlife, 192

Cabins at state parks, 168, 181, 239–40, 246,
   252
Caledonia State Forest Park, 54–55
California: acreage of state parks in, 213;
   Angel Island State Park, *159;* Anza-
   Borrego State Park, 217; Big Basin
   Redwoods State Park, 57–59, 69; bond
   issue for state park acquisition, 106; forest
   preservation, 57–59, 79; Golden Gate
   National Recreation Area, 203; historic
   preservation, 59; lodging at state parks,
   238; mission statement for state parks,
   226; site-selection criteria for state parks,
   177; state park commission, 106, 116; state
   parks foundation, 247; statistics on state
   parks in, 262–63; survey of state parks,
   108; system planning for state parks, 105,
   106, 108; taxation, 245; Yosemite Valley
   state park, 30–33, 35–36, 40, 46, 57, 106,
   250
California Historical Landmark League, 59
California Redwood Park. *See* Big Basin
   Redwoods State Park
Cammerer, Arno, 115–16, 135, 137, 153, 164
Camp David, 147

Camping and campsites, 136, 168, 235–36,
   240, 246
Camp Release, 40
Canada, 209–11, *210*
Caparn, Harold, 113
Carhart, Arthur, 88
Carter, Jimmy, 204
Carver, John, 184
Cathedral Gorge, 103
Catlin, George, 10
Catoctin property, 147
Catskill Forest Preserve, 214
Catskill Mountains, 10, 38n10, 53
CCC. *See* Civilian Conservation Corps
   (CCC)
Central Park (New York City), 6, 10, 22, 30
Central plaza in Spain, 6
Chadron State Park, 100–101
Cheaha State Park, 137
Cheraw State Park, 137, 147
Cherry Creek State Park, 168
Chugach State Park, 217
Citizen support groups, 247
City parks. *See* Local parks
City planning, 6
Civilian Conservation Corps (CCC), xiii,
   125, 127–41, *133, 136, 144,* 145–49,
   151–56, 159, 163, 167, 182, 193, 234,
   237–38
Civil War (War between the States), 11
Clark park property, 53
Classification: of parks, 145, 151, 176–77; of
   recreation, 18–22
Clawson, Marion, 19–20, 21, 185, *198,*
   198–200, 202
Cleveland Metropolitan Park System, 91
Clinton, DeWitt, 37
Coca–Cola, 247
Colonial America, 16–17
Colorado: acreage of state parks in, 213;
   Cherry Creek State Park, 168; Garden of
   the Gods, 35; intervention by National
   Conference on State Parks (NCSP), 172;
   lottery, 245; Royal Arch, 35; state parks
   board, 168; statistics on state parks in,
   262–63
Colorado State University, 231, 232
Commerce Department, U.S., 165

Commercialization and overdevelopment of state parks, 179–81, 250
Commission on Uniform State Laws, 92
Committee of Fifteen, 183–85, 189
"Common Ground for Common Goals" conference, 203–4
Commons, 6, 16, 17
Comprehensive Employment and Training Act, 243
Conard, Rebecca, 70, 82
Conference on State Parks. *See* National Conference on State Parks (NCSP)
Congress, U.S.: and Area Redevelopment Act, 190; and Bureau of Outdoor Recreation, 187, 188, 189; and Civilian Conservation Corps (CCC), 164; and Flood Control Act (1944), 165, 167; and Hetch Hetchy dam controversy, 75; and Housing Act (1964), 190; and Land and Water Conservation Fund Act, 191–92, 194; and Mackinac Island, 35; and mineral and hot springs, 28–29; and national parks, 1, *5*, 26, 61, 74, 76, 77–78, 117; and New Deal, 125–26, 140; and Outdoor Recreation Act, 189, 255; and Outdoor Recreation Resources Review Act, 185–86; and Park, Parkway, and Recreational Area Study Act, 140, 147–53, 156, 163, 183; and park funding, 163–65, 184, 186; and Recreational Demonstration Areas (RDAs), 146; and Resettlement Administration, 146; and surplus federal real property, 165, 167; and Yellowstone National Park, 33–34, 74; and Yosemite National Park, 32; and Yosemite Valley grant to California, 30–31, 33
Connecticut: Mount Tom, 61; parks of deer, 16; site-selection criteria for state parks, 177; state park commission, 61–62, 91; state parks during World War II, 161; statistics on state parks in, 262–63; system planning for state parks, 105; Turner's contributions to state parks in, 227, 228n4
Conservation, 71, 74, 75, 166. *See also* Preservation
Conservation Foundation, 229–30, 244, 259
Conservation Fund, 215
Convention and meeting facilities, 239

Cook County Forest Preserve, 178
Coolidge, Calvin, 94–95, 178
Corporate partnerships, 247
Corps of Engineers, 167, 168
Cost-recovery ratio, 248, 263, 265
Cougill, Kenneth, *173*, 186, 187
Coulter, Stanley, 67, 113
Council of State Parks, 54
County parks. *See* Local parks
Cowles, Henry C., 80, 86, 90, 91
Cox, Laurie Davidson, 15, 113, 174, 175, 176, 227n4
Cox, Thomas R., 61, 68, 70
Crafts, Edward, 185–86, 188–89
Crater Lake, 35
Crawford Notch State Park, *25*
Creek Indians, 28, 103
Cumberland Falls, 103, 118, 238
Cumberland River, 118
Custer, George A., 61, *62*
Custer State Park, 63–64, 161, *162*, 214, 217

Dakota Indian War (1862), 40
Dale Hollow Lake State Resort Park, *239*
Dalles Interstate Park, 52, 55
Delaware: and Civilian Conservation Corps (CCC), 135; Fort Delaware, 168; statistics on state parks in, 262–63; Trap Pond, 135, 167
Dells of Wisconsin, 55, 57
Depression years. *See* Great Depression; New Deal
DeTurk, Charles, *173*
Devil's Lake, 55, 57
Douthat State Park, *133*, 137
Droop Mountain Battlefield State Park, 104
Drury, Newton, 164, 169
Du Pont, T. Coleman, 118

Economic incentive: for national parks, 75; for state park movement, xii, 88, 105, 221
ECW. *See* Emergency Conservation Work (ECW) program
Eisenhower, Dwight D., 185
Elmer, Arthur, *173*
Emergency Conservation Work (ECW) program, 116, 125–26
Enfield Glen park property, 53

England, 6, 15–16
Eppley Institute for Parks and Public Lands, 209
Eugene T. Mahoney State Park, 237
European parks, 6
Evaluation. *See* Self-evaluation by parks
Evans, James, 178
Everglades National Park, 69
Evison, Herbert: on automobile and state parks, xii; and Civilian Conservation Corps (CCC), 129; leadership role of, in National Conference on State Parks (NCSP), 88, 90, 113, 129; at meeting for creation of National Conference on State Parks (NCSP), 80; and National Conference on Outdoor Recreation, 95; and National Conference on State Parks (NCSP), xii, 119, 169; and National Parks Association of Seattle, 80; at National Park Service, 119, 129; photograph of, *142;* on role of state parks, 115
Expenditures for state parks, 167, 168, 212–13, 263, 265

Fall Creek Falls, 217
Family Fun, 216
Farm Security Administration, 146
Farwell, Mrs. F. C., 80
Fechner, Robert, 126–28, *127,* 131, 132, 134, 140, 149
Federal Emergency Relief Administration, 44
Federal Inter-Agency Committee on Recreation, 165, 178
Federal Power Commission, 118
Federal Provincial Parks Council (FPPC), 209–11, *210*
Federal Security Agency, 140, 165
Federated Societies on Planning and Parks, 98–99
Fees for state parks, 102, 114, 213, 245–46
Fisher, Carl, 65
Flickinger, V. W., *173,* 184–85
Flood Control Act (1944), 165, 167
Florida: acreage of state parks in, 213; Civilian Conservation Corps (CCC), 137; Everglades National Park, 69; Gold Medal Award for state parks in, 218, *218;* Highlands Hammock State Park, 137; in-

tervention by National Conference on State Parks (NCSP), 172; John Pennekamp Coral Reef, 217; Landrum as state park director in, 207, 208; lodging at state parks, 252; Miami Beach, 65; Paradise Key, 68–69; Royal Palm State Park, 69; statistics on state parks in, 262–63; taxation, 244
Florida Federation of Women's Clubs, 69
Forest and Reclamation Services, U.S., 75
Forest preservation: in California, 57–59, 79; in Georgia, 103; in Massachusetts, 45; and National Conference on Outdoor Recreation, 95–96; and National Conference on State Parks (NCSP), 87–88, 112; in Nebraska, 100; in New Hampshire, 42; in North Carolina, 68; in Pennsylvania, 42–43, 54–55; in Vermont, 101–2
Forest Service, U.S., 88, 92, 117, 128, 150, 185
Fort Abraham Lincoln, 60, 61, *62*
Fort Delaware, 168
Fort Frederick, 60
Fort Mackinac, 44
Fort Massac, 59, 60
Fort Michilimackinac, 44
Fort Washington, 55
FPPC. *See* Federal Provincial Parks Council (FPPC)
Franconia Notch, 217
Fremont, John C., 9, 30
Friends of Our Native Landscape, 80
Frommer's America's 100 Best-Loved State Parks, 216
Funding: from Conservation Fund, 215; and fees for state parks, 102, 114, 213, 245–46; and financial self-sufficiency for state parks, 249–51; from Land and Water Conservation Fund, 191–94, 215; and lotteries, 245; from Nature Conservancy, 215; for recreation, 186, 206; for state parks, 154, 156, 163–65, 167, 184, 186, 187, 190–94, 206, 215, 223, 242–51; and taxation, 244–45; from Trust for Public Land, 215

Game refuges, 103
Garden Club of America, 80
Garden of the Gods, 35
Garrison, Lemuel "Lon," 202–4

Gasoline shortage, 242, 248
Gateway National Recreation Area, 203
Genesee River gorge, 53
Geological Survey, U.S., 75
George Washington National Forest, 128
Georgia: forest preservation, 103; Indian Springs, 10, 28, *29*, 45, 101; Jekyll Island State Park, 214; lodging at state parks, 238; state parks during World War II, 160; statistics on state parks in, 262–63; Vogel State Park, 103
Gettysburg Battlefield, 11, 21
Gibbs, Mary, 42
Gift shops, 246, 247, *248*
Golden Gate National Recreation Area, 203
Gold Medal Awards program, 217–19
Grand Canyon, 9, 75, 80, 205
Grand Teton National Park, 45
Great Depression, 119–20, 124–27. *See also* New Deal
Great Smokies, 68
Greece, 15, 17
Greenleaf, James, 113
Green Springs, Va., 11
Greylock Park Association, 45–46
Grinnell, George Bird, 75
Gwinn, Abner, *173*

Hamlin, Chauncey J., 97, 99
Harbaugh, W. H., 50
Harding, W. L., 81
Harlan, Edgar R., 81, 82, 111
Harrison Bay State Park, 137
Hasbrouck House (Newburgh, N.Y.), 11
Hawaii: intervention by National Conference on State Parks (NCSP), 172; park areas in, at statehood, 168; statistics on state parks in, 262–63
Held, Burnell, 198
Heritage Conservation and Recreation Service, 206
Hetch Hetchy dam controversy, 75
Heyburn, Weldon B., 61
Heyburn State Park, 61, *63*
Highlands Hammock State Park, 137
Highway rest-stop programs, 147
Highway wayside areas, 101, *102*, 147
Hill, Andrew P., 58

Historic preservation, 10–11, *12*, 21, 59, 168. *See also* specific historic sites
Hotels and other lodging, 136–37, 168, 179, 181, 237–40, *239*, 246, 252
Hot/mineral springs, 10, 28–29, *29*, 45, 101
Hot Springs National Park, 29, 101
Housing Act (1964), 190
Houston, Sam, 39
Hudson River, 51–52, 237
Huttleston, L. L., 179

Ickes, Harold, 152, 158, 164
Idaho: Cox on park program, 70; Heyburn State Park, 61, *63*; statistics on state parks in, 262–63
Illinois: Cook County Forest Preserve, 178; Fort Massac, 59, 60; Illinois Beach State Park, 195; lodging at state parks, 238; Park Commission, 59–60; Starved Rock, 60; statistics on state parks in, 262–63
Illinois Beach State Park, 195
Indiana: conservation department, 65, 67; Lieber's contributions to state parks in, 227, 228*n*4; lodging at state parks, 238; McCormick's Creek Canyon, 64–65; state park commission, 64; statistics on state parks in, 262–63; Turkey Run, 65, 93
Indiana University, 209
Indian Springs, 28, *29*, 45, 103
Inland Waterways Commission, 50
Interior Department, U.S., 69, 76, 78, 129, 148–50, 158, 184–85, 187, 188, 189–90, 204, 205. *See also* National Park Service (NPS)
International Union for Conservation of Nature and Natural Resources, 252
Iowa: Backbone State Park, 71; board of conservation, 71–72, 85; mission statement for state parks, 225; motivations for state parks during early twentieth century, 69–72; National Conference on State Parks (1921), 70, 81, 82; statistics on state parks in, 262–63
Iowa Academy of Science, 71
Iowa Conservation Association, 71
Iowa Park and Forestry Association, 71
Iowa State Historical Department, 81
Ise, John, 32, 35

Itasca State Park, 40–42, *41,* 47, 48, 217
Izaak Walton League, 185

James, Harlean, 120–23, 169, *173*
Jekyll Island State Park, 214
Jennings, May Mann, 69
Jenson, Jens, 80
Jillson, Willard Rouse, 103
John Pennekamp Coral Reef, 217
Jones Beach State Park, 216

Kanopolis State Park, 168
Kansas: funding for state parks, 249;
   Kanopolis State Park, 168; statistics on
   state parks in, 262–63
Kennedy, John F., 187, 188
Kentucky: Cumberland Falls, 103, 118, 238;
   Dale Hollow Lake State Resort Park, *239;*
   lodging at state parks, 238; state park
   commission, 103; state parks during
   World War II, 161; statistics on state parks
   in, 262–63
Kikuko, Princess, 38
Kingery, Robert, 163, *173*
Knetsch, Jack, 198
Koenemann, Ed, *210*
Korean War, 165–66

Labor Department, U.S., 126–27, 128
Lake Chatcolet, 61
Lake Hope State Park, *173*
Lake Murray State Park, 137, 147
Lake Texhoma State Park, 166, *166*
Land and Water Conservation Fund
   (LWCF), 191–94, 201, 215
Land and Water Conservation Fund Act, 191
Landis, Kenesaw, 158
Land Planning Committee, 143–45
Landrum, Ney C., 207–10, *210,* 216
Lane, Franklin K., 1, 76, 78
LaPage, Wilbur, 231–32
Lathrop, Harold, 163–64
Laws on state parks, 86–87, 91–92, 140,
   147–53, 156. *See also* Congress, U.S.; New
   Deal; and specific laws
LeRoy Percy State Park, 137
Letchworth, William Pryor, 53
Lewis and Clark Caverns, 137, *139*

Lewis and Clark National/State Monument,
   118
Licking Reservoir/Buckeye Lake, 59
Lieber, Richard: death of, 171; on financial
   self-sufficiency of state parks, 250; and
   National Conference on Outdoor
   Recreation, 95; and National Conference
   on State Parks, 80, 93, 113, 122, 140, 169,
   171, 228n4; photograph of, *66;* on relationship of state and national parks, 140;
   Sauers as protégé of, 178; as state park
   practitioner, 65, 67, 227, 227–28n4, 237;
   and Turkey Run State Park, 65, 93; and
   unified approach to state parks nation-
   wide, 257; on World War II's impact on
   state parks, 161–63
Lincoln Woods, 60–61
Little Big Horn, Battle of, 61
"Living history" presentations, 241, *242*
Local parks, xi, 4, 85, 96, 136, 174, 184, 224,
   255, 256
Lodging at state parks, 136–37, 168, 179, 181,
   237–40, *239,* 246, 252
Longfellow-Evangeline State Park, 137
Lorimer, George Horace, 75
Lotteries, 245
Louisiana: Civilian Conservation Corps
   (CCC), 137; Longfellow-Evangeline State
   Park, 137; state parks during World War
   II, 161; statistics on state parks in, 262–63
Louisville Times, 118
Lowry, William, 250
LWCF. *See* Land and Water Conservation
   Fund (LWCF)

Macaulay, Thomas, 7
Mackinac Island, 35, 44, 214
Mackintosh, Barry, 75
Maine: Aroostook State Park, 137; Baxter
   State Park, 214, 217; Civilian Conservation
   Corps (CCC), 137; statistics on state parks
   in, 262–63
Maintenance and operation of state parks,
   229
Manassas Battlefield, 11
Man-made recreational facilities, 236–37
Marinas, 236
Maryland: Catoctin property, 147; corporate

partnerships with state parks, 247; forests, 60; Fort Frederick, 60; Patapsco Reserve, 60; statistics on state parks in, 262–63; taxation, 244

Massachusetts: forest preservation, 45; great ponds of, 16; Mount Greylock, 45–46; statistics on state parks in, 262–63

Mather, Stephen Tyng: as businessman, 76; and California redwoods, 79; as director of National Park Service, 1–2, 76–79, 119, 123, 206; illness and death of, 119, 122, 177; and lodging at state parks, 238; and National Conference on State Parks, 2, 79–92, 94, 100, 111–13, 119, 122, 147; as National Conference on State Parks chairman, 119; photographs of, *xviii, 93;* on relationship between state parks and national parks, 79, 84–85, 114–16, 147; speeches and radio talks by, 113; and standardization of state park legislation, 86–87, 91–92; and state parks, 79, 84–86, 91–92, 99–100, 104, 106, 108, 110, 114–16, 206, 257; and state park survey, 99–100; youth of, 76

McBride, Thomas, 70–71

McCormick's Creek Canyon, 64–65

McCurdy, Dwight, 228–29

McEntee, John, 140

McFarland, J. Horace, 76, 80

McIntosh, Chief William, 28

McKinley, William, 74

Meeting and convention facilities, 239

Mena National Park, 117

Miami Beach, 65

Michigan: acreage of state parks in, 213; corporate partnerships for state parks, 247; funding for state parks, 249; Mackinac Island, 35, 44, 214; statistics on state parks in, 262–63; Traverse City State Park, 235–36; Yankee Springs State Park, 147

Midwest State Park Association, 171

Military, 127, *159,* 161, 162. *See also* World War II

Millard, Everett L., 92

Miller State Park, 42

Mineral/hot springs, 10, 28–29, *29,* 45, 101

Minnehaha State Park, 39–40

Minnesota: Camp Release, 40; and Dalles

Interstate Park, 52, 55; Itasca State Park, 40–42, *41,* 47, 48, 217; Minnehaha State Park, 39–40; park property acquired in early twentieth century, 55; statistics on state parks in, 262–63; St. Croix State Park, 147; system planning for state parks, 105–6

Mission and role of state parks, 115, 197–200, 221, 224–27, 254–55, 259–61

"Mission 66" program, 183

Mississippi: Civilian Conservation Corps (CCC), 137; LeRoy Percy State Park, 137; statistics on state parks in, 262–63

Mississippi River, 50

Missouri: Arrow Rock Tavern, 103; Big Spring, 102; statistics on state parks in, 262–63; taxation, 245

Mont Alto Forest Reservation, 54

Montana: Civilian Conservation Corps (CCC), 137, *139;* intervention by National Conference on State Parks (NCSP), 172; Lewis and Clark Caverns, 137, *139;* Lewis and Clark National/State Monument, 118; statistics on state parks in, 262–63

Montgomery Bell State Park, 147

Monuments, national, 76

Moran, Thomas, 10

Moran State Park, 62

Morgan, J. P., 51

Morse, Thomas W., *173*

Morton, Rogers, 204

Moses, Robert, 54, 106

Mott, William Penn, 202–3

Moundsville, 21

Mount Greylock, 45–46

Mount Laurel State Park, 60

Mount Mitchell, 68

Mount Olympus (Olympic), 75

Mt. Philo State Forest Park, 102

Mount Tom, 61

Mount Vernon, Va., 11, 21

Muir, John, 9, 32–33, 75

NASPD. *See* National Association of State Park Directors (NASPD)

National Association of State Park Directors (NASPD): and Canadian Federal Provincial Parks Council, 209–11; and competitive award for state parks, 217–18; creation and growth of, 196, 201, 206–12; and federal activity in urban parks, 204; leadership of, 203, 207–8, 216, 259; membership of, 233–34, 259; and National Conference on State Parks (NCSP), 196, 197, 203, 206–7; and National Recreation and Park Association (NRPA), 197, 207–8; and policies for state parks, 228; purpose and role of, 211–12, 258–59; and revenue generated by state parks, 252; and self-evaluation by state parks, 231–32; separation of, from National Society for Park Resources (NSPR), 208; statistical surveys of state parks by, 208–9, 212, 259; and visitor programs, 241

National Conference on City Planning, 98, 119–20

National Conference on Outdoor Recreation (1924), 23, 94–98, 99

National Conference on State Parks (NCSP): and active (or physical) use of state parks, 177–80; and administration of state parks, 175; and American Planning and Civic Association, 119–20, 196; annual meetings of, 86, 90, 112–13, 170; assessment of effectiveness of, 111–23, 171; board of directors of, 118, 121, 123, 169–70, 173, 183, 184, 195; and Bureau of Outdoor Recreation, 187–88; and classification of state parks, 176–77; conflict within, 112; and Cumberland Falls in Kentucky, 103, 118; decline and end of, 194–97, 202–3, 206; executive committee of, 90, 113, 119, 121; executive secretary and other staff members of, 90–91, 94, 99–100, 113, 119, 120–21, 169, 196; and federal aid for state parks, 163–64; and Federated Societies on Planning and Parks, 98–99; during Great Depression, 119–20; headquarters location of, 19–20, 99, 196; incorporation of, 119; intervention by, in state matters, 172; issues considered by, 113–16, 172–81, 202–3; leadership of, 86, 90, 113, 118, 119, 121, 122, 169, 197, 228n4; and Lewis and Clark National/State Monument, 118; Lieber's leadership of, 80, 93, 113, 122, 140; and Mather, 2, 79–92, 94, 100, 111–13, 119, 122, 147; membership of,

122–23, 171–72; and Mena National Park, 117; name changes considered by, 196, 203; and National Association of State Park Directors (NASPD), 195–96, 197, 203, 206–7; and National Park Service (NPS), 122, 169–70, 195; and National Recreation and Park Association (NRPA), 196–97; during 1940s–1950s, 169–81; organization and governance of, 90–94, 121–22; and overdevelopment and commercialization of state parks, 179–81; and Parks for America program, 184; and policy for state parks at state level, 227–28; publications by, 114, 170, 171, 196; and publicity for state parks, 99–100; purpose of, 91–92, 111–13, 119, 121–23, 155, 195, 203, 253; regional meetings of, 113, 170–71; and relationship between state parks and national parks, 114–16; selective advocacy by, 116–19; and site-selection criteria for state parks, 177; and standardization of state park legislation, 86–87, 91–92; and statistics on state parks, xii, xiii, 108–10, 208, 212; and surveys of state parks, 97–100, 108–10, 209, 212; and Theodore Roosevelt National Memorial Park, 117–18; unofficial slogan of, 88, 233, 255; and World War II, 157, 160–62, 170

—1921 meeting: accomplishments of, xiii, 82, 86–89; attendance at, 2, 82, 87; Chicago meeting before, 79–80; conflicts during, 112; date and location of, 2, 70, 81, 82; and forest preservation, 87–88, 112; and Mather, 2, 79–90, 100, 111, 112, 147; Mather's agenda for, 84–86, 90, 111; participants at, 82, 87; program for, 83, 84; and resolution on annual conferences, 86, 90; and standardization of state park legislation, 86–87; title of, 82; and tourism, 88

—1922 meeting: ix, 86, 92, 93
—1923 meeting, 93
—1926 meeting, 51, 93, 93
—1928 meeting, 106
—1931 meeting, 38
—1937 meeting, 150
—1946 meeting, 170
—1955 meeting, 181
—1962 meeting, 195–96
—1965 meeting, 197

*National Geographic's Guide to the State
   Parks of the United States,* 216–17
National Geographic Traveler, 216
National monuments, 76
National parks: acreage of, 4, 147, 257; and
   Civilian Conservation Corps (CCC), 133;
   economic value of, 75; inauguration of,
   with Yellowstone National Park, 5, 10,
   33–35, 74; influences of, on state parks,
   xiii; legislation on, 1, 26, 61; Mather as
   administrator of, 1–2, 76–79, 84–86, 123;
   and "Mission 66" program, 183; preservation value of, 74–75; and Recreational
   Demonstration Areas (RDAs), 145–47;
   regional distribution of, 257; relationship
   between state parks and, xi, 24–25, 79,
   84–85, 114–16, 174, 204–6, 255–57; revenue generated by, 252; and Theodore
   Roosevelt, 49–50, 75; self-evaluation by,
   231; standards for, 1–2, 77–79, 84–85,
   115–16, 117, 123, 177, 259; takeover of, by
   state parks, 205; urban recreation projects,
   203, 204; and U.S. Congress, 1, 26, 61, 74,
   76, 77–78, 117. *See also* specific parks
National Parks and Conservation
   Association (NPCA), 205
National Parks Association, 80
National Park Service (NPS): Albright as
   director of, 115, 119, 129, 135, 206; Bureau
   of Outdoor Recreation versus, 187–88,
   194, 206; Cammerer as director of,
   115–16, 135, 153, 164; and Civilian
   Conservation Corps (CCC), 129–40, 146,
   151, 153–56; and Committee of Fifteen,
   183–85, 189; and "Common Ground for
   Common Goals" conference, 203–4; criticism of, 195; Drury as director of, 164,
   169; and federal aid for state parks, 156,
   163–65; and Land and Water
   Conservation Fund (LWCF), 192, 194;
   legislation establishing, 1, 26; Mather as
   director of, 1–2, 76–79, 119, 123, 206; and
   "Mission 66" program, 183; Mott as director of, 202–3; and National Conference on
   State Parks, 122, 169–70, 195; and
   National Park–to-Park Highway, 80; and
   National Resources Board report on recreation, 143, 149–50; opposition to Mena
   National Park in Arkansas, 101, 117; and

overdevelopment and commercialization
   of state parks, 180; and Park, Parkway, and
   Recreational Area Study Act, 148–49, 163,
   183; *Park and Recreation Progress Yearbook*
   by, 170; and Parks for America program,
   183–85; and *Parks for America* report,
   189–90; and Recreational Demonstration
   Areas (RDAs), 145–48, 153; and relationship between state and national parks, 79,
   84–85, 114–16, 174, 204–6; and
   Resettlement Administration, 146; and
   revenue generated by national parks, 252;
   and state legislation on state parks, 140,
   152; and state parks, xiii, 85–86, 115,
   138–40, 146, 156, 163, 164–65, 174,
   183–85, 195, 204–6, 233, 234; *Study of the
   Park and Recreation Problem of the United
   States* by, 156, 158, 174, 175, 183; survey of
   recreational areas by, 148–52, 156, 167,
   183; and urban recreation projects, 203,
   204; Walker as director of, 204; Wirth as
   director of, 129, 181, 183–85, 189–90, 195,
   206; and World War II, 158
National Park-to-Park Highway, 80
National Production Authority (NPA),
   165–66
National Recreation and Park Association
   (NRPA), 196–97, 232
National Recreation Association, 7, 172, 180
National Resources Board, 142–43, 146, 148,
   149–50, 151, 176, 183
National Society for Park Resources (NSPR),
   197, 203, 206, 207–9
National Sporting Goods Association's
   Sports Foundation, 217–19
National system of parks, 255–56
National Youth Administration, 148
Nature Conservancy, 215
NCSP. *See* National Conference on State
   Parks (NCSP)
Nebraska: Chadron State Park, 100–101;
   Eugene T. Mahoney State Park, 237; forest
   preservation, 100; state park board, 101;
   statistics on state parks in, 264–65; taxa-
   tion, 245
Need for state parks, ix
Neff, Pat, 104
Nelson, Beatrice Ward. *See* Ward, Beatrice M.
Nelson, Wilbur, 109, 119

Nevada: Cathedral Gorge, 103; game refuges, 103; statistics on state parks in, 264–65; Valley of Fire State Park, *136*

Newburgh, N.Y., 11

New Deal: Civilian Conservation Corps (CCC), xiii, 125, 127–41, 145–49, 151–56, 159, 163, 167, 182, 193, 234, 237–38; Emergency Conservation Work (ECW) program, 116, 125–26; end of, 153–56; Federal Emergency Relief Administration, 44; Federal Security Agency, 140; Land Planning Committee, 143–45; National Resources Board, 142–43, 146, 148, 149–50, 151, 152, 176, 183; Public Works Administration, 142, 144; Recreational Demonstration Areas (RDAs), 143–48, *144,* 153; Resettlement Administration, 143–44, 146; Roosevelt's creation of, 124–27; Work Projects Administration, 145, 148

New Hampshire: acreage of state parks in, 214; Crawford Notch State Park, *25;* forest preservation, 42; Franconia Notch, 217; funding for state parks, 249; Miller State Park, 42; mission statement for state parks, 225; Pack Monadnock, 42; statistics on state parks in, 264–65

New Jersey: acreage of state parks in, 213; Bass River State Forest, 60; corporate partnerships with state parks, 247; establishment of state parks in early twentieth century, 60; Mount Laurel State Park, 60; Palisades Interstate Park, 51–52, 53, 69, 79, 80, 93; statistics on state parks in, 264–65

New Jersey Federation of Women's Clubs, 51

New Mexico: Bottomless Lakes State Park, 137; Civilian Conservation Corps (CCC), 137; statistics on state parks in, 264–65

New York City: Central Park, 6, 10, 22, 30; Gateway National Recreation Area, 203; Riverbank State Park, 237. *See also* New York State

New York State: Adirondack Forest Preserve, 214; Adirondack Mountains, 10, 38*n*10, 53; Catskill Forest Preserve, 214; Catskill Mountains, 10, 38*n*10, 53; Civilian Conservation Corps (CCC) program, 134–35; Clark park property, 53; corpo-

rate partnerships for state parks, 247; Enfield Glen park property, 53; Genesee River gorge, 53; Jones Beach State Park, 216; lodging at state parks, 238; Niagara Falls, 37–39, *39,* 46, 48, 53; Palisades Interstate Park, 51–52, 53, 69, 79, 80, 93; Saratoga Springs, 53; State Council of Parks, 54; statistics on state parks in, 264–65; St. Lawrence park property, 53; system planning for state parks, 105, 106; Thatcher park property, 53; Washington Headquarters State Historic Site, 30. *See also* New York City

New York State Council of Parks, 54, 106

Niagara Falls, 37–39, *39,* 46, 48, 53

Niagara Reservation State Park, 38–39, *39,* 46, 48, 53

Noble, John W., 32

Nolen, John, 56–57, *56,* 60, 177

Nonprofit organizations, 247

Norbeck, Peter, 64

North Carolina: acreage of state parks in, 213; forest preservation, 68; Mount Mitchell, 68; statistics on state parks in, 264–65; taxation, 245

North Dakota: Badlands in, 117–18; Fort Abraham Lincoln, 60, 61, *62;* and Roosevelt National/State Park, 117–18; statistics on state parks in, 264–65

NPA. *See* National Production Authority (NPA)

NPCA. *See* National Parks and Conservation Association (NPCA)

NPS. *See* National Park Service (NPS)

NRPA. *See* National Recreation and Park Association (NRPA)

NSPR. *See* National Society for Park Resources (NSPR)

Oak Mountain State Park, 147

Odegaard, Charles "Chuck," 203, 207

Ohio: Cleveland Metropolitan Park System, 91; Division of Parks, 59; Gold Medal Award for state parks in, 218; Lake Hope State Park, *173;* Licking Reservoir/Buckeye Lake, 59; lodging at state parks, 238; marinas in state parks in, 236; statistics on state parks in, 264–65

Oil shortages, 241–42, 244, 248
Oklahoma: acreage of state parks in, 214; Civilian Conservation Corps (CCC), 137; Lake Murray State Park, 137, 147; Lake Texhoma State Park, 166, *166;* lodging at state parks, 238; state parks during World War II, 161; statistics on state parks in, 264–65
Olmsted, Frederick Law: and New York City's Central Park, 6, 9, 22; and Niagara Falls, 38; and planning, not administration, of state parks, 227*n*4; Yosemite Valley state park, 30, 31
Olmsted, Frederick Law (younger), 108, 174, 176, 177, 227*n*4
OPEC (Organization of Petroleum Exporting Countries), 241–42, 248
Orcas Island, 62
Oregon: administration of state parks in, 221; Cox on park program, 70; Crater Lake, 35; funding for state parks, 249; Sara Helmick State Park, 101; Sodaville Mineral Springs, 101; state highway department, 101; statistics on state parks in, 264–65; wayside areas, 101, *102*
Organization of Petroleum Exporting Countries (OPEC), 241–42, 248
ORRRC. *See* Outdoor Recreation Resources Review Commission (ORRRC)
Ouachita Mountains, 101, 117
Ouachita National Forest, 117
Outdoor recreation. *See* Recreation
Outdoor Recreation Act, 189, 255
Outdoor Recreation Resources Review Act, 185–86
Outdoor Recreation Resources Review Commission (ORRRC), 23, 184, 185–91, 198, 199
Outsourcing of activities and services, 247
Overdevelopment and commercialization of state parks, 179–81, 250
Ozark National Scenic Riverways, 102

Pack, Charles Lathrop, 96, 99
Pack Monadnock, 42
Pagosa Springs, 35
Palisades Interstate Park, 51–52, 53, 69, 79, 80, 93

Pammel, Louis, 70–71, 80, 90, 91
Paradise Key, 68–69
Park, Parkway, and Recreational Area Study Act, 140, 147–53, 156, 163, 183
Park and Recreation Progress Yearbook (NPS/NCSP), 170
Park Practice (NPS and NCSP), 170
Parks: classification of, 18–22, 145, 151, 176–77; in colonial America, 16–17; common denominator for, 17–18; derivation of term, 15–16; European tradition of, 6; historical perspective on, 15–17; and historic preservation, 10–11, *12,* 21; local parks, xi, 4, 85, 96, 136, 174, 184, 224, 255, 256; national system of, 255–56; origin of, 3–4; and playground movement, 7–8, 17; preservation movement and American frontier, 8–10, 17; progression to park systems from, 26, 104–8, 152, 175–76; public perceptions of, 14–15; recreation/parks relationship, 18–20, 259–60; responsibility for, 22–25; as urban landscape features, 6; writings on, 11–13, 70. *See also* Local parks; National parks; State parks
Parks Canada, 210–11
Park Service. *See* National Park Service (NPS)
Parks for America program, 183–85
Parks for America report (NPS), 189–90
Park systems, 26, 104–8, 152, 175–76
Patapsco Reserve, 60
Patapsco River, 60
Payne, John Barton, 79, 81, 86, 90, 92–94, 95, 97, 117, 119
Peeler, Ruth, *173*
Penfold, Joseph, 185–86
Peninsula park property, Wisc., 57
Pennsylvania: Caledonia State Forest Park, 54–55; forest preservation, 42–43, 54–55; Fort Washington, 55; intervention by National Conference on State Parks (NCSP), 172; mission statement for state parks, 225; Mont Alto Forest Reservation, 54; statistics on state parks in, 264–65; system planning for state parks, 105; Valley Forge, 43, *44,* 48, 55; Washington Crossing, 55

Pennsylvania Parks Association, 105
Pepper, Claude, 164
Pepsi, 247
PERC. *See* Political Economy Research
    Center (PERC)
Perkins, George W., 51
Peterson, J. Hardin, 164
Petit Jean State Park, 101, 117
Philadelphia, 6
Planning: nationwide outdoor recreation
    plan, 255; for state parks, 229; state recre-
    ation plans under New Deal, 143
Planning and Civic Comment, 120
Playground movement, 7–8, 17
Policy on state parks at state level, 227–30
Political Economy Research Center (PERC),
    250
Politics factor in state park movement,
    221–24
Powell, John Wesley, 9
Preservation: in ancient civilizations, 15;
    convergence with recreation movement as
    possibility, 22–23; historic preservation,
    10–11, *12,* 17, 21, 59, 168; national parks'
    value for, 74–75; natural area preservation
    and American frontier, 8–10, 17; and
    Progressive Era in early twentieth century,
    48–49; and state park movement, xii,
    48–49, 260–61. *See also* Forest preserva-
    tion
President's Commission on American
    Outdoors, 23
Progressive Era, 48–50
Publicity for state parks, 99–100, 216–19
Public Law 85–470 (Outdoor Recreation
    Resources Review Act), 185–86
Public Law 87–27 (Area Redevelopment
    Act), 190
Public Law 87–70 (Housing Act), 190
Public Law 88–29 (Outdoor Recreation Act),
    189, 255
Public Law 88–578 (Land and Water
    Conservation Fund Act), 191–94
Public Law 616 (on surplus federal real
    property), 167
Public parks. *See* Local parks; National parks;
    Parks; State parks
Public Works Administration, 142, 144

Purdue University, 67
Puritans, 7, 16–17

Quinn, Frank, *173*

Rating of "best" state parks, 215–19
RDAs. *See* Recreational Demonstration Areas
    (RDAs)
Real estate transfer tax, 244–45
Recreation: in ancient civilizations, 15; and
    Bureau of Outdoor Recreation, 187–89,
    194, 195, 206; classification of, 18–22; con-
    vergence with preservation movement as
    possibility, 22–23; and Coolidge, 94–95,
    178; definition of, 18; and Federal Inter-
    Agency Committee on Recreation, 165,
    178; and Land and Water Conservation
    Fund (LWCF), 191–94, 201; in mission
    statements of state parks, 225–27; and
    National Conference on Outdoor
    Recreation (1924), 23, 94–98; National
    Resources Board report on, 143, 146,
    149–50, 152, 176; and Outdoor Recreation
    Resources Review Commission, 23, 184,
    185–87; and Park, Parkway, and
    Recreational Area Study Act, 140, 147–53,
    156, 163, 183; parks/recreation relation-
    ship, 18–20, 259–60; and playground
    movement, 7–8, 17; separate federal
    agency on, 65; state parks and outdoor
    recreation needs, 177–80, 198–200; state
    recreation plans under New Deal, 143;
    user-oriented/resource-based distinction
    in, 20–24, *25. See also* Parks; State parks
Recreational Demonstration Areas (RDAs),
    143–48, *144,* 153
Redwood forests, 57–59, 79
Reservoir projects, 165, *166,* 167, 168
Resettlement Administration, 143–44, 146
Resort parks, 238–40, *239*
Resource-based recreation, 20–22, 24, *25*
Resources for the Future (RFF), 185, 198,
    202
Rest-stop programs, 147
Retail shops, 246, 247, *248*
Revenues from state parks, 245–46, 248–52
RFF. *See* Resources for the Future (RFF)
Rhode Island: acreage of state parks in, 214;

Lincoln Woods, 60–61; Metropolitan Park Commission, 60; statistics on state parks in, 264–65

Riverbank State Park, 237

Rockefeller (Laura Spelman) Memorial, 98–99

Rome, 15

Roosevelt, Franklin, xiii, 124–27, 128, 141, 143, 146, 153, 158, 159–60. *See also* New Deal

Roosevelt, Theodore, 6, 9, 49–50, 57, 74–75, 94–95

Roosevelt National/State Park, 117–18

Rothrock, J. T., 43, 54–55

Royal Arch, 35

Royal Palm State Park, 69

Sales tax, 245

San Jacinto Battlefield, *12,* 30, 39, 104

Santa Anna, 39

Sara Helmick State Park, 101

Saratoga Springs, 53

Sauers, Charles G. "Cap," 101, 113, *173,* 174, 178–79, 237

Savannah, 6

Save-the-Redwoods League, 106

School lands, 63, 63*n*7

Scoggin, Lewis G., *173*

Seaton, Fred, 183, 184

Self-evaluation by parks, 230–32

Sempervirens Club, 58

Sequoiadendron giganteum (Sierra redwoods), 57–58

Sequoia sempervirens (redwood trees), 57–59

Shankland, Robert, 77

Shoshone Tribe, 45

Site-selection criteria for state parks, 177

SIU. *See* Southern Illinois University (SIU)

Smith, Ralph Sidney, 58

Snowmobiles, *235*

Sodaville Mineral Springs, 101

South Carolina: Cheraw State Park, 137, 147; Civilian Conservation Corps (CCC), 137; funding for state parks, 249; statistics on state parks in, 264–65; wayside areas, 147

South Dakota: Custer State Park, 63–64, 161, *162,* 214, 217; proposal by, for takeover of national parks in, 205; state park board,

64; state parks during World War II, 161; statistics on state parks in, 264–65; Wind Cave National Park, 63

Southern Illinois University (SIU), 228–29

Spain, 6

Sporting goods tax, 244

Sports, 7–8, 158, 236–37

Sports Foundation's Gold Medal Awards, 217–19

Standards for national parks, 1–2, 77–79, 84–85, 115–16, 117, 123, 177

Starved Rock, 60

State laws on state parks, 86–87, 91–92, 140

State Park Anthology (NCSP), 114

State park directors, 195–96, 222–23, 254. *See also* National Association of State Park Directors (NASPD)

State parks: acreage of, 4, 137, 147, 167, 193, 194, 212–15, 262, 264; appearance of, as important, 220; assessment of current situation of, 251–61; attendance at, 160, 167, 168, 212–13, 240, 246, 263, 265; changes in, during 1980s and 1990s, 233–52; and Civilian Conservation Corps (CCC), 131–40, 147–49, 153–56; classification of, 176–77; and corporate partnerships, 247; cost-recovery ratio for, 248, 263, 265; definitional confusions about, 108, 214, 258; diverse approaches to, xiii, 256–57; in early twentieth century, 48–73; economic incentive for, xii, 88, 105, 221; expansion of, after World War II, xiii, 165–68; expenditures for, 167, 168, 212–13, 263, 265; financial difficulties for, in 1970s–1990s, 242–49; funding for, 154, 156, 163–65, 167, 184, 186, 187, 190–94, 206, 215, 223, 242–51; interstate initiatives in, during early twentieth century, 51–52, 72; lack of critical attention to, 12–13; lodging at, 136–37, 168, 179, 181, 237–40, *239,* 246, 252; man-made recreational facilities at, 236–37; and Mather, 79, 84–86, 99–100, 104, 106, 108, 110, 114–16; mission and role of, 115, 197–200, 221, 224–27, 254–55, 259–61; and National Conference on Outdoor Recreation, 94–98; need for, ix; in 1960s, 182–200; in 1970s, 201–19, 241–49; in nineteenth cen-

tury, 27–47; norms for, xiii, 257–58; organizational placement of, in state government, 175, 221–22, 263, 265; and outdoor recreation needs, 177–80, 198–200; outsourcing of activities and services by, 247; overdevelopment and commercialization of, 179–81, 250; overview of, xi–xiii, 26; policy at state level on, 227–30; and politics factor in, 221–24; and Progressive Era, 48–50; publicity for, 99–100, 216–19; rating of "best" state parks, 215–19; and Recreational Demonstration Areas (RDAs), 143–48, *144,* 153; relationship between national parks and, xi, 24–25, 79, 84–85, 114–16, 174, 204–6, 255–57; revenues from, 245–46, 248–52; self-evaluation by, 230–32; site-selection criteria for, 177; South lagging behind in, during early twentieth century, 68, 137; standardization of legislation on, 86–87, 91–92, 140, 152; statistics on, xii, xiii, 26, 108–10, 135–38, 147, 167, 168, 183, 194, 208–9, 212, 240, 259, 262–65; surplus federal real property for, 165, 167–68; surveys of, 97–100, 108–10, 148–53, 156, 167, 183, 209, 212–14; system planning for, 104–8, 152, 175–76; takeovers of national parks by, 205; taxation for, 244–45; and tourism, xii, 105, 168, 181, 221, 227; transportation to, xii, 60; unsuitable projects as, 223–24; user fees for, 102, 114, 213, 245–46; visitor programs at, 240–41, *242;* and World War II, 152, 155–63. *See also* National Conference on State Parks (NCSP); National Park Service (NPS); and specific states and state parks
State recreation plans, 143
St. Croix River, 52, 55
St. Croix State Park, 147
Stegner, Wallace, 4
Stinchcomb, W. H., 90, 91
St. Lawrence park property, 53
Study of the Park and Recreation Problem of the United States (NPS), 156, 158, 174, 175, 183
Sumer, 15
Surplus federal real property, 165, 167–68
Surveys of state parks, 97–100, 108–10, 148–53, 156, 167, 183, 209, 212–14

System planning of parks, 26, 104–8, 152, 175–76, 255–56

Taxation, 244–45
Teller, Henry M., 34
Tennessee: Civilian Conservation Corps (CCC), 137; Fall Creek Falls, 217; Harrison Bay State Park, 137; lodging at state parks, 238; mission statement for state parks, 226; Montgomery Bell State Park, 147; state parks during World War II, 160; statistics on state parks in, 264–65
Tent and trailer campsites, 136, 168, 235–36
Texas: acreage of state parks in, 213; funding for state parks, 249; San Jacinto Battlefield, *12,* 30, 39, 104; state parks board, 104; state parks during World War II, 160; statistics on state parks in, 264–65; taxation, 245
Thatcher park property, 53
Theodore Roosevelt National Memorial Park, 117–18
Thompson, Ben, 150
Tilden, Freeman, 108
Time magazine, 198
Tobacco tax, 245
Tobey, Russell, *173*
Torrey, Raymond H., 51, 98, 99–100, 108, 109, 113
Tourism, xii, 75, 88, 105, 168, 181, 221, 227
Trap Pond, 135, 167
Traverse City State Park, 235–36
Treman, Robert H., 53
Trust for Public Land, 215
Tubac Presidio, 168
Turkey Run State Park, 65, 93
Turner, Albert M.: as Connecticut state park practitioner, 62, 91, 174, 177, 227, 227–28n4; and National Conference on State Parks (NCSP), 90, 91, 113; photograph of, *107;* and site-selection criteria for state parks, 177; and system planning for state parks, 105

Udall, Stewart, 184–85, 188, 189–90
University of Chicago, 80, 86
Urban America, 196
Urban planning, 6
Urban recreation projects, 203, 204

User fees for state parks, 102, 114, 213, 245–46
User-oriented recreation, 20–24
Utah: mission statement for state parks, 225; statistics on state parks in, 264–65; Territorial State House, 168

Valley Forge, 43, *44*, 48, 55
Valley of Fire State Park, *136*
Van Wyck, Oze, 80–81
Vaux, Calvert, 6
Vermont: acreage of state parks in, 214; forest preservation, 101–2; funding for state parks, 249; Mt. Philo State Forest Park, 102; statistics on state parks in, 264–65
Veterans Administration, 127
Vietnam War, 241
Virginia: Civilian Conservation Corps (CCC), 128, *133*, 137; Douthat State Park, *133*, 137; George Washington National Forest, 128; Gold Medal Award for state parks in, 218; statistics on state parks in, 264–65; wayside areas, 147
Visitation statistics for state parks, 160, 167, 168, 212–13, 240, 246, 263, 265
Visitor programs, 240–41, *242*
Vogel State Park, 103
Volunteer programs, 247

Wagner, Harold, *173*, 176
Walker, Ron, 204
Wallace, Tom, 118, *120*, 122, 178
Wall Street Journal, 250
War between the States, 11
Ward, Beatrice M., 90–91, 94, 99–100, 109, 113, 117, 119
War Department, U.S., 44, 127
Washington, D.C., 6
Washington, George, 11
Washington Crossing, 55
Washington Headquarters State Historic Site, 30
Washington State: Cox on park program, 70; Moran State Park, 62; Orcas Island, 62; State Board of Park Commissioners, 62; statistics on state parks in, 264–65
Water and reservoir projects, 165, *166*, 167, 168
Water sports, 236, *236*

Watoga State Park, 104
Wayside areas, 101, *102*, 147
Weir, L. H., 7
Welch, William A., 80, 90, 93, 95, 97, 227–28n4, 237
Wells, William W., *173*
West Virginia: Droop Mountain Battlefield State Park, 104; lodging at state parks, 238; State Forest, Park, and Conservation Commission, 104; statistics on state parks in, 264–65; Watoga State Park, 104
Wilbur, Ray Lyman, 116
Wilson, Woodrow, 2, 81
Wind Cave National Park, 63
Wind River Reservation, 45
Wirth, Conrad: and Association of Southeastern State Park Directors, 171; and Bureau of Outdoor Recreation, 187, 188; and Civilian Conservation Corps (CCC), 129, 146, 152–53; as director of National Park Service, 129, 181, 183–85, 189–90, 195, 206; and federal funding for state parks, 164; and National Conference on State Parks (NCSP), 169–70, 171, 183, 197; and National Resources Board's report on recreation, 143; and Park, Parkway, and Recreational Area Study Act, 151, 152–53, 183; and Parks for America program, 183–85; and *Parks for America* report, 189–90; photographs of, *130, 142, 173*; and Recreational Demonstration Areas (RDAs), 146; retirement of, 190, 195, 197; and state legislation on parks and recreation programs, 140; and statistics on parks, 136; support of state parks by, 206, 257; and survey of recreational areas by National Park Service, 151, 152–53; on wayside areas, 147
Wirth, Theodore, 90, 95
Wirth, Walter, *173*
Wisconsin: administration of state parks, 56–57; conservation commission, 57; and Dalles Interstate Park, 52, 55; Dells of, 55, 57; Devil's Lake, 55, 57; nineteenth-century State Park, 36–37; park property acquired in early twentieth century, 55–57; Peninsula park property, 57; site-selection criteria for state parks, 177; statistics on state parks in, 264–65; Wyalusing, 57

Work Projects Administration, 145, 148
World War II, 152, 155–63, *159*
Wright, George, 143
Wyalusing, 57
Wyoming: acreage of state parks in, 214; Big Horn Hot Springs Reserve, 45; statistics on state parks in, 264–65; Yellowstone Park and Wyoming Territory, 33–35

Yankee Springs State Park, 147
Yellowstone Basin, 9, 11, 28

Yellowstone National Park, *5,* 10, 33–35, 40, 45, 74, 75, 80, 86, 238
YMCA, 8
Yosemite National Park, 31, 32, 33, 75, 238
Yosemite Valley, 9, 10
Yosemite Valley state park, 30–33, 35–36, 40, 46, 57, 106, 250
Young Adult Conservation Corps, 243